"For years I was burdened by a deeply gloomy out-look. Life seemed drab, dull, depressing. One day I griped bitterly to a co-worker, 'What's the use of anything? Why live?'

"She exploded, 'Know what's the matter with you? You want to be unhappy. You make your unhappi-ness yourself!' "

Those shocking words from an angry co-worker started Samm Sinclair Baker on a conscious search for happi-ness. Over twenty years ago, he began discovering and setting down detailed "how-tos" and exercises.

The results changed his life. They can change yours.

CONSCIOUS HAPPINESS
How to Get the Most Out of Living

by Samm Sinclair Baker

BANTAM BOOKS · TORONTO · NEW YORK · LONDON

CONSCIOUS HAPPINESS

A Bantam Book / published in association with Grosset & Dunlap, Inc.

PRINTING HISTORY
Grosset & Dunlap edition / January 1975
Bantam edition / July 1976

ISBN 0-02356-X

Published simultaneously in the United States and Canada

Bantam Books are published by Bantam Books, Inc. Its trademark, consisting of the words "Bantam Books" and the portrayal of a bantam, is registered in the United States Patent Office and in other countries. Marca Registrada. Bantam Books, Inc., 666 Fifth Avenue, New York, New York 10019.

To Sue
who enjoys
and shares
and inspires
conscious happiness

Contents

1. What Conscious Happiness Can Mean for
   You 1
2. What Is True Conscious Happiness? 16
3. Your Approach to Conscious Happiness 27
4. Living "The Glorious Life That Is Within
   You" 33
5. Gaining New Awareness 43
6. Appreciating and Strengthening Your
   Individuality 68
7. Self-Quiz: Seeking and Finding Your
   Personal Truth 93
8. Doing What You Want to Do 109
9. Setting and Reaching Your Most Fulfilling
   Goal 133
10. Recognizing and Developing Your Creativity 155
11. The Joys of Work and Achievement 170
12. How You Can Gain Increased Optimism,
   Enthusiasm, Humor 190
13. Giving Love and Friendship—Helping Others
   and Yourself 212
14. Finding Inner Peace—Rewards from Beauty
   and the Arts 234

Contents

15. Unworthy, Wasteful Emotions: "You Make Most of Your Unhappiness Yourself" .. 252

16. Dealing Affirmatively with Troubles, Illness, Death 274

17. Making the Most of Marriage, Children, Family Life 295

18. How to Grow Older Enthusiastically, Exultantly, Ecstatically 314

19. Welcome to Your Future of Conscious Happiness 329

Conscious Happiness

1

What Conscious Happiness Can Mean for You

"CONSCIOUS HAPPINESS" is free. It can enrich your life tremendously—yet it doesn't cost you a cent from now on. But nobody else can pay for it and give it to you as a gift. You must earn it yourself by wanting it enough so that you work at it daily. Once you attain it, you can keep and enjoy its great benefits for the rest of your more rewarding life.

Lincoln said bluntly: "Most folks are about as happy as they make up their minds to be." Achieving happiness, the sense of uplifting, enduring awareness that I call *conscious happiness*, isn't that simple. You can't usually just make up your mind to be happy—and presto, there it is, a full and sustaining part of you.

It would be a sublime solution if the miracle could be accomplished by willing and wishing it so—and as a result you were liltingly, effusively happy, bubbling all over . . . forevermore. It doesn't happen that way. It can't and it shouldn't since gains which come too easily usually don't sustain themselves.

So don't expect to grasp conscious happiness totally

with that instant, intense revelation that Sartre called "a burst of realization." Occasionally, yes. Always, no. Can you attain conscious happiness eventually? It's not only possible but probable, and beginning right now. But you must exert effort. Ben Franklin cautioned: "All the Constitution guarantees is the pursuit of happiness. You have to catch up with it yourself."

You have to work at it eagerly and continually to gain and solidify your conscious happiness, as with anything else worthwhile. The trying and achieving is part of treasuring what you attain. When you do enjoy conscious happiness, when you feel the sweet assurance within you, permeating your every living moment—then it can lift and sustain you for the rest of your life.

Just "Inhale and Exhale"?

It has been said that "all you have to do in order to enjoy life is to inhale and exhale." Not true. It takes much more than that for even the most optimistic individuals. You can and should be aware of the large and small opportunities for enjoyment in living, alive to the actual and potential beauty and bounty that surround you—*if you will look and see*. If.

You can gain a new, better way of judging and seeing things and handling everyday living. The beauty of a perky robin, for example, doesn't lie just in the creature itself but must also exist in the mind and eyes of the person who looks at it. Otherwise the apathetic reaction may well be, "So it's a robin, a bird. So what?"

You will find the "hows" of attaining conscious happiness as you absorb these pages. An individual who had profited greatly from reading asserted, "A book is that most precious of all things, one human being reaching out to communicate with another." Here is a direct, ardent reaching-out to you.

Gaining from this book is up to you as you start by adopting the simple but basic desire *to be reborn every day*. A radiant lady, educator Mary Susan Miller, explained, "I decided that all of a sudden 'tomorrow' was *today*. I could no longer permit myself to delay by saying that 'I'll change my outlook tomorrow.' I began that day to seek conscious happiness—and each today has been infinitely better ever since."

She laughed, flinging her arms wide. "See how easy it is? I greet each day as a new adventure, a new challenge, instead of as an added burden. Certainly troubles come along, but I handle them rather than break under them. I keep reminding myself that each dawn brings with it an opportunity—because I've never lived this day before. You see, I've learned that I'm here to use and try to enjoy this day, the here and now, regardless of what may come later that I can't foresee."

She looked thoughtful, searching for the right self-expression. "I still lack the same material things as before, but the difference is that I don't let the negatives get me down. As a result, I'm doing better in all of living, including my job, and getting ahead faster."

She concluded slowly, "It's not just 'positive thinking' —far more important is positive *doing*. Mostly, with conscious happiness, I keep trying to be all that I can be. I never give up. . . ."

You Radiate Conscious Happiness

It's undeniable: When you feel conscious happiness within, it shows and glows on your face. Conscious happiness helps you feel better, therefore look better. You reveal your new deep understanding and resulting sense of exultation in the way you stand proudly, your entire aspect, even your posture, uplifted. It begins with the realization and then the determination, at any age, that there is no desirable or viable alternative to looking ahead and making the most of each today and tomorrow.

A very few individuals are born with a superlative gift for music, art, writing, mathematics, science, or another specialized pursuit. But each person is born with *the gift of living*—which can be developed into a gift of joy by pursuing that goal consciously and constantly. Painter and teacher Victor Candell told me, "Anyone can be an artist at being *alive*."

Each of us is born with a natural feeling of elation and optimism which is lost by too many in growing up. It's a precious euphoria that you regain when you gain conscious happiness. It is yours for the taking from within yourself, and then making it whole and lasting.

A friend, Helen H., who had moved abroad wrote, "I'm practicing your 'conscious happiness.' Each day passes too quickly but without regret, because tomorrow beckons even more invitingly. I'm doing the best I can, squeezing the most out of each day's living, *and being aware of it every minute*."

Research Study on Happiness

It's not easy to research "happiness"—but a study was undertaken at the University of Chicago by the psychology department about 10 years ago. A total of 2006 women and men were surveyed in four different towns. Of these individuals, only 24 percent said they were "very happy"; 59 percent were "pretty happy"; the remaining 17 percent were "not too happy." Now, over a decade later, the "unhappy" percentage figure probably has increased considerably while the "very happy" (those who I'd say possess conscious happiness) probably has decreased beyond the low 24 percent figure.

The following findings emerged from the study, as reported in the *New York Times*: "A pioneering study on the average American 'in pursuit of happiness' has concluded that happiness depends on the positive satisfactions in life, not on the absence of negative experiences or even on the amount of bad experiences."

This major point was emphasized: "A person can feel very depressed because of many negative forces, such as dissatisfaction with his job or marriage, and yet describe himself as being very happy *because his positive satisfactions are greater*."

The director of the study stressed: "It is the lack of joy in Mudville, rather than the presence of sorrow, that makes the difference. . . . Happiness is a resultant of the relative strengths of positive and negative feelings rather than of the absolute amount of one or the other."

In essence, the study affirms two basic points of supreme importance to you and your attainment of conscious happiness, proposed here repeatedly: First, *accent the positive*, as you work toward eliminating the negative as much as possible. Second, *set your goals realistically*, not for 100 percent bliss, but for 51 percent or as much more as you can achieve of positive feelings and attitudes.

"One single positive weighs more . . . than negatives by the score." With that attitude, setting your course accordingly, carrying through energetically and without surrender to negatives, *you can attain conscious happiness*. Regardless of any research results, your concern is individual. Aldous Huxley pinpointed it: "There's only one corner of the universe you can be certain of improving, and that's your own self."

The experience of many others like you proves that such achievement can be yours. Realize that you possess a prime asset that sets man apart from the lower animals: the human's ability to be a positivist in action and in thoughts and emotions.

Your Choice: Happiness or Unhappiness?

A historian points out, "Through the ages of man, *unhappiness* has always been and still is fashionable among a good many seemingly intelligent people. Fostering such an attitude serves only to make and keep those individuals unhappy. They wouldn't have it any other way."

Writing in *Esquire*, Dorothy Parker described an artist appearing "as nearly happy as anyone ever gets to be." She added quickly, "I know that few of the gifted can accept that as a compliment ('So she says I'm shallow, does she?'), but I mean it to please, and that's why I envy him."

There it is, the sophisticated apology for even suggesting that a person is happy. In such a group, an individual remarked during a discussion, "Well, *I'm* a happy man." The woman at his elbow asked with a frown, "What's the matter, you some kind of a nut?" She strode away lest she be contaminated by adjacency to happiness.

For many, not all, of the "elite," an aspect of grimness or depression is considered admirable. But in one's world of real, personal living, such pseudo gloom is utterly self-defeating and therefore stupid as it wastes the gift of time.

I expect to convince you, as I have many others, that it's not a sin to be happy. This is not a book "about" happiness in the abstract. It will reveal to you exactly *how* you personally may gain and sustain the greatest possible happiness every day for the rest of your life. What you attain is much more than just "happiness"—it is being conscious of every opportunity and possibility for happiness always.

A pale-faced man with a fixed expression, obviously bored even with talking, told others, "My idea of happiness is an absence of pain and trouble." Questioned whether he experiences much elation, he shook his head negatively, "No, I rarely feel a sense of happiness." He added proudly, "Only idiots are happy." I interjected, "That kind of idiot I want to be."

The key clue to a jaded individual's unhappiness is usually his determinedly negative, even antagonistic attitude. This is often marked by a blank, non-smiling, even "dead" aspect. Belligerent pessimism is not a very satisfying way of life generally. On the other hand, dour actor George C. Scott was quoted as saying, "I think a certain amount of controlled unhappiness is probably a good thing." Again, you decide for yourself.

As noted, there is no assurance that you can achieve happiness just by wanting it. But you can be certain that you'll miss a lot of readily available joy if you close your eyes to the possibility or turn away from it. You'll miss a great deal of pleasure if your outlook is basically, "I just haven't the disposition or capacity to be a happy individual. I'm not the type."

That's probably true if your disinterested or listless attitude results in your refusing to become aware of or take advantage of available joys you possess or that come your way inevitably, as happens in greater or lesser degree for everyone. "It's no use," you may insist gloomily, "I'm a loser."

That hopeless, self-defeating focus is nullified if you will make the effort repeatedly to assert instead, "The best times are ahead because I'll make them the best. I

7

seek to be happy from now on, and I'll work at it." You'll find out in detail later how four words—"I'll make things better!"—can work wonders for you.

Concentrating on unhappiness is as obtuse and wasteful as throwing away a whole apple because a part of it is rotten. Instead you could enjoy the rest which you might find is sweet and delicious. Editor Norman Cousins stressed another application: "The most costly disease in America is not cancer or coronaries. The most costly disease is *boredom*—costly for both the individual and society."

That doesn't mean that you adopt a devil-may-care "why worry?" or "no worry" attitude toward living as you exist in a constant state of mindless elation. Your responsibility to yourself and others, a thinking responsibility, is essential as a foundation for self-respect. But you stop worrying needlessly and ineffectually in the sense of building tragedies of trifles instead of proceeding positively toward solutions. Facing up helps to eliminate burdensome, empty fear.

Author G. K. Chesterton suffered a long period of deep depression. He finally emerged from the abyss with a strong, revivifying conviction as he asserted that "the fact of existence is in itself wonderful."

Eleanor Roosevelt declared: "Life was meant to be lived, and curiosity must be kept alive. One must never, for whatever reason, turn one's back on life." That would be a squandering of time, and time is given to be used, not wasted.

There was a popular book titled *Life Begins at Fifty*. But life "begins" not at forty or thirty or twenty or fifty or at any other numerical point. Life begins and should be lived to the full every day, regardless of age. If you don't follow that personal course, you are letting much of life and yourself go down the drain. I noted in my diary: "I'm much more alive at fifty than I was at twenty.

That's not because fifty is better, but at twenty I just didn't understand the full potential available from living, as I understand and practice it now—thanks to my development of conscious happiness."

First you must believe in being happy, in that strong possibility for yourself. One day I had a date for lunch with an acquaintance, Tom W., who prided himself on being a realist, his synonym for pessimist. I knocked on his door, heard a grunt which I took to mean, "Come in." He looked up from his desk with an automatic frown. I called out, "Hi! What a great day—"

"What are *you* so happy about?"

"Why not? I'm alive. I feel happy. I believe in being happy. How about you?"

"Oh, hell, I'm disgusted with myself and everything else."

"Y'know, you *believe* in being depressed. Doesn't make you feel good, does it? Or—do you enjoy being unhappy?"

"I don't see anything to be happy about."

"You're alive—that's enough of a start for being happy. All you have to do is *believe* in being happy—and then you work at it to make it come true. Why not give it a chance?"

"Nobody Has the Right to Look So Happy."

One evening during the writing of this book, I encountered a friend, noted psychiatrist Dr. Milton Rosenbaum, at a dinner party. He said, "I almost called you last Tuesday. I was driving down a quiet street—Beach Avenue—and saw you walking along. Just walking. I slowed for a bit and watched you."

"Sorry. I didn't see you."

"I know, but I watched you anyhow. You were pretty

9

busy. As you walked, you glanced up and around at the trees, at the sky, at gardens that you were passing. All the while you had an alert, pleased half-smile on your face. You looked happy, deeply happy, as though enjoying every minute as you walked."

"Well," I shrugged, "I like to walk—"

He grinned, then tried to look severe, "Nobody has the right to look so happy. I almost stopped to ask you how you do it, and whether you really have the feeling, the awareness of being a happy individual."

I hesitated because I hate to sound like a Pollyanna or a preacher or a do-gooder. Then I answered, "Yes, I'm aware—because I work at it. I've developed for myself what I call 'conscious happiness.' I believe that most anyone who wants to can acquire and enjoy conscious happiness—granted pretty good health, average well-being, and lack of overwhelming personal tragedy."

He nodded. "Makes a big difference in your life, doesn't it?"

"It has made all the difference in the flavor and deep enjoyment I get out of living every day. In that walk, for instance, I consciously delighted in an hour of looking at flowers and trees and blue sky, breathing in clean, refreshing air. Instead I might have had a dull time pushing one reluctant leg ahead of the other."

"It's a conscious choice you've made then?"

"Yes." I thought for an instant. "I think that just about every individual has the choice—conscious happiness versus unrewarding apathy or worse. What do you think?"

He paused, his professionalism advising caution. Then he touched his forehead in salute: "More power to you. Keep doing what you're doing. It works for you. Just keep doing what you're doing."

I do. I keep trying. I keep working at it. And I find it ecstatically worthwhile—as you will.

A Way of Living . . . Better!

You will find stated in these pages—presented as clearly and simply as possible—a way of living, thinking, and acting that I (and others my life has touched) have developed through years of productive, rewarding, happy living. This practice should also serve you best.

It is this procedure which can have you awaking each morning to face the day eagerly and optimistically. The development of conscious happiness for yourself, through the detailed suggestions here, can help you look forward more enthusiastically to the rest of your life, starting today. You can gain the joyous anticipation that each day will be most fulfilling—at least providing the lift that "I'll try to make it so. And if I fail today, I'll try to make tomorrow better."

Trouble comes inevitably and repeatedly to practically everyone. That's one reason why it's not only desirable but essential always to seek out and recognize happiness —and enjoy it, making the most of it as it happens, as you help to make it happen.

"Of all things you wear, expression is the most important." How you look at life affects fundamentally how you look at others and how you look to them. People usually gravitate toward the happy person because joy is more desirable and catching. Just as surely, gloom and pessimism are unwanted and repellent. Asked why he usually tried to appear optimistic, Harry Truman replied bluntly, "Who wants to be with a grouch?"

Whatever your problems, you can look and feel most attractive and alive if a sense of conscious happiness is deep within you. It shows in the aware, interested look on your face, the springy way you walk, the eagerness with which you greet each day and handle every day's living.

11

An outflow of enthusiasm often lights up even a drab undertaking.

"Since I developed a sense of conscious happiness," a friend, Ann R., explained, "I've been better able to endure and emerge from tragedies that have hit me—the loss of my husband, severe illnesses of loved ones as well as my own health problems. I manage to go on steadfastly, without falling apart. And I have the strength to find some joy, even if slight, in every day. I don't know how I could have gotten along without that reinforcement of the spirit."

Expanding Your Capacities

This book is intended to help reveal to you the joys of living to the fullest possible extent. As a result, you will open yourself wider, feel more, savor every possible instant, every smallest sight, to the utmost of your abilities and capacities. You will probably come to realize that your attainments of all kinds never have and never will reach their "fullest possible extent." Always you can expand and achieve still more, to find more, feel more, enjoy more.

The potentials are all there for you to embrace, and to add to your ever-increasing enjoyment of life—to step up the zest that you draw from the hours of each day. Thus you add to yourself many more moments to savor, to remember and cherish, which will feed your ever-growing consciousness always.

Of course this doesn't signify shallow "ha-ha" happiness, a constant whirl of gay partying and raucous, perhaps empty, laughter. Primarily the focus here is for you to enrich yourself increasingly with the inner enjoyment of everything possibly worthwhile: the momentary, flashing, thrilling sight of a surging wave . . . the sound of a child's soft murmur . . . the inspiring emotion of feeling for an instant the warmth in the eyes of a passing stranger.

These are the ever-occuring fragments that can lift you each day, that can ennoble you if you will keep yourself open for opportunities and seek them watchfully. Inevitably you will then find them, hold them in your lasting remembrance as gems of living. These are available to all just for the looking, recognizing, and accepting.

It doesn't matter how burdened and depressed you may be by personal, very real, oppressive troubles—as everyone is at times. The little, sometimes seemingly insignificant extras that can make the gloomy day brighter nevertheless are there for the taking, enjoying, and then treasuring forever.

Strengthening Your Individuality

Striving for conscious happiness definitely does *not* mean becoming bloodless, devoid of thoughts or ideas, or fitting into a mold. Precisely the opposite. You'll discover as you read and absorb and think through your conclusion for yourself that you, as an individual, will build and strengthen your own individuality. You will fortify your self-reliance and self-respect.

Thus you can gain a more invigorating and sustaining sense of self, and belief in yourself. When you come to terms with yourself in this way, honoring your individuality adequately, you will be more likely to recognize and appreciate the individuality rather than the alikeness of others. You will get along better with yourself and with others. Suddenly or gradually, you should find yourself saying, as Thoreau did: "I can see beyond the range of sight."

Thereby your entire outlook can be extended and expanded, lifting your spirit as your view of life and your way of living change for the better. You learn not to be so involved with the business and details of living that you don't have time to live. With this more open, more flexible, maturated outlook, you should be able for the rest of your days to think and feel and see "beyond the range of sight."

You *can* make things better, along the lines of Thoreau's insistence: "I know of no more encouraging fact than the unquestionable ability of man to elevate his life by a conscious endeavor." Ben Franklin agreed: "We can make these times better, if we bestir ourselves." The precepts here will stir you up so that you bestir yourself for the better—always.

You can be certain that the joys of gaining conscious happiness can enrich you whatever you are, wherever you may be. This struck me particularly when I, an American born and bred, met a foremost Norwegian concert pianist, Jan Henrik Kayser, and his sparkling wife, Anna Moren, aboard the cruise ship *Argonaut*. Although we differed in nationality, background, and language, and were decades apart in age, we sparked to each other instantly as our eyes met.

Sailing Norway's magnificent fiords, we laughed and danced together, exchanged thoughts and ideas excitedly. Thus we learned conclusively that there is no really insurmountable language or other barrier. For we were all four (including my Natalie) interested, exultant individuals—as you are, or can be. And each of us possessed and was eager to share the all-important human quality available to everyone, to you: *love of living*.

* * *

I can't sum up the preceding more succinctly than to relate my bedside visit with a dear friend, Marie Killilea. She wrote the inspiring best-seller Karen, *about the* heroic struggle against her daughter's cerebral palsy. Now Marie herself was afflicted with a crushing illness which kept her constantly bedbound.

Conquering her suffering, she told me, "Samm, I'm one of the luckiest people in the world. I have the loving support of my family and friends. Through the window I can see my beloved trees, birds, sky. I'm living, breathing, reading, talking, blessing the gift of each moment, every day. I'm so happy to be alive. . . ."

"You're happy," I murmured, "because you make it so."

Her beautiful eyes glowed. She said simply, "Everyone can."

You can.

2

What Is True Conscious Happiness?

A CARTOON IN *The New Yorker* showed a saleswoman in a greeting card store going berserk and screaming: "*Greetings* out there, all you *Happy* people! *Happy Birthday! Happy Anniversary! Happy Graduation! Happy! Happy! Happy!*" That, of course, is manufactured "h-a-p-p-i-n-e-s-s," no relationship to conscious happiness which is the deep, supportive inner joy you seek.

Nor does conscious happiness mean constant cheerfulness. Attaining conscious happiness is not so much setting a destination as practicing the ways and means of getting there. Working on that daily cultivates and builds in you a productive, optimistic viewpoint. But your basic attitude becomes not that "things will get better if I hope and wait long enough." Instead, your approach is that "I'll try consciously and determinedly, I'll exert my energy constantly toward *making things better*."

Ridiculing the whole idea of being truly happy, a glum-faced night club comedian paused during his act whenever his alarm wristwatch rang. He'd bark a brief, explosive laugh—and explain, "I make it a point to laugh every so often, on schedule." Then his face would transform into a mask of deep gloom again. Unfortunately it doesn't help much to laugh unless you really mean it—not "on schedule."

A psychiatrist, Dr. Theodore I. Rubin, put the question, "What exactly is happiness?" Then he answered: "Well, to me, happiness is feeling good. Other simple ways of describing happiness include: being at peace with oneself; feeling comfortable; enjoying self-acceptance; being basically pain- and tension-free. As simple as it is to define, happiness is not simple to find and even less simple to sustain."

He noted further: "While happiness is certainly not everything in life, it is an enormously important facet of human existence. Happiness is, to many, the feeling that makes life truly worthwhile."

Explaining his personal concept, novelist John Buchan wrote: "Peace is that state in which fear of any kind is unknown. But joy is a positive thing . . . something goes out from oneself to the universe, a warm, possessive effluence of love. There may be Peace without Joy, and Joy without Peace, but the two combined make happiness."

You may have your own simple or complicated definition of happiness. Many who are asked reply uncertainly something like this: "Happiness is feeling good—depending on what makes each person feel good." Just trying to define and shape it is a step toward acquiring conscious happiness. Significantly: "The foolish man seeks happiness in the distance; the wise grows it under his feet."

Pianist Artur Rubinstein said at age eighty-five: "We are given a short life. . . . What we know is what our sense tells us—flowers, love, poetry, music. People think money, success, power are necessary. No! It's so absurdly stupid. I need only one flower in that corner there to be happy."

What do you need?

Conscious happiness means squeezing every possible bit of joy out of every hour, every day. It means being conscious of and uplifted by every scrap of good feeling that comes your way—or that you can bring about each day. This may add up to only a few minutes or lots more of conscious happiness each day. However small or large your daily portion may be, you savor and use it and enjoy it to the full.

"Life Is Not a Lollipop"

A father refused to give a sweet to his three-year-old. "But, Daddy, if I can't have a lollipop, I'll be unhappy," the child insisted. The thoughtful man said carefully, "Johnny, sooner or later you'll learn that happiness isn't a lollipop."

Nor is happiness what some self-serving advertisers have proclaimed: "Happiness is a $49 mattress" . . . "Happiness is a new bathroom" . . . "Happiness is a quick-starting car" . . . "Happiness can be the color of her hair."

If you think that happiness is something as inconsequential as something sweet at the end of a stick, or "the color of her hair," or some other minor self-gratification—then, of course, you are underrating happiness and yourself. Those fleeting little titillations are among the things that true happiness is not. Nor is it the spasm of laughter at a comedian's joke (though that is fun and may help).

You won't find conscious happiness in dictionaries offering explanations in definitions such as: "Characterized by luck or good fortune; prosperous . . . pleasure or satisfaction . . ." Happiness—conscious happiness—in the meaning of this book is gut-deep, something you develop and *live* every day.

You think about conscious happiness, learn it, relish it, work at it. Conscious happiness becomes part of you not only by echoing and repeating the phrase but by what you do, how you live, by your actions toward others, your interchanges with everyone, *and the awareness of the resultant deep-rooted joy within yourself*. Once conscious happiness is part of you, it can lift and sustain you every day of your better, more fulfilling life.

"Pure Pleasure"

Living each day with an awareness of and a striving for conscious happiness brings with it moments of sheer exhilaration. They add up to what one reasoning individual called "pure pleasure . . . that intoxicating state in which the whole man finds himself centered on and in a sensation of having just been born—and having just been set free—and having been born for the freedom he is feeling."

The same is true for women as well as men, of course, and for every age and stage of living.

In short, attaining conscious happiness gives you a repeated sense of rebirth, that uplifting feeling of being *new*, free, soaring in spirits, especially and thrillingly alive. This feeling of almost bursting with quiet ecstasy is an exhilaration that you must have experienced at some time. You will savor it more often in the future—and in a more fulfilling and lasting way because you will be conscious of enjoying and appreciating the sensation more deeply, more significantly.

To some degree, this rebirth carries with it a sense of

19

emerging, of "coming upstairs." As Congreve commented tongue-in-cheek, "I came upstairs in the world, for I was born in a cellar."

An elevator starter in Radio City ("Call me Joe") greeted everyone daily with a bright "Good morning!" He was asked by a grumpy tenant, "How the hell do you stay so damned cheerful every day?"

The smiling man replied, "If I'm grouchy, I'm the guy who loses out. 'Cause I get unhappy and so does everybody else around me. I figure it's up to me to enjoy my life, nobody else is gonna do it for me. It's the only life I've got. And I'm enjoying it 'cause I say to myself when I wake up, 'Look, here's another day. I've never had this day before. So let's see what happens, and let's make the most of it.'"

"Don't you ever feel just plain lousy so you can't brighten up?"

Joe explained, "What's the use? I just don't give in. I know that some people think it's smart to feel that life is lousy. I decided that I'd rather be stupid—but happy. It's that easy: I decide each morning to be happy today. Otherwise I'd waste the day, see?" He tipped his cap as the frowning tenant left the elevator—"Have a good day."

There's a story about one good fairy telling another, "I stopped bringing good luck to that lady I'm in charge of —because she never noticed when she had it." You must be conscious of your happiness or it is likely to be invisible or evaporate. You must be aware of what goes on about you and get excited about life. If you don't bother to count your blessings, then you may not even know they exist.

To attain happiness, some have proclaimed: "What you think, you become." And: "You can if you think you can." It's more complex than that. Nor is it effective just to nail on the wall the common placard: "Think."

Think what? Think how? Thinking, of course, must be directed productively or it may dissipate in space and vapidity.

Furthermore, you must realize that there is not just one level of happiness but many levels, shifting levels, all differing somewhat. You will come to recognize, to be conscious of what is most likely to make *you* happy as an individual. What you read here is aimed to help you achieve and retain conscious happiness on your personal levels.

The Target, The Goal

This book examines, probes, and proposes to help you attain and sustain conscious happiness for yourself primarily. There are no "must" instructions, but possibilities, choices, alternatives. Not only attaining but truly sustaining conscious happiness is the emphasis and the goal. And, as a most valuable by-product, you engender a sense of conscious happiness for those about you.

Honored essayist Walter Lippmann wrote that he approached life "not as something given but as something to be shaped." A character in a novel observed, "Each day we have one day less, every one of us. And joy is the only thing that slows the clock." It helps to realize that "each day is a lifetime in miniature," teeming with opportunities for happiness or alternatives to despair.

Yes, time is the most precious and priceless element each of us owns—to use, not to let slip away and lose, as too many people do. Think—are you among the latter? Are you allowing time to pass by unused? Have you a feeling of lack and yearning? "Time is on my side," a young man asserted. His older friend advised, "Time is only on the side of the one who uses it."

In a short story, John Updike described a rooster's

morning greeting: "He flops up on his roof with a slap like a newspaper hitting the porch and gives a crow as if to hoist with his own pure lungs that sleepy fat sun to the zenith of the sky. He never moderates his joy, though I am gradually growing deafer to it. That must be a difference between soulless creatures and human beings: creatures find every dawn as remarkable as all the ones previous." Emulating the rooster is part of conscious happiness.

True, each day is yours if you awaken with the eager attitude that "this day is mine to make the most and the best of. I won't let it waste away as just so many more empty or dreary hours. The choice is mine in facing this day: *use it or lose it.*"

Then each night before sleep you can say, "I made the most of this day. I enjoyed what was possible in it." But you must strive toward that realization purposefully. A talented woman with this viewpoint, my wife, Natalie, told me after an exhausting day of painting at the easel in her studio, "I don't know whether I've advanced much or accomplished anything new in painting—but anyhow, I enjoyed myself today."

How Can You Gain Conscious Happiness?

It can't be stressed too much that attaining conscious happiness isn't just a goal you dream about and achieve automatically. Here you'll find ideas, specific ways, clear paths you can follow to the desired personal fulfillment that conscious happiness brings as its reward. But you must exert effort to reach that goal.

It's not an easy, overnight, miraculous achievement. You can't just throw off and ignore all burdens, cares, and personal problems and responsibilities through the shallow, devil-may-care attitude that "You only live once!" Old troubles and new roadblocks and challenges persist, and you don't live fully even once—unless you strive for it.

On the other hand, some people, many people, live as though they had made and are supporting a decision to be unhappy for the rest of their lives. A frowning cynic professed, "I always start the day with a smile—to get it over with!"

Neither the flippant, non-productive approach nor the pervadingly pessimistic outlook pays off. Only a positive, energetic attitude can be truly supportive. Picasso said, "Everything exists in limited quantity—even happiness." It is up to each individual to create his own; it is up to you.

If this book, or any of its elements, can convey to only one person, to *you*, what embodies conscious happiness, how you can gain and own it, how it can help you live most fully and exultantly—then that will be sufficient reward for all concerned.

Even if just once a day you feel "extra good," enjoying a sense of special gratification from what goes on about you and within you, that's a great bonus. Perhaps rereading a few lines or more from this book now and then may help to lift you during a particularly difficult situation or at an especially grueling pressure point. That alone would make it worthwhile for you (and for me).

A Person-to-Person Linkage

Everything set down throughout these pages endeavors to help you on a person-to-person basis. I'm not a psychiatrist or psychologist or any kind of doctor. I respect such professionals but I'm not one by education or training.

This book isn't addressed to anyone who is emotionally ill as any kind of a "cure." All such persons should have qualified professional help.

I've been a textile laborer, retail clerk, mill foreman, student, university instructor, business executive—and now full-time writer. I've done a lot of living on many levels—and have attained conscious happiness. I've written this book over a period of more than twenty years for you who seek to get the most out of each day and through all of life—to get *more* out of living.

You'll find quotes from many noted and obscure people, not always identified by name lest meaning be obscured by an excess of detailed references. Certainly the individuals quoted briefly would be delighted to have their significant, often inspiring thoughts passed on to you—if they can help you in any way to greater happiness.

In total, this isn't solely the statement and evocation of a personal philosophy, but much more. Through the years, in planning this volume, the thrust has been to help provide a clear connection for you to what many thinking, caring individuals, including myself, have learned and expressed meaningfully for you. The comments of others are added here to inform, inspire, and enrich you—and lead you to *your personal grasp and possession of conscious happiness.*

A Simple Experiment

Please try this simple little experiment in conscious happiness, no special talents or equipment required. I tried this each term when conducting classes in creativity and writing at New York University, and found that the students were alerted and affected beneficially:

The next chance you get, on a bright moonlit night, look up at the moon. Don't just glance up, but really fix your gaze upon it. Let your mind and your vision open wide to feel the faraway, mysterious glory . . .

Then, as you gaze aloft, think of the deeply felt, uplifting words written by poet Walt Whitman:

> *Lo, the moon ascending.*
> *Up from the East, the silvery round moon.*
> *Beautiful over the housetops;*
>   *ghastly, phantom moon, immense and*
>   *silent moon . . .*

Feel the sight of the moon filling your eyes and your head and your being. Now realize the thrilling, rewarding difference when you look and absorb and enjoy *consciously*. As you know so well, the same moon has been up there in the sky night after night before. But this time you looked at it purposefully for enjoyment. As a result, you experienced exceptionally uplifting emotions in those very pleasurable moments that you wouldn't have felt and appreciated otherwise.

Try it yourself the next moonlit night. It works. Look around. Give of yourself. Feel. Every day, from the moment you arise, apply this attitude of searching and discerning that leads to conscious happiness. It can become a natural, rewarding, sustaining part of your daily living and achieving. It can enrich your life and the lives of all around you.

*   *   *

Don't confuse conscious happiness with the simplistic, nebulous blather about "finding oneself" without much thinking about it. I don't know what such glib "finding" means, nor does anyone else who mouths the word thoughtlessly. The expression is too vague, too easy.

The purpose and function of this book rather is to

help you recognize, realize, and respect the best that you are and can be—and to make the most of it.

Please check again major points in this chapter:

1. *Realize that deep conscious happiness is not surface ha-ha happiness.*

2. *Determine to exert not only your will but your energy toward making things better for yourself and for those around you.*

3. *Seek the uplifting sense of "rebirth" that comes with attaining conscious happiness.*

4. *Understand that time is a priceless asset—and the target here is to use it, not lose it.*

5. *Appreciate that a positive, forward-moving attitude, not pessimism, pays off.*

6. *Read with the assurance that each word in this book is set down to help you personally.*

7. *Try the "moon-gazing" experiment—see how surely it works for you.*

8. *Above all, approach this book with an open, searching mind, with the eager expectation that you will read and learn here—step by step—how to achieve and enjoy your greatest possible potential for very real and sustaining conscious happiness every day from now on.*

3

Your Approach
to Conscious Happiness

VOLTAIRE WROTE: "We never live; we are always going to live." From now on you can determine to live—more fully, and your most rewarding way of life. That prospect will develop and expand as you evolve your personal, unfolding, permeating sense of conscious happiness, helped by the guidelines here.

Through the years, starting with a personal gloomy outlook which I found unsatisfying, unproductive, and self-defeating, I have helped myself and many others to reach and keep as a way of life this intimate personal joy and sustenance that I call conscious happiness. Just targeting and repeating those two words as a constant reminder can be reinforcing: *conscious happiness.*

Some people have gained the essence of conscious happiness independently—whether they call it by that name or not, or most likely by no name at all. You can acquire and benefit greatly from conscious happiness too—if you want it enough. Just reading about it here is a promising beginning since it indicates desire and willingness on your part. Personal involvement is a key essential, of course.

A woman, Elaine C., who had practiced and achieved conscious happiness said, "It has kept me balanced and functioning in spite of adversities of every kind, involving health, family and business problems, all heaped on me at once. You know how that can happen—troubles accumulating in a chain reaction, piling on as if to test or break a person ..."

Remembering, she shuddered, "Time after time, my imbued sense of conscious happiness—trying to find and hold the good in each day, however little it might be—kept me fighting back, never giving in. Otherwise, as in the past, I'd have moaned, 'What's the use?'—and I'd have slid into melancholy or worse, spoiling the well-being of my family and friends, as well as my own."

It has been said: "We want to live by each other's happiness . . . not by each other's misery." By being consciously happy, you radiate your inner cheer to others. They feel better accordingly, and they like having you near and being with you.

Just *trying* will bring you worthy rewards right from the first moment. The pursuit of conscious happiness gains much of its joy and fulfillment from the striving and the involvement alone—from the "happiness of pursuit." Isn't it wise to try to spend time joyously rather than indifferently or unhappily?

Your Beginning

You start with the conviction that life is good. And then you set out to make it better, whatever the obstacles, no matter how many inevitable setbacks you encounter.

You may be familiar with the challenge in the Bible: "I have set before you life and death, blessing and curse. Therefore choose life, that you and your descendants may live." Which have you chosen consciously? Or haven't you thought about it? Have you been living, enduring, trying to survive the blows and buffeting? Are you ready to "choose life"?

A learned gentleman of sixty-one, my friend Harry Slater, who had a pervadingly gloomy view, was suddenly overwhelmed by a severe illness which brought with it terrible pain, dizziness, blurred vision, and other destructive afflictions. After lingering near death for weeks, he was saved by a brain tumor operation. Recuperating, still weak but improving day by day, he declared, "For the first time in my lengthy and mostly wasted life, I have the positive charged-up feeling that it's good to be alive."

He shook his head, "My enormous regret is that it took me so long to get around finally to enjoying each day as much as possible. What a loss, dissipating all the unsatisfying, depressing decades when I could have made them different if I tried . . . " He brightened, "But now I know that it's never too late to begin. And as each day begins anew, I'll be looking up, not down. I'll be trying, not giving in to my old morbid tendencies."

There is no question about the truth of the summation by comedian Joe Lewis: "My life has been a yo-yo. I've been up, and I've been down. And, believe me, up is better." Agreeing, you ask logically, "Sure, but how can I manage to be *up*? And then how do I stay up—not all the time but enough of the time, even hopefully most of the time?"

You start by being at least expectant and reasonably determined that you can lift yourself up, no matter how low you may feel. Or perhaps you have a vague but aching yearning to enjoy a more satisfying existence, a nagging void to fill within you, an elusive perception that "I know there must be more to life than this."

Be assured that "hope can carry us aloft . . . hope, and a certain faith." That means faith in yourself primarily— a belief in yourself that you can develop if you don't have it now. And in addition, as always, you must work at attaining happiness, as suggested on these pages.

Jefferson wrote in a letter to Lafayette: "We are not expected to be translated from despotism to liberty in a featherbed." Nor should you expect to be transformed from the despotism of gloom to the liberation of conscious happiness by lying around and waiting for it to happen. You are going to make it happen.

It takes energy, fortitude and tenacity to attain and maintain conscious happiness. Joubert, an author in Napoleon's time, wrote to a woman he loved: "One must learn to love life. . . . I perceive in you the most beautiful of all forms of courage, the courage to be happy." Certainly you have it within you if you will exert your energies and mentality at developing and sustaining your innate personal *courage to be happy.*

A "Lifetime Guarantee"?

Complete happiness from now on—"guaranteed"? No, absolutely and definitely not. Enduringly "perfect" happiness doesn't exist. There is no living state completely free of problems or cares, ever joyous and lilting, with no downs. No one can promise you that and fulfill the pledge.

Even if it seemed desirable to find such unvarying bliss and perfection, it wouldn't be satisfying or complete. Everything would stay at one lofty level, no further ups, no dips, no changes, no variety. You'd miss the spice of intangible excitement, the stimulating expectancy of having something more, something challenging to look forward to and to strive for. The result would be impossibly dull and ultimately a tiresome, dragging, unhappy existence.

Life is a continual learning process. Each stage is another step in the process. All problems can't ever be eliminated, but your positive, courageous, searching attitude of conscious happiness can reduce and accommodate the number and especially the effect of heavy, unavoidable burdens. You'll find that usually, happiness doesn't lie in the mere fact of having what you want—but in adjusting yourself to cope more rationally and effectively with the problems that occur. Then you seek to savor whatever good exists in each day, however small that beneficence may be.

There is no intention here, not the slightest, to lead you to ignore and bypass the ills and evils that exist in the world and in daily living. While you care about and fight for a better way of life for yourself and for all, you realize that fundamentally—whatever controversy and struggle buffet you and swirl about you—you can function most effectively when you are imbued with the inner peace and joy of conscious happiness.

How Much Happiness?

Fortified thus in your deep inner being, you are better equipped to cope with the trials and pressures of living. And, as a further extension of the increased self-possession and strength you have gained, you are better able to help others as well as to derive the utmost from each day for yourself, your family, all who come in contact with you.

How much of the time can you rationally expect to be happy? Freud suggested that even as little as 51 percent happiness, and 49 percent unhappiness, is a balance worth achieving. Please dwell on that a moment. Remember: 51 percent happiness, not 100 percent.

Even the marginal happiness of 51 percent can be ex-

hilarating if you make this your way of life, your credo.
Please read the following words aloud, believe them, then
work to make them come true for you from this day on:

> I will live consciously aware of every tiny bit of hap-
> piness I can find in each day . . . and that I can
> squeeze out of each developing and existing and on-
> coming moment.

*   *   *

Points for Emphasis:
   1. *Target and repeat often the two words: conscious
      happiness.*
   2. *Trying brings you rewards immediately.*
   3. *Start with the conviction that life is good.*
   4. *Develop the "courage to be happy."*
   5. *Realize and understand troubles that exist and
      recur—and always exert yourself to overcome
      them.*
   6. *Work toward and adopt the conscious happiness
      credo.*

4

Living "The Glorious Life That Is Within You"

"WHEN I WAS in my early teens," lovely, glowing Alice Binder of Paterson, N.J., said quietly, "I picked up a novel from a library shelf and took it home. I can still feel the green binding imprinted with dark red ink, the linen slightly ragged at the edges from the friction of hundreds, perhaps thousands of hands. I wonder how many readers held that book, perhaps caressing it as I did the many times later when I reread it . . ."

She mused, "The book was titled *The Happy Mountain* by Maristan Chapman. I haven't been able to locate it since. But I'll never forget the first lines, which propelled me into a lifetime of excited anticipation and awareness. They went something like this: 'Live! Live the glorious life that is within you. . . . There is such a little time that your life will last, such a little time . . .'"

She took a deep breath and went on, "The key words to me were '*within you* . . . the glorious life that is *within you*.' The lesson to me was that I couldn't depend on any outside force or individuals to sustain me—that I must reach within me for an inner force, depend on my own being for the sustenance that spells happiness. There, and only there—*within me*—could I find my personal recognition and potential for the fullest enjoyment of life."

She pondered for a few seconds, her eyes reflective yet sparkling in their depths. "That perception of my personal responsibility for myself has helped me ever since. It has enabled me to endure troubles hopefully as I tried to conquer them. But more than that, it has encouraged me to live eagerly and even exultantly, and to be happy, consciously happy . . . most of the time. I wanted 'the glorious life' within me, and I've tried ever since to make the most of every possibility."

You can achieve the same knowledge—that, above all, ultimately and always, you must live and grow within yourself—as well as along with others, giving and taking. Then you can recognize and appreciate more fully the wonders in the world about you. That perception is something you owe yourself. It's an obligation to yourself to make the most of each existing and approaching moment of every day.

"Why Are You So Happy?"

The question was addressed passionately to a bright, smiling lady, Joan Toulouse, by an envious friend. The woman thought about it, her smile lingering as she concentrated. Then she said slowly, "I *have* to be happy. Nobody else in the world is going to be happy for me. I must do it myself. If I don't, then I won't be happy at all, or at any rate as happy as I could be."

She went on, "If I didn't bring out the positive, optimistic feeling in myself, then I'd be numb. I'd be nothing. Or I'd be painfully unhappy. To expend my days and my life on numbness or dreariness or nothingness is, I figure, just plain stupid." She grinned brilliantly, her face lighting up, "So I recognize and accept and make the most of my responsibility to be happy and to stay happy." Joan paused, nodded her head: "So most of the time, I am happy. I can't and don't expect more than that."

A scholar explained to an interviewer, "I was born with nothing but brains and a deep, stifling sense of unhappiness. I had to learn to use my brains to fight depression and become a happy person enjoying life. If I hadn't, my brains and my life would have proved quite worthless."

This profound individual used his brains to switch himself away from a sense of depression. *How about you?*

A Readily Available Ingredient

Conscious happiness is an element that anyone can add to season and improve his or her life. A major league baseball star, Ernie Banks, was playing the game joyously and well at age thirty-nine, long past the time when most other professional athletes fizzled out and quit. A reporter watched Banks finish a tough session and heard the team's manager ask him anxiously, "You all right, Ernie?"

Big grin. "Yeah, man, I feel great."

The writer noted, "Banks looks great, too, and he has a great attitude which infects everyone around him." He went on to tell about one wet, frosty day late in the season when the team found the ball park grounds covered with slush. Everyone griped but Ernie remarked cheerfully, "Good day to play."

The reporter commented, "Banks constantly says such things and looks at life in a completely positive manner, repeating, 'Can you believe we get paid to play baseball? Each day is brand new.' Maybe that's the attitude that keeps Banks so youthful. . . ."

Yet that's quite an uncommon posture for an athlete to adopt, as well as for individuals in any walk of life. It needn't be. It shouldn't be. The difference for you can be in looking around you, regardless of the obstacles or problems that beset you, or the forbidding "slush" that's around you, and deciding, "Great day to play."

Lincoln put it another way: "I do the best I know how —the very best I can; and I mean to keep doing so until the end." You couldn't ask more than that of yourself— but you can ask that much. And then, no matter what, you can feel good about whatever happens—and stop kicking yourself around. Make sense?

It's true: "The one certain way of making things worse than they are is saying that they are worse than they are."

Focusing on Conscious Happiness

Suppose you decide that you want to be very rich. Thinking about it, analyzing what it takes, you learn that one of the prime requisites for becoming rich is to want one thing more than practically anything else: in this particular instance, money. Individuals with that over-powering lust and drive for wealth frequently care more about money than for the love and welfare of family, friends, or anyone else.

But . . . they don't just dream or muse about acquiring money. Rather, they focus just about all their thoughts, energies and activities on gaining money, then more money, always more money. "That's the name of the game," a multi-millionaire said bluntly. In most cases, if they want it enough and try hard enough to amass money, they become rich.

Are these driving men and women happy then? Not necessarily. You can be sure that conscious happiness (far more valuable and sustaining than money) is much more readily obtainable than masses of money. But you must decide: "How much do I want happiness?"

If you want conscious happiness enough, you'll endeavor daily by your thoughts and actions to attain it. You'll work at that goal untiringly. Then you'll persist in maintaining and increasing your sense of well-being and uplift each day—and through all the beckoning years ahead.

The uplifting sensation isn't something vague and mysterious. It's not "a gift of the gods." It's a gift from you to yourself, a gift that you construct for yourself. You never let up in sustaining and fortifying this precious possession. On the other hand, the longer you possess conscious happiness, the more it increases automatically.

You discover this pervading sense of well-being in little things primarily. You must come to the realization—and then the conviction—that every normal function of living holds some small delight. You will find it by looking for, recognizing, and then cherishing each nugget of delight, tiny as it might be.

The total increases for you as you accumulate each treasured amount day after day. It all adds up and endures in the sustaining warmth which assures you that you possess the self-made gift of conscious happiness. You'll anticipate each day as a new opportunity, a fresh beginning—as you realize and recognize it as such. A banker emphasized: "Today is ready cash; spend it well."

It's an expanding joy to keep working at building conscious happiness as a natural, recurring part of you once you gain it. The first black big leaguer, Jackie Robinson, titled his touching autobiography *I Never Had It Made*. He learned the hard way that he could never let up.

Robinson had to keep trying, a realistic, challenging fact of living for him, for you, for everyone. You must keep "making it" every day. And if today was terrible, you exert yourself to make tomorrow better. You know that the events of any day are never so awful that you can't find at least a few moments of brightness and relief in all the hours—if you look for and make yourself aware of them deeply.

In a Tennessee Williams play, a character says, "Life is an unanswered question, but let's still believe in the dignity and importance of that question." So what if one can't answer the towering, all-encompassing question of "life"? You gain nevertheless when you are conscious of living as alertly as you can as you are seeking the best answer for yourself. The worst thing is just to walk languidly or dejectedly through life, ignoring the possibilities.

Somehow, as you actively search, or simply keep your perceptions wide open, you get the enlivening feeling that the answer may be just ahead, just one more seeking step ahead. Keep in mind wise Clarence Darrow's advice: "The pursuit of truth shall set you free—even if you never catch up with it." Similarly with the pursuit of happiness—but you can have much greater assurance that you *will* "catch up with it."

"Everything to Live For"

When a person dies today, at practically any age, unless he or she was terminally ill or destitute or desperately unhappy, someone is likely to sigh, "Too bad . . . he had everything to live for." But—how about you right now, whatever your age? Have you "everything to live for"— and yet are not living for everything every day, with all the strength at your command?

If your answer is a sad recognition of that lack, why are you permitting time to slip by so negatively, so wastefully? Why are you allowing one day to dwindle into the next— unfulfilled, and therefore relatively *unlived*?

Usually there is no reason for this deplorable loss except that you are not aware, not trying, not consciously drawing from each day the fullest happiness attainable. Again, the fault and the loss are yours. Correcting that is up to you—nobody else can assume the responsibility or repair the ongoing damage to yourself.

If you are missing the daily opportunity for greater happiness, isn't it time for you to change that listless pattern? *Now?* You can find at least some of the increased joy and gratification you yearn for—by looking for it, recognizing it, grasping it. *Beginning today.*

The clues to gaining maximum happiness from each day are there for you to uncover and employ as sustenance for your daily living. Seemingly small things await your notice and resultant delight: The graceful flight of a bird across the sky. The warmth of a pleasant human voice. The joy derived from caring for someone, helping someone, even a passing stranger. There are actually an inexhaustible number of signals and signs through life every day, awaiting only your perception, acceptance, and participation.

A news story told of a woman who had been held hostage by terrorists for seventeen nerve-racking hours. Constantly threatened with death, she was finally released unharmed. It was reported that "she clutched a wine glass and danced as she shouted, 'I didn't know it was so good to be alive.'"

Those are such simple words, a seemingly obvious expression—"good to be alive." Yet when was the last time you said those words? Please ask yourself right now: "In spite of the negatives that confuse and batter me, do I appreciate how good it is to be alive?"

Going a step further, ask yourself this: "When was the last time I said that 'it's good to be alive'?" Please think about it for a minute or two. Then consider whether you are making the most of the possibilities and potentialities for happiness in each day's living—as you can by your own decisions and positive action.

Reviewing her long years, a woman in her fifties, Esther

B., said, "What a wonderful life I've had. . . ." Then, with a slight shake of her head and a voice tinged with regret, "I only wish I'd realized it sooner." She brightened suddenly and laughed, "There I go again, wasting time on laments. From now on I'm going to enjoy every possible minute of my 'wonderful life' still to come."

From now on, you can and hopefully will do the same. Starting this instant you can begin discovering the potential for greater happiness within yourself and in each day as it comes. It's your volition—make up your mind toward that upward course. Then follow through eagerly, not wavering from your determined purpose.

Yours to Find Every Day: "The Beauty That Lives"

You can form and set your viewpoint this way: to seek the positives in living rather than to overlook or deny the good by moaning about the bad—as too many people do. When you stop concentrating on how awful things are, go a step further and ask yourself, "How can I make each day better for myself—and for others?"

One way you proceed is to appreciate and cherish life—not just acquiesce or merely accept. That is, hold dear, treat the gift of time with respect and anticipation. Regard the hours as extremely valuable for your productive purposes.

With that approach, you will recognize "the grave beauty of what lives and dies"—instead of complaining, as so many do, that what is beautiful and alive now will soon be dead. What a waste that depressing viewpoint is. The person who focuses on dreariness and the eventual death of all living things and moments is living half-dead, is missing out on *the beauty that lives*.

A courageous actress, Nancy Walker, beset in her career

by many downs as well as ups, finally attained firm stability. Asked how she had endured the stresses, she said that in spite of all the pain and defeat during her struggles, she realized that "every moment that I lived got me to this moment. . . . I believe tremendously in the energies of life. To me, the world is a miracle."

In spite of everything depressing that has been besetting you, as happens to everyone recurrently, is the world "a miracle" for you? It can be. You have company in your effort. You are not alone. Millions visible and unseen about you are enduring tribulations. You can decide to be a determined survivor and more, as many have done.

Shakespeare wrote of a character filled with hope: "The sun shall not be up so soon as I try the fair adventure of tomorrow." You can train yourself to acquire and sustain a sense of anticipation so intense and fortifying that you can hardly wait for day to begin so that you may exert your wakeful efforts to enjoy that day, each day, most fully. You will awaken with a thrilling sense of expectation for "the fair adventure" of today and tomorrow. . . .

At that point, and from then on, you will possess and experience and profit from *conscious happiness*.

Some people who are imbued with it now murmur, "It was right there available for me all the time. But nobody ever told me. Nobody ever pointed it out and showed me the way." Now you can be started on your way, but *you* must take the first step in the journey. The longest or shortest trip cannot be begun without that first step . . . then another and another until you reach your rewarding destination.

Conscious happiness basically must be firmly founded and then emanate from *within yourself*. In addition, it derives from your contacts with others and reflects its benefits on them—along with the great bonuses for yourself. You must consciously want and seek and strive for it, developing attitudes and abilities which result in the at-

41

tainment of it. That inner realization and its resultant actions form the keystone.

There is a rather common but nonetheless significant statement: "Today is the first day of the rest of your life." Cellist Pablo Casals said at age ninety-three: "Each day I am reborn. Each day I must begin again as a rediscovery of the world of which I have the joy to be a part." What will this day be for you? Discovery? Rediscovery? What will you make of this day?

Finding the ways to conscious happiness can help you make the most of today and tomorrow, and all the days and years ahead. You want to—or you wouldn't be reading this book. "The beginning is half the whole." It is vital to look forward always, not focusing on the end but on your new beginning.

This can be your beginning. . . .

* * *

High Points to Recheck:

1. *Remind yourself daily to "live the glorious life that is within you."*
2. *Realize that being happy stems from your personal decision and volition—nobody else's.*
3. *Make it a prime, everyday priority to attain and practice conscious happiness.*
4. *Think it over: Are you really, actively living up to your full potential for the greatest enjoyment of each day?*
5. *Recognize all the clues to gaining even the slightest happiness from every day.*
6. *Look forward consciously, eagerly to "the fair adventure of tomorrow."*

5

Gaining New Awareness

CURIOSITY IS THE food of the mind. By being aware, curious, by probing and investigating your mind—which is you—you can enjoy the most satisfying feasts of living. The banquet is all laid out before you each day. If you care enough, you will partake of the offerings, and feed your mind and body well. If you don't even bother to look at and consider the possibilities, visible and invisible, you are the loser.

"To be alive is a fine thing," Edna Ferber wrote. "It is the finest thing in the world, though hazardous. It is a unique thing. It happens only once in a lifetime. To be alive, to know consciously that you are alive, and to relish that knowledge—this is a kind of magic. . . .

"Millions of people never once in their lifetime reflect on the stupendous fact that they are alive. They merely live. They walk talk work play love hate and die a little daily without marveling at these fascinating processes."

Unlike those who enjoy "this kind of magic" which I call conscious happiness, the unknowing, unfeeling people are missing out on the greatest joys of living—being alive and experiencing it.

In which category do you place yourself? If among "the unfeeling," shouldn't you switch to achieving conscious happiness—*immediately?*

A historian commented about Franklin D. Roosevelt that he was "alive—and keen about everything"—and that this eagerness was a key quality in carrying him through even the most troublesome of times and events. "His character *resonated* with the surge and flow of human experience," and he never veered from the conviction that "life is meant to be lived to the utmost."

Certainly the same curiosity that killed a cat can get you into trouble if you use unsound judgment or don't exert reasonable caution. But there's a vast difference between searching into matters with careful discernment and jumping off the deep end at every whim. It can be just as harmful to be overly cautious: "Prudence keeps life safe, but does not often make it happy."

Too few people, perhaps not you at this point, have a renewing interest and exultation in each day's living. Alertness, awareness, excitement, appreciation—all are really the savory meat and drink of living, as those who possess the questing spirit know.

A twenty-year-old college student, Karen Cornell, searching for her most fulfilling way of life, cried out, "I know I am young with high aspirations and values, but don't tell me to compromise. I've got to fight this internal battle through. If one doesn't approach life wide-eyed and with great expectations, then what is there to live for?" Much is left—but with too passive an approach, too much can be missed.

An alert curiosity is one of the things that keeps an individual ageless. A world-famous cosmetician, Pablo Manzoni, affirmed this to me: "Feeling alive, alert and interested—and reflecting it; that's one of the most valuable 'beauty secrets' you can ever possess."

In a luncheon interview with Bette Davis, it was reported: "She attacked her salad as if she had just discovered food, then demanded that the waitress come back. 'Get me the recipe for this marvelous salad,' she said, and then switched to other subjects. 'The trouble these days is, there is no enthusiasm any more. It's a bore to watch people pretend to be bored. Why do they bother? Whatever I do, I do with all my heart.'"

In the same vein, Laurence Olivier advised: "Keep your bloody eyes open, all your senses open. You never know what might be useful . . . discovering things, what is there more important to do in the world?" Look about you. Myriads of things are happening, good things as well as bad. It becomes obvious that if you permit yourself to be bored, you simply are not paying attention.

An alert, eager mind is an open mind, always seeking, not prejudging. Dave Garroway noted: "Approaching reality with an open mind, attempting to see it in its pure form—this, to me, is truly the Art of Observation. . . . With an open mind and the willingness to accept reality, it would be possible to live every day as though it were a lifetime, which in a way it is. . . . Growth represents learning, learning represents awareness—and awareness is life." And the more aware you are, the more alive you are, the more you get out of life.

It's so easy to widen your horizons. A couple, the Waltons, purchased an old house on the shore of a lovely lake. They complained for years that the view from the living room was restricted because the window was so narrow. "Open it up," a friend urged, "it's as simple as replacing that slit with a big picture window." When they did, it revealed the glorious vista of trees and water and reflected sky, lifting their spirits each day.

The Waltons wondered, "Why didn't we do it before, why didn't we widen our view?" Similarly, is your outlook on life narrow and circumscribed? If so, why wait to open your mind with a new picture window that will enable and spur you to see more and participate more, as never before? It's much easier than breaking through the wall of a house—and even more gratifying.

Opening your mind right from the moment of waking up each day helps you to look at that day as new and untouched. You are the first to *touch* your day—"whose golden touch could soften steel and stones." You can make it a rewarding habit to approach the hours with the realization that it is your personal responsibility to try to make the day a pleasant rather than a trying experience.

With diligent awareness of all the good things, the little as well as big things, as you touch each hour, you are likely to sustain conscious happiness that day and every day. *Touching* this way—fully alive, awake and alert to the potential of every minute—is a first step to grasping the utmost day after constantly improving day.

"Every Day Is a New Beginning; Every Morn Is a Man Made New"

Would it take some kind of disaster to prove to you the inestimable value of increasing your awareness of all wonders available to you? Too often this rewarding sense of wide-open participation in living comes only after a person has faced death through severe sickness or smash-up.

A grim young man, Bob D., maintained a somewhat common attitude of acting uninterested in anything, even dispirited. He explained when asked, "I don't see much sense in living." Driving recklessly at top speed on his motorcycle, he suffered a horrible accident. After weeks of touch-and-go, and more than a year of mending and re-cuperation, Bob told a former buddy, "Each morning now when I wake up, I open my eyes, stretch my body and tell myself joyfully, 'Thank God, I'm alive!' "

Why should it take a crisis like this to convince many individuals to be grateful for being alive, to become aware of and enthusiastic about that simple fact? Furthermore, even with many such almost-victims, the euphoria doesn't last. Unless one achieves the recognition and acceptance of conscious happiness as an *enduring* way of living most fully, he might slide right back into the same old grimy, unsatisfying groove. "None so blind as those who will not see."

It's easy to feel alive and discover the riches in each day if you seek them, if you try. Remember that the cost of this great, repeated reward is little or nothing in dollars. The price of admittance is mostly in three words: *openness to experience*. It's as simple as looking around you. Something new is always happening. New challenges. New prospects. Only if you are willing to see them can you make the most of them for yourself and for others. Instead of *beware*, you accept the challenge to *be aware*.

Please try this exercise in being fully alive, alert, awake, all your senses open, receptive, and functioning at top power:

Look—as though your eyesight might dim at any minute . . .

Listen—as if your ears would fail at any time and close out all sounds, a beloved one's voice, a bird's song, music . . .

Touch—with the fierce possibility that at any instant you could lose the ability to feel . . .

Employ all your senses avidly as though they might perhaps desert you in the oncoming split second. How *alive* you are now, utilizing your senses fully! You can hold on to and foster that ecstatic gain always—if you will.

Being fully alive is like opening a door to a wonderful new house. As you proceed, the expectation and the rewards increase. You press on, opening doors to inviting, revealing rooms, each one providing a glorious added prospect. As you step over each threshold, you experience new insights, new thrills of discovery. You are experiencing to the utmost the enjoyment of "the adventure of the human mind" and imagination.

One brilliant morning I was having my breakfast coffee in the backyard as I read an absorbing book. Hearing a sharp clang, I glanced around to see the garbage collector going about his work—a short, stocky fellow with cigar jutting jauntily between his lips. I called out a greeting. He looked up while handling the messy refuse. He grinned and said, "Man, this is the kind of day that it's great to be alive!"

Doesn't it pay to stop feeling gloomy, worrying and complaining—long enough to enjoy what you now have? Then the more you gain, the more you'll relish and revel in what you have.

A little-educated but brilliant woman I'd never met in person became a friend through long correspondence when she wrote to me about one of my books. She had attained conscious happiness, primarily through her own living experience. In one letter, at year's end, Mercedes Boyle stated:

"I'm so glad that you feel you've gained something from my commonplace comments, and weren't bored. Doggonit, I react emotionally to people and things that affect me. Then I'm often haunted that I've permitted myself to become too excited about something that may be small or foolish. It's like getting more out of life than I dare to believe . . .

"However, I'm getting over that, I'm letting myself swing, and enjoying it tremendously. I rationalize and console myself that if I didn't become happily emotional and excited, I wouldn't absorb stimulating colors, sights, sounds, and experience sensations that delight me. I'm afraid that I'm trying to round out the old year by grasping it and squeezing it to death instead of letting it slip quietly away because I shall never have it again. . . .

"I find each day too short for all the thoughts I want to think . . . all the walks I want to take . . . all the books I want to read . . . all the friends I want to see. The longer I live, and more than ever now at eighty, the more my mind dwells upon the beauty and wonders of the world. I don't want to let the old year go. . . .

"Then I lift up as I look forward to the new year. I'm filled with the hope that I'll always have with me the power of a dream, the anticipation of today and tomorrow. And I know that I'll exert all my personal power to give my family and friends pleasure—and to help make all our dreams come true."

It's always there to energize you: *the power of a dream.* Today, tomorrow, from now on.

The Fervor of Participating

A character in a novel cried out to the heavens: "But I am human, a warm being that feels pain, that sings, that dies." And lives, dares to live the glorious life that is within. Seek, search, make choices. Discover other enthusiastic people, catching, sharing, and spreading the fervor of participating.

It isn't necessarily the big things that delight you deeply. J. B. Priestly urged attention to "the minor pleasures of life. . . . Enjoy golden moments brought by little things—delight in city streets—the smell of roasting coffee—the sight of a noble fish outside a fish-monger's shop, reminding me of all the oceans of the world—a child laughing—a piano playing in a strange house—the smell after a

49

shower. How one of these things can light up and change a whole day!" And lift one for a lifetime: anyone, *you*.

You may have heard it said one way or another that life is a cup which is handed to you. What you do with it governs the worth of that cupful. You can spill it and waste it all, and so it has little or no value for you. Or you can drink it slowly, appreciatively, savoring each swallow, enjoying it totally for the priceless gift it is. The cupful can become a miracle—but not if you are indifferent to its worth.

Art critic John Canaday, assessing the work of Grandma Moses after she died at age 101, concluded that she was not a very great artist according to the standards of excellence through the centuries. But he noted that she had a very special talent: "Her magic was that she knew how magical it was to be alive, and in her painted records of her life she managed to relay some of the magic to the rest of us. . . .

"She was a human being who painted directly from a life that she relived from day to day. If she plunged no esoteric depth, she warmly reflected some of the simplest and most ordinary and hence most magical aspects of the experience upon which all of us must rise or fall, the experience of meeting the world on the terms it presents to us." Do you know how magical it is to be alive, to participate, conveying the sense of the magic to others by your presence?

An appreciative sculptor, Louise Nevelson, said about Picasso on his ninetieth birthday: "You feel that he gives birth to himself every day. There's nothing stale. Through his creativity he doesn't touch old age." How rewarding it is to greet each day as though you were giving birth to yourself anew.

A life of *non*involvement, of staying completely out of activities and action and participation, is certainly wasted. It can't compare in personal rewards with trying. Even if you fail at times, many times, at least something happened, moved you, proved that you are alive and living and striving, not just surviving.

Do You Stop and LOOK Consciously?

Next time you are walking outdoors, please stop where you are, where you walk—*stop*. Concentrate your senses consciously—let the sights and sounds and smells play over your emotions like a vibrating bow on the strings of a cello.

Stop—as I did one morning amidst the buildings in the crowded midtown streets of New York City. I had walked past these buildings hundreds of times on the way from train to office. I had walked past, almost unheeding.

But this morning, I told myself, "Stop. Look around as though you are a visitor from a foreign land, come to see for the first time what there is to see here." I looked—almost straight up into the sky as my eyes climbed the towering sides of the building directly before me. Then I turned slowly, looking ahead and up, enjoying impressive, majestic sights I'd scarcely noticed before.

Within the circle of my slowly-turning gaze, I saw a magnificent jumble of shapes, squat buildings, tall towers, the strong, ragged skeleton of a new gigantic structure under construction. I drew in a breath deeply as my emotions were aroused by the overwhelming sight. I walked on with a springier step, my mind churning with renewed interest and awakening. I had consciously seen and experienced a glory within and all about me, something I'd bypassed unconsciously so many wasted times.

I was reminded of a day over a score of years before when I lived for a time in the tiny village of Grottoes in the mountains of northwestern Virginia. As I had done each day for months, I walked across fields at dawn toward

51

a small textile mill in a tiny village where I worked. Usually I moved mechanically across this stretch of land, still half-asleep. But somehow this morning an especially exquisite bird call, or some other exceptional sound, brought me to vivid consciousness.

I stopped in the tall, damp grass to look for the bird. I gazed up, wide-eyed now, into a majestic tree, then slowly turned, fully aware of nature's glorious sights and sounds . . .

All around me, the lofty Blue Ridge Mountains stretched and rolled, graceful and somehow thundering against the white-blue, then dawn-pink sky. I breathed more deeply of the sweet, clean, cold morning mountain air. My emotions sang with the music of the birds, as never before.

Yet I had passed this way so many times and noticed little, walking through almost wholly unaware of the thrilling beauty always there to fill one's eyes. I'd fallen far short of William Blake's assertion: "To see a world in a grain of sand, and a heaven in a wild flower."

Now again, years later, in the city as then in the country, I became aware of the extra dimensions of emotional and sensual enjoyment open to me, to everyone, to you. And to savor them, all you need do is to stop and look—*consciously*. I determined never to forget the ready, constant availability of such enormous pleasures again.

The extras are occurring all about you, for those who observe, who care. A wide-eyed friend, a normally very quiet lady, Marilyn Smith, told me this story:

"Riding into the city on an early train a few days ago, we stopped at a station. From my window seat facing east, I looked at the giant bridge crossing the parallel river just a block away. At that instant, the sun—a giant orange-red, flaming ball—pushed through the murky haze and was framed as in a painting right in the center of the four-square construction of the bridge. I quivered, my emotions soaring from the beautiful sight. . . ."

She laughed. "I couldn't contain myself. I turned to the tall, heavy woman next to me and said, pointing, 'Look at that glorious picture!' She glanced up from the magazine she was reading, then shrugged with a 'so what' expression, and turned back to her magazine. I felt like some kind of a nut, and was uncomfortable for the rest of the trip."

She flushed, and continued, "Going up the elevator of my office building, I met a man from my firm who often took the same train. I couldn't resist asking whether he'd seen the glowing winter sunrise. Tom said that he hadn't noticed. Silently we left the elevator together. I squirmed with embarrassment, thought that I'd better keep my big mouth shut from then on. . . .

"But the next day Tom popped into my office, his face aglow. He erupted enthusiastically, 'Hey, coming in on the train this morning, I made it a point to watch the sun rise. Brother, what a thrill! Thanks for tipping me off.'" She grinned. "Imagine, he shared my enjoyment. That gave me a thrill too."

To See or Not to See

Marion B., a woman imbued with conscious happiness, related: "A business associate of my husband's visited us one Sunday afternoon. I'd never met Ted although he and his family had moved to our suburb about a year ago. As I showed him around our gardens, I asked whether he had much interest in nature. He said hesitantly, 'Well, I guess I haven't had much time to pay attention. But I'd like to know more.'"

She went on, "I'm excited about every flower and bush

and tree, as you know, so my enthusiasm took over. As we walked, I pointed out different varieties, then paused and gestured, 'That's my favorite, that glorious copper beech tree. See how the gray twisted trunk is wrinkled like elephant skin. The leaves turn red and green and copper and gold with the changing seasons. At the slightest breeze, they dance and kind of tinkle like little bells. . . .'

"My companion reacted, 'Wow, what a rare tree! I've never seen one like that. It's sensational. You're to be envied.' He left a little later. Shortly after, the phone rang. Ted's voice came through excitedly, 'Hey, Marion, I've just walked around our place, and guess what—we have a copper beech tree! Not as big as yours, but it's beautiful, exquisite. I just never bothered to notice it before. . . .' "

The world is filled with copper beeches and other wonders. But they exist only if you bother to notice them. They thrill you only if you are aware and think about and care about them.

In instructing writers, John MacDonald urged: "You must go through the world at all times looking at the things about you. Texture, shape, style, color, pattern, movement. . . . There are people who have eyes and cannot see. I have driven friends through country they have never seen before and have had them pay only cursory attention to the look of the world. Trees are trees, houses are houses, hills are hills—to them."

Similarly I have noted this sad phenomenon (sad for the individuals themselves) in our home which has huge windows facing the sea. Some visitors enter, glance out, and murmur, "Oh, there's the water." Then they turn their backs on the scene, and start chattering.

Compare that blank attitude with the reaction of a truckman who delivered a package and exclaimed, "Wow, look at those waves, that blue sky—hey, see those gulls swooping—wow!" Leaving, he turned for a last lingering look and said, "That's a beautiful sight, makes me feel good I saw it—I'll never forget it."

A best-seller novelist who wrote primarily about city life moved to a beautiful country area. Within a year he came back to a towering apartment house. "I couldn't stand the miserable country," he explained in a lecture hall, "because there was nothing to see but trees. And once you've seen a tree, you've seen them all." My companion murmured, "How sad for him."

What's your attitude? "Oh, there's the water" . . . or . . . "Wow!" The "wow" approach makes all the difference between getting little or nothing out of what you see and gaining huge enjoyment and the exciting, constantly recurring emotional lift of being fully alive, involved, and appreciative.

One person can see a gorgeous garden, and to her it's nothing but stuff growing from the earth. Another, an enthusiastic gardener, bent down, plucked one green blade, and held it up: "Look," he exclaimed, "how beautiful— a single blade of grass emerging from the soil is a miracle." Miracles are where you look for them and recognize them. But if you don't look, you'll never find them. If you let a day pass without that alert search and recognition, you are the loser. How sad for you.

Make a Little List

Here's a little game you may find helpful: At the end of a typical day, just before bedtime, take a pad and pen, and think over what happened during the day. Consider what you saw, what you did, where you went, from your first waking moment. Then start writing down all the possibilities that occurred for helping you to feel good.

Was the sunrise or even the morning scene outside your

window, whatever it was, especially bright, pretty, interesting?

Was breakfast, or lunch, or any meal particularly tasty or appealing or fun?

Did you run into someone, or speak to anyone on the phone or in person who was very pleasant, forthcoming, stimulating?

Did you accomplish something special, no matter how small?

Go on and on with your list, regardless of how tiny or insignificant any detail might seem. You will find invariably, however commonplace the day may have appeared, that things happened from which you could have gained a sense of joy—of conscious happiness. And if you didn't, as many people don't, it was because you weren't fully aware and alive to the occurrences and the possibilities. Why not?

Will you try to notice and make the most of the little things from now on—as they happen?

There is so much going on which you can perceive and absorb with one or more of your senses to bring you added delight. A simple, scientific experiment has proved repeatedly that people are not aware consciously of much of what exists about them. Compared with what is noted by the subconscious or unconscious mind, the difference is stunning.

In a common test, the subject is taken into a room and left there without any instructions other than that she will be called for an interview in a few minutes. Within about five minutes she is brought to another room. There she is asked to write down on a pad, as quickly as possible, a list of objects that she recollects having seen in the first room while waiting. She might list about twenty items within a few minutes.

She is then hypnotized by a qualified professional. Under hypnosis, she is given pen and pad again, and asked to make a similar list of objects seen in the first room. This time, while hypnotized, with her unconscious mind released freely, she would probably list as many as two hundred or more items as compared with the previous listing of only twenty or so.

The point is that the person who is fully aware and alive consciously of the most that is going on about her, will gain a larger "listing" from every waking moment. Such alertness leads you to increased appreciation of sights, sounds, smells, and impressions of all types. It's a kind of galvanized dreaming with your eyes open. That expansion multiplies your enjoyment and fortifies your always expanding sense of conscious happiness.

How Enthusiasm Sparks Enjoyment

"Nothing great was ever achieved without enthusiasm," Emerson asserted. That doesn't refer to shrieking, screaming, mindless frenzy. Nor does it embody rash or wild enthusiasm which may distort sound judgment. *Productive enthusiasm* arises from being alive, aware. It means developing a spirited outlook tempered by insight and thought, to foster living joyously and energetically.

There is no gain in pretending to appear blasé, surfeited, above-it-all. If you don't *care* about what is going on around you, then others are likely to find you tiresome. On the other hand, when you exude a zest for what is happening, and help make it happen, others are attracted to you. More important, enthusiasm feeds upon itself and reenergizes your spirit.

Feeling life, enjoying life, and showing it—that alone enriches you and radiates to those about you, inciting comments such as: "It's a joy to be with her." Genuine, appealing enthusiasm is the product of sincerity, not of artificiality or phoniness. A part of every great theatrical star through the centuries has been a perceptible air of inner interest and enthusiasm which is often called *charisma*.

This can't be affixed superficially like putting on a false face. You can develop and reflect it by nurturing a wholehearted zest for living and enjoying each moment—revealing your ever-present sense of conscious happiness. You feel it. You believe it. You live it. You show it. You speak it.

Essayist Eric Bentley wrote: "If I use enthusiastic language, it is because I really feel the enthusiasm, not that I wish to sell anything to anyone." No, you don't try to impress anyone with your enthusiasm. You develop and practice it openly primarily for your inner reward. Feeling it and enjoying it is extraordinary compensation in itself. It can make a decisive distinction between just existing indifferently or living joyously.

When does one benefit most from developing and using the quality of enthusiasm? Right now, today, tomorrow, whatever age you are. Greeting and employing each day with zest instead of apathy becomes a habit that strengthens and enlivens you for at least some part of every day thereafter. It's a habit worth building from this moment on. An enthusiastic, interested person is inevitably a more interesting individual.

As a university professor, I asked a brilliant student what motivated her. Judy W. explained, "It's easy for me because I get interested in almost anything. On any assignment, I dig in enthusiastically because I want to find out everything I can about the subject. My main drive is not to get a good grade but to add to my fund of information, to handle the challenge, to solve the puzzle."

Clearly what makes this young woman an effective and interesting person is that she's interested in people, places, problems, in just about everything. One of her class assignments was to write a ten-page report on China. She dug in, became so involved that she wrote eighty pages, explaining, "It's such a fascinating project—I didn't begin to scratch the surface of the possibilities." Most others in the class barely reached the ten-page total, many complaining, "The subject is so dull."

Who gained most? The same applies to so many things you encounter each day. Whether you find them exciting or drab depends greatly on your approach and viewpoint: "fascinating" or "dull"? Choosing the latter attitude results in living only halfway—or less. You can enjoy a perpetual high without drugs *by getting high on life*.

Bored? Two Kinds of People

A friend who was concerned that so many people don't seem to be fully alive or are frequently bored concluded that the world is divided into two kinds of people: those who *feel*, and those who don't. Archibald MacLeish emphasized: "To feel emotion is at least to feel. The crime against life, the worst of all crimes, is *not* to feel." Experiencing boredom is a crime against yourself.

Others have suggested that the two classes of people are those who are *for* things, and those who are *against*. Being *against* is self-defeating; being *for* is nourishing. You will note invariably that an individual becomes more interested in you when you are interested in him or her. If your attitude is negative or apathetic, you are depriving yourself. Voltaire asserted that "the spectator forgives everything except dreariness."

A bitter, deeply unhappy woman admitted, "I hear nothings, I speak nothings, I take interest in nothing, and from nothing to nothing I travel gently down the dull way which leads to becoming nothing." Even though grammatically two negatives may make an affirmative, a string of nothings ends up only in more nothingness.

The opposite attitude, the anti-boredom, conscious happiness way, results from interest in practically everyone and everything. If you don't reach out to enjoy other people and what they have to offer, it's your misfortune. Being awake to the possibilities, reaching out and touching, you inevitably amass gains.

Consider whether boredom isn't your own fault, usually for being so absorbed with yourself and your own problems, real or imaginary, that you have no interest in others. Think about this: A bore was defined by Ambrose Bierce as "a person who talks when you wish him to listen"—while you talk to him only about what concerns you personally.

An alert, successful man explained that one reason he was interested in people was, "I simply won't allow myself to be bored. If I find that someone appears very dull to me, I ask myself why, what is lacking in that individual or in me that results in this sense of ennui? Then I get so immersed in finding out why I am bored that I'm no longer bored at all."

Isn't that little gambit worth trying next time you're feeling bogged down by someone? The fault might simply be lack of enough interest on your part. Soon after you start probing acutely, you might uncover an interesting personality—or at least enjoy a stimulating period, attempting discovery.

There is something shameful about anyone allowing herself to be bored and thus letting a segment of time drift away listlessly. Actor Robert Ryan noted that after he learned he had an inoperable cancer he became fully alive—"Now that I know I'm on borrowed time . . . I have a whole different feeling about what are the good things. I see trees and flowers and pretty girls. I see beauty that I used to be oblivious to. I see things with a much fresher eye. And actually, life is much better enjoying it day to day."

I met Ryan not long before he died, at a dinner party. I found him to be one of the seemingly happiest and certainly one of the most aware and interested human beings I've ever encountered. Everything and everybody caught his attention. Nothing and nobody bored him. A sense of smiling radiated from his face. His eyes twinkled. He was *alive*. People gravitated to him.

How terrible it would be if any one of us had to be sentenced to death before we would be awakened fully and not permit boredom to take over even for an instant. There certainly are better formulas against detachment and indifference. One is to fight against them actively, consciously, by looking at people and things with wide-awake interest instead of apathy.

Turn it around, battle against lethargy and for exultation. A psychology professor said he was on his way to lecture a class on the subject of "boredom." An associate suggested, "Why don't you reverse it—and talk to them instead about 'elation'?"

Jack London wrote: "I would rather be ashes than dust. I would rather that my spark would burn out in a brilliant blaze than be stifled by dry rot. . . . The constant function of man is to live, not to exist." If you feel bored, blame yourself—and act to change it by determining to feel alive. Then you can't help but to be alive and love it.

How to Stay "Happy as a Child"

"Why can't I be happy as a child," a woman sighed as she watched her spirited youngster. "Where has all my laughter gone?" Nobody is born bored. Babies seem born to be happy. Not long after coming into this world they start smiling, gurgling, giggling. This would seem to be the natural state of living, a state of joy.

Some children retain this condition, this radiant feeling,

and reflect it into their teen years, and sometimes—as I urge here—into the adult years right to the end of life. Sadly, many, perhaps most, individuals lose the sense of wonder and elation early.

Why can't this state of anticipation and delight continue "forever" for all of us? "It's impossible," most people reply. "The blows of living hammer us down, sadden us, deaden us. Losing the natural sense of happiness of the very early years is inevitable, utterly unavoidable."

Obviously for too many individuals this observation is correct. But there is much you *can* do to prevent the sadness and deadness from setting in—by striving consciously each day to be aware, reaching, looking, seeing. To the very young, this pervading feeling of happiness comes naturally, is as much a part of living as breathing. But growing older, enduring disappointments, surrounded by listless or dejected people, you must work at it in order to retain or recapture an optimistic, eager viewpoint.

A youthful grandmother, my wife Natalie, told how our grandson, four-year-old Mike, lived at our home for two weeks while his mother and father were vacationing. They were returning on Monday. The day before, late Sunday afternoon, she visited some friends with Mike— the Hausers. The hostess' brother and parents arrived for a visit. They came in tired and dispirited, and sagged into chairs with a collective sigh.

Mike greeted them merrily. He chattered with them, grinned continually. He burst into song spontaneously several times while enlisting their help in putting together a child's jigsaw puzzle. Upon leaving a couple of hours later, he hugged and kissed them enthusiastically. They followed him and waved at him merrily, laughing at the faces he made back at them as they crowded the doorway.

A few days later, Natalie received a letter from the hostess' mother, Elsie Nordlinger, stating in part: "I had to tell you how enchanting we all found Mike to be. And

I want to send you my most sincere sympathy that you had to return him to his parents. I had been in bad humor over minor trifles. Mike changed all that. Since the visit I've found myself bubbling and smiling at unexpected moments as his bright radiance sweeps over me in recollection. If only I could always feel like that and never let everyday burdens, including relatively unimportant ones, overwhelm me and get me down. . . . "

It's not possible for most grownups or even adolescents to "always feel like that." But this one thing everyone, you, can do: *you can try*. And, surprisingly often, it's effective —so much so that feeling alive, expectant, appreciative of what you possess that is good, becomes a habit.

Author Santha Rama Rau wrote: "My young son picked up what looked to me like a pebble and, spellbound with wonder, stood gazing at it. I peered over his shoulder to see what could absorb him so profoundly. By way of explanation, he said, 'Look! It's so *white*.' It occurred to me then that, as our complicated civilization claims us, we lose that sense of discovery and amazement with which children see the most everyday things. We lose the capacity to enjoy what is known as 'the simple pleasures.'"

You need not lose that capacity if you *will* not, if you resolve to "use your common senses" from now on—and then follow through without letup. The joy that was in you at birth—grab it, hold it, use it. Recapture and strengthen the bursting gaiety you enjoyed as a very young child, even though you may not remember it. This sense of ever-present quiet delight becomes always greater as you achieve and practice conscious happiness.

Physical as Well as Emotional Well-Being

"Today I have grown taller from walking with the trees." There is no question, having experienced and noted the proof repeatedly, that being physically lively and exercised—as much as possible within your personal limitations—is an enormous asset. It helps you to maintain the essence of being mentally alert and successful as you practice conscious happiness. Even Diogenes observed: "By constant exercise one develops freedom of movement—for virtuous deeds."

By exercising, I don't mean becoming a muscle man or an Amazon. There are many good forms of easy exercising to tone your body and mind. You begin by respecting and making the best use of your physique—if only by straightening up, sitting, standing, and walking "tall." A slumping body tends to induce a slumping mind, and vice versa.

Psychiatrists have pointed out that the difference between getting a mental patient to sit straight instead of slumped is only a few inches—but it can make a world of difference in one's mental attitude. If the individual accomplishes that little difference, he or she has made an important advance. The same benefit of straightening up is true for everyone.

Please try it right now as you sit: Head erect . . . chin up at right angles to your neck . . . shoulders back . . . chest lifted forward and upward . . . diaphragm pulled in (abdomIN!) . . . spine straightened. Now you are sitting tall—physically, emotionally, and mentally you tend to "grow taller." The same happens when you stand and walk erectly and energetically, consciously using your lengthened body and enjoying the sense of vigorous movement.

Shakespeare wrote about "the rich advantage of good exercise." And he provided a helpful, healthful tip in stressing, " 'Tis the breathing time of day." Every minute provides a better "breathing time" when you breathe deeply, consciously, aware of specific benefits.

Here's a quick, helpful little exercise: Sitting or standing tall, breathe in deeply through your slightly open mouth to a slow count of five . . . then exhale vigorously through your nose. Repeat this slow, measured breathing five or ten times. Go through this routine many times during the day and evening. (Even better—raise your arms as you breathe in; drop your arms quickly as you exhale.) You'll expand your lungs, improve your breathing and calorie-burning efficiency, and you'll feel brighter and better. So easy, yet so valuable.

Do you really use your body and free your mind by *walking enough* (unless you are incapacitated, of course)? An observer noted that "walking is a form of touching, and being touched, through the whole body. Walking is like making love to the landscape and letting it love you back. Walking is a feeling of well-being . . . our best thoughts come to us when walking."

And when you walk, you benefit most when you walk aware, alive, energetically. Feel the vigorous push in the ball of your foot against the ground or pavement, heel rising. Enjoy the springiness of forward motion, making every step count in boosting your zest in activity, spurring you to be physically and mentally alive.

Statesman Charles Yost commented: "There is more to be felt and learned about the world and oneself in half an hour's walk up a country hillside than in a flight around the earth at twice the speed of sound." That's true whether you walk in city, suburb, country, wherever you are. Author Jerome Weidman noted, "Gazing at passing faces as I walk down a single crowded city block, I see a dozen short story plots." Robert Frost quipped: "I have walked many miles with my dog. It has done me a lot of good. I hope it has my dog."

Move—as much as possible. Take the advice of Dr. Irwin M. Stillman who is slim, vigorous, seldom still at age seventy-nine: "Don't sit if you can stand. Don't stand if you can walk. Don't walk if you can run!" Dr. Irving J.

Kane, chest specialist, urges you to exert and profit from the "natural exercises that come with easy laughter, humming, singing, and whistling—they all help healthy lung function." Aristotle called laughter "a bodily exercise precious to health."

Move about. Look about. Use your body. There are many books and articles about exercising, readily available. Exercising equipment is always right at hand—the ground, pavement, stairs.

Your goal: *Mens sana in corpore sano*, a sound mind in a sound body—pursued daily to the utmost of your capacity. "Good health and good sense are two of life's greatest blessings." You don't just inherit them, you must work for them—*consciously*. And you will gain great and sustaining rewards—*actually*.

* * *

Poet *e. e. cummings* expressed the quality of "*aliveness*" vividly when he wrote of a woman he knew: "Her very presence emanated an honour and a glory: the honour of spiritual freedom . . . and the glory of being, not (like most extant mortals) really undead, but actually alive."

And after a visit to Paris some years ago, he enthused: "Everywhere I sensed a miraculous presence, not of mere children and women and men, but of living human beings; and the fact that I could scarcely understand their language seemed irrelevant, since the truth of our momentarily mutual aliveness created an imperishable communion."

Not just "momentarily mutual aliveness" but everpresent, enduring awareness and participation can be yours if you will practice these precepts as detailed in the preceding:

1. Learn to greet each morning as the beginning of

a new, challenging experience, to "give birth to yourself every day."

2. Exert this three-way exercise constantly: A. Look B. Listen C. Touch.

3. Keep reenergizing yourself with "the power of a dream."

4. Enjoy the fervor and revitalizing benefits of participation.

5. Take time to stop, perceive, and feel consciously.

6. Check yourself periodically with the "listing game."

7. Practice productive enthusiasm daily.

8. Develop a searching attitude so that you are never bored.

9. Recapture the uplift of childlike joy.

10. Keep active in body as well as in mind.

6

Appreciating and Strengthening Your Individuality

A CREED INSCRIBED on a green marble slab in Rockefeller Center begins: "I believe in the supreme worth of the individual and in his right to life, liberty, and the pursuit of happiness." Do you regard yourself highly enough and specifically as an *individual?* Do you believe in and find daily sustenance in your supreme worth? Affirmative answers are essential for your conscious happiness.

A scientist asserted: "Honor yourself as an individual. You are the survivor of millions of years of winnowing out, despite decimation by predatory animals, disease, disaster." An ancient philosopher, accepting his responsibility, stated: "He (God) hath entrusted me with myself." And it followed that he endeavored to make the most of that trust.

But . . . *do you really trust and honor yourself as an individual?*

Please consider the question and your answer thoughtfully, thoroughly. If your reply is a forceful affirmative, then undoubtedly others recognize your worth and honor your individuality. If negative, then it becomes vital and imperative that you expand your mind and spirit to build up, respect, and take pride in your individuality.

Your *sense of self*, your self-regard, may be the most important ingredient in enjoying conscious happiness. You must feel positively that you are not "people," you are a person, an individual, unique, different, totally *you*. No one except yourself can erase your personal identity, if you recognize and hold it firmly.

As you appreciate your individuality, you recognize and respect increasingly the individuality of others. It follows that if you esteem yourself, you are more likely to like or love yourself, and accept that "thou shalt love thy neighbor as thyself." But unless you rate yourself high, it is difficult to respect or like your neighbor or life itself.

Fundamentally you set the value that others place on you. If you underrate yourself, others are likely to do the same. If you mark yourself down, believing you are doomed to failure, then such a defeatist attitude practically makes failure inevitable. But if you feel and reflect confidence, that factor is a keystone in building your conscious happiness.

A dictionary defines *keystone* as "the central wedge-shaped stone of an arch that locks the others together." That's how important I consider one's self-realization and self-esteem to be in making the most of your totality for getting the greatest rewards from living for yourself and your loved ones, friends, acquaintances—for practically everybody with whom you come in contact.

You, like every other individual, are a complex person. But do you appreciate your intricate as well as intrinsic worth? It has been said that "the essence of tyranny is the denial of complexity." If you underrate yourself, then you tyrannize and demean yourself, and thereby cause others as well to regard you as less than you are.

This often results in self-inflicted depression and misery,

or at least in a lack of the uplifting elation with which you are entitled to live your days. There is a witticism that you should make one person happy each day—even if it's yourself. Why not yourself, as well as others?

Whatever you are, you are someone, an individual with special characteristics and abilities which you should honor —no matter how humble you may think you are. Edward Everett Hale recognized his individual worth in stating: "I am only one, but still I am one. I cannot do everything, but still I can do something." Such self-esteem is completely the opposite of the narcissism, the exaggerated self-love of the person who can only adore himself.

Of course you gain knowledge and benefits from others. But self-reliance, along with self-approval, grow from inside yourself, rooted solidly and soundly in your own strength and convictions. You must basically and ultimately count and rely on your independence, rather than dependence on someone else. Then you can enjoy life fully, imbued with your sustaining conscious happiness, no matter what severe external forces may press upon you.

I have learned through long experience and repeated proof that the self-respecting individual who won't be demeaned can't be demeaned. That person is always fortified by courage, pride, and an unswerving self-assurance that is supported by self-knowledge. And, such a one possesses admirable forbearance and regard for others which links with a lack of fear. That one can be you.

The Importance of Your Individuality

A valedictorian, our daughter Wendy, warned: "Everyone needs to develop his individuality and thus enrich his life. This is increasingly important in order to keep mechanical existence in a technological society from becoming more dominant than you as an individual in that society." As a corollary, seeking and accumulating stimulating knowledge helps to build your individuality, and to fortify inner respect for your worth. You honor yourself and cannot be submerged as just another unit in a mass.

You must realize the truth of this if you feel, as many do, that the individual has very little choice in a mechanized, computerized society keyed increasingly toward bigness. It has been stressed by many thoughtful leaders, as asserted by Chief Justice Warren, that "The greater our scientific and technological advances become, the more emphasis we must put on the importance of the individual."

Remember that even the largest mass of people or biggest business is composed of and motivated by *individuals*. As an advertising agency president at one stage of my career, I was asked by a reporter, "What is the chief ingredient in your company's success?" I answered without hesitation, "People—the effective individuals who work here. Without those individual abilities and efforts, no enterprise can succeed, regardless of its size."

"I Am an Individual. . . ."

A highly intelligent widow, Sandra F., was upset at the realization that her young adult son and daughter, both of whom had married and left home, were feeling sorry for her. They felt a sense of having abandoned her, leaving her alone and lonely. Pondering the problem, wanting them to realize that she was able to live pleasantly on her own, wishing to lift the heavy sense of responsibility from them, she wrote duplicate letters to them including these statements:

"When I was about to marry your Dad, he told me, 'Darling, you're a whole person, and I love you fully. But if you ever stop being an individual, we'll stop making it,

71

because we'll become bored with each other.' I've never forgotten that. I live with the consciousness of that admonition. Now, once and for all, I want you to realize this:

"Beyond being a mother and a wife, I am and always have been an *individual*. I have always believed that, fundamentally, if I am not myself, if I don't strive and honor and respect myself as an individual, then I am nothing. Nothing for myself. Nothing to and for those I love. I have always believed, and more strongly now than ever, that each woman, as well as man, must always appreciate and affirm her individuality. Please understand and respect that as my right and prerogative."

What happened when the young people received that letter? Sandra told me, "They were thrilled. Each called and said, 'Mom, you're terrific. You've freed us from an overwhelming burden of feeling responsible for you. We love you and respect you more than we knew possible—for your individuality, and your strength in being and liking yourself.' "

Robert Louis Stevenson put it this way: "To be what we are, and to become what we are capable of becoming, is the only end of life." No one else has fingerprints or lip prints exactly like yours. No one thinks precisely the way you do. There is no disputing that you are an individual, an entity. It's up to you to recognize and make the most of it—no one else can do it for you.

A historian noted that no matter how intricate a political system may be, it always comes down to human beings. Comparably, no matter what outside pressures and complications may beset you, the ultimate resolution depends on you, the individual. How you think, react, and act determine the result—and the amount of joy you derive from personal volition.

It pays to take the time to be yourself and to learn to

like yourself as an individual. It's a big step toward making you a more feeling, stronger, more effective person. Give attention to knowing yourself, not subjugating yourself to others. Think things through, consider, then decide from your depths of knowledge and deliberation to *be yourself*. That feeling is one of the greatest, most supportive, and most rewarding elements in living.

A minor politician recommended, "If you want to get along, go along." That isn't true of politics or for you or for anyone else. Those in government who have won enduring acclaim didn't just "go along." They created and carried through worthy individual initiatives. Weakness, falsity, going along—all result in a loss of self-esteem—and if you lose that, you lose everything.

Sakharov, the Soviet scientist who courageously protested repression in Russia, asserted: "You always need to make ideals true to yourself. You always have to be aware of them, even if there is no direct path to their realization. Were there no ideals, there would be no hope whatsoever. Then everything would be hopelessness, darkness—a blind alley."

A novel delineated what happened when a woman discovered her value as an individual: "She realized that her own pride of accomplishment was important . . . and for that she made no apology because the feeling, good, bad or indifferent was part of herself—and to no other person did she owe the fealty that she did to herself." Actor Michael Constantine tells of a proud woman who worked as a domestic and always demanded respect, asserting, "Nobody makes me feel inferior without my permission."

One thing certain: Nobody in the world is better qualified than you to be yourself. Picasso said, "Actually everything depends on oneself. It's the sun in the belly with a million rays." Centuries back, around 300 B.C., Antigonus wrote: "Wonders are many on earth, and the greatest of these is man." Honor yourself, for you are a "wonder," a human being, you have a sun in your belly. Never forget that individuality is an enormous and universal privilege—your privilege.

When you appreciate your individuality, you perceive more clearly the totality of life. According to John Gardner: "The cynic says, 'One man can't do anything.' I say, 'Only one man [or woman] can do anything.' One man, interacting creatively with others, can move the world.'" Cooperate with yourself, cooperate with others. It's readily possible when you know and are yourself. Only "neurotics are sure that no one understands them—and they wouldn't have it any other way."

Conductor Pablo Casals kept after his orchestra to play Bach "with honor." Consider that phrase in regard to your sense of self, your respect for yourself. *Do you regard and treat yourself and other individuals "with honor"?*

Knowing and feeling the certainty of your individuality can fill you with exultation. Comedian Godfrey Cambridge cheered, "I'm part [of it all], and want to feel the whole world is my kin. I just want to be a man. Life is a joy. I dig it." *Do you dig it?*

Finding the Right Balance

You tend to get into trouble if you overrate yourself—because then you fall short of goals, letting down yourself and others. But it's as bad to underrate yourself since you accomplish and gain far less than you are capable of—and you lose possibilities and self-esteem. Understanding and respecting yourself, and not expecting too much or too little of yourself—that's the gauge, the balance one should strive for constantly, realistically, neither conceitedly nor humbly.

Abe Lincoln assessed the measure of his efforts practically and unashamedly as a guide for you: "If the end brings me out all right, what is said against me won't amount to anything. If the end brings me out wrong, ten angels swearing I was right would make no difference."

"If I am not myself . . . then I am nothing." People of genius found their way to the studio of author and art patron Gertrude Stein in Paris. What was her secret? She explained to a friend: "I write to please myself. I write to please no one else in the world but myself, and so I please myself completely. And in doing that, I please a few others completely. I please them so completely that each one goes out the door and becomes my messenger. . . .

"What *you* try to do is to please everybody. And when you try to please everybody, you end up by pleasing nobody completely." It has been said that there are a thousand forms of mind. You cannot be or accommodate to all of them. Your prime responsibility and sustenance is simply and clearly to be yourself.

Assessing Yourself Accurately

Do you put yourself down, undeservedly? Excess humility can be a serious fault, getting in the way of your self-respect and happiness. Without sound self-esteem, there can be no sense of solid self-fulfillment. For years, as a young man, when I was complimented on my work or for accomplishments in other areas, I'd shrug it off, "It was nothing—anybody could do it."

Then I'd feel like a fool, a victim of self-deception, ashamed for myself. Because it wasn't "nothing," it was *something*. And I should have honored myself accordingly. I had worked, sweated, as few people would, and I produced. Finally I realized that it's much more honest and honorable to take merited credit for things well done. "Anybody" didn't do it—*I* did it—and you must credit yourself for accomplishing something worthy. *Do you?*

Modesty for the sake of proportion, understanding, and balance—*yes*. Humble for the sake of being subservient, resulting in being unappreciative of self—*no*. A short man had a poor opinion of himself because of his size; he was told by a wise friend, "It doesn't matter how short or tall you are. What counts is how big you are *inside your head.*"

Overrating yourself so that you set your sights too high can be equally self-damaging, as touched on earlier. You have to know—through honest self-assessment—what you can and cannot do. If you expect more of yourself than you are capable of, then you have erred in two ways: You have failed by reaching for more than you could handle. And you haven't achieved what you could have accomplished readily within your sizable capacities.

An illuminating example is the story about a small boy whose hands and knees were always covered with scrapes and bruises from falling down. As he picked himself up from the sidewalk for the umpteenth time, a neighbor asked, "Tommy, how do you manage to fall down so often?" The boy grinned, "It's easy. *I keep trying to run faster than I can run.*"

From my earliest recollection, as soon as I could hold a pencil, I knew that I wanted to be an author. I wrote and wrote more, more, more toward that end. As I matured, I decided that I would be a great novelist. Try as I did, over a period of years, I couldn't write a superb novel. I came to realize unwillingly that I didn't have that particular special ability.

Having assessed myself accurately, based on my experiences, I began to write nonfiction books because publishers asked me for them. The books were very successful, but still I felt a bit frustrated. Finally I concluded, "Don't overrate yourself. Face it, you can't be everything, you'll never be a Tolstoy, Faulkner, Hemingway. So be yourself. Concentrate on the books that fulfill your basic writing aim: to help people live happier, more rewarding lives." That self-recognition and acceptance both of my limitations and my real special abilities became an essential part of my achieving conscious happiness.

Rex Stout acknowledged similarly that he had to give up his dream of being a general novelist because he wasn't good enough at it. When he concentrated on his facility which made him a superior mystery novelist, he became a much happier man. The same applies to you, whatever your work or other pursuit. Greater enjoyment develops from being the most that you can be, but not demanding more than you are.

There is only disillusionment and despair in trying to convince yourself and others that you are something that you are not. Shakespeare stated it positively:

> This above all: to thine own self be true,
> And it must follow, as the night the day,
> Thou canst not then be false to any man.

A hard-working man who wasn't happy with his way of life examined his character and actions to determine whether the problem stemmed from his own faults or those of his environment. He discussed this with a friend, commenting, "I guess you can't fit a square peg into a round hole."

"That's true, I suppose," his friend nodded. "But you can always try to reshape the peg."

The thoughtful man considered this. "There's another approach," he said slowly. "I can try to reshape the hole."

There is rarely much satisfaction or benefit in trying to

fit yourself into an uncomfortable mold for the sake of conforming, settling on what is average or normal. A proud individual asserted, "I'm a fugitive from the law of averages." Remember the soldiers' definition of SNAFU: Situation Normal, All Fouled Up.

Assessing Yourself

How can you assess yourself accurately?

First, you realize that only you can divine your individuality truly, and that you must work toward that honestly and unwaveringly. How? A fine artist, but a greater teacher, Hans Hofmann, wrote a book, *Search for the Real.* His main premise was that the artist had to search out what was real in the subject for himself, and paint it accordingly, to produce his best work. No copying a "popular" style. No pretending. No overstating.

Similarly, as you look into yourself fairly, candidly— *search for the real.* Only you can find and know the real you.

When is the right time to search for what you are as an individual, to assess, to act?

The time is now, from this minute, and from now on. Albert Schweitzer said, "Truth has no special time of its own." But every minute, all of time, is the right time for your search and pursuit of the real. Schweitzer's philosophy, as he stated it, was "reverence for life." And he acknowledged, as each of us must, "I am a life." His beloved associate, Erica Anderson, said of him, as you must of yourself, that "he accepted life with all its possibilities" —*and made the most of it.*

The joys of self-discovery have been summed up this way: "Find out what is really important to you. Then sing your song. You will have something to sing about, and your whole heart will be in the singing."

Using the Externals

Are you comfortable with yourself? A big part of evaluating and respecting yourself, your abilities and resources, is to be at ease with yourself. You must be, and can be, to achieve and enjoy full conscious happiness. Then, no matter what external forces and circumstances may upset you, there is always yourself, your inner being, to turn to, and from which to gain sustaining solace and support.

The externals, the physical things around you, can be an ever-present, enduring mainstay. Noting and benefiting from your surroundings purposefully can be a tremendous help. Often it is at least a temporary, sometimes lasting solution for handling oppressive unease. These externals become yours personally, for your aid. All you have to do is be aware of them and put them to your self-serving use.

I have found it necessary through the years to find support again and again by fixing upon and enjoying whatever there is around me. When I lived in a tiny deep-country village as an adolescent, looking out the window at the hills in the distance lifted me when I felt low. Mountains and sky—seeing them, recognizing their beauty and absorbing their radiance—that saved me from a threatening sense of tragedy and despair due to being young, unsure, and wanting.

In my early twenties, I went to a big city to make my way toward business success—hopefully. Nothing came easily. I scarcely earned enough to get by. Many nights I sat in my small rented room, with only a couch, bureau, chair, and tiny sink as furnishings. But I managed to be at ease with myself instead of breaking apart due to poverty and loneliness.

How? I sought company in books borrowed from the library. I submerged myself in their pages, found fellowship there. And often I stood at the one narrow, grimy window in my room, studying the contours of the old red brick buildings across the street, looking sharply aloft at the rooftops, noting the shapes of crooked chimneys which soon seemed like friends.

After I made some headway and married, we moved to an old house in a crowded suburb. Burdened by the responsibilities of supporting a family and handling oppressive business problems, again I found relief within myself, using the externals. I gained comfort from working in our garden and, when indoors, gazing out often at the few shrubs, a cherry tree, clouds in the sky. Such simple, lovely sights settled me down so that I'd be at ease with myself, better able to comfort and care for my loved ones.

And now, with children grown, we've found a home on the sea, and the outside vastness of sky and water combining give me a sense of ease and elation within as never before. Each morning, before settling into work in my office at home, or after the day's efforts, I find at least a few minutes to sit by the picture window, listening to a favorite Bach or Mozart recording—heaven indeed . . .

To the rhythm of the music, I watch the flow of the waves of the sea, gulls drifting against the far sky in a moving ballet. Always the externals, whatever they may be, always there wherever you are, have supported me. Awareness of my surroundings, and whatever they offer, has fed my spirit, kept me at ease, and fortified the sense of conscious happiness that has sustained and uplifted me unfailingly.

You can use "the externals" in similar ways to help develop and expand the balm of self-knowledge and of being comfortable with yourself. The externals may be city life, country, woods, gardens, water. You need only want to look and feel—and then do it, and keep on doing it wherever you are at any time. This is a vital part of conscious happiness, yours for the taking, free for the using and enjoying daily and increasingly.

You can also exert your "internals," your inner will, courage and strength, to make yourself a happier and more effective individual. All kinds of miracles can happen, emotional and physical—not always, but sometimes— *when you exert enough volition.*

In an indicative instance, a young man suffered a form of sclerosis, a type of tissue disease which sapped the strength which had been his pride. He lost the use of his arms; his legs weakened drastically. He seemed doomed to live in an iron lung. One day he told his father, "I'm determined to regain the use of my arms and legs, to be healthy again—starting today." He exerted his dwindling strength day by day increasingly, with superhuman determination and application.

He started to improve after a while, bit by bit. Now, some time later, he is vigorous, healthy, living a normal life. His doctor was asked, "Would you call this a medical miracle?"

The physician shrugged, "There is simply no judging the power of psychological effect of personal will and volition. It doesn't occur often, but unpredictable 'miracles' do happen in a very few cases, bringing joy to the doctor as well as the patient." He smiled delightedly. "Whatever works, I'm for that!"

Responsibility for Your Individuality

A young man asserted: "The day I stopped blaming my parents for my condition and accepted responsibility for my own acts was the day I began to grow up." Each person benefits from recognizing and utilizing his or her individuality—and from accepting responsibility for the ensuing self-expression. If the accountability is not assumed, then "individuality" becomes just a word, an evasion, not something of real value and sustenance to that person. A wit stated, "Freedom of speech does not mean calling collect."

Winston Churchill's challenge applies to every human, to you: "Enter upon your inheritance, accept your responsibilities . . . do not be fobbed off with mere personal success or acceptance." When you make personal decisions, isn't it fair that you shoulder full personal obligation for the outcome, good or bad? According to Sartre, "We are responsible for what we are—that is the fact."

And you must face that fact in order to strengthen and sustain yourself. If you want to possess and maintain the vital personal reward in being yourself, you must also bear the responsibility for what you do, the results of how you conduct yourself. If you blame others for disastrous consequences of your own acts, you are not a whole individual but only an evasion—and true conscious happiness necessarily eludes you.

It is an easy way out, a convenience, to blame your own failings or lacks on other persons and events. But you will never really respect yourself as an admirable individual until you acknowledge that you are the originator and cause of your problems when that is the case. Brooding over your mistakes is destructive. Recognizing, accepting responsibility, and correcting errors is constructive, builds you up instead of tearing you down.

Conversely, you can and should take full credit (certainly within yourself, at least) for results and accomplishments due to your own acts. Too much modesty, which is false modesty, is self-disparagement. That, in turn, is self-corroding. It is your responsibility to recognize your worth as well as to bear failures deriving from your own actions. Emerson advised, "Make the most of yourself, for that is all there is of you."

However, if you further yourself at the expense of others, by unfair and unkind treatment of others, you demean yourself, and you can't hide it from yourself. That leads to unconscious *un*happiness which gnaws at you from within. Your own safety is threatened if you set fire to your neighbor's house. It is not only far more desirable and practical, but absolutely essential that as you build yourself up, you don't tear down another. That is your accountability for others, but primarily it is a responsibility for your own solid and lasting benefit.

Nicholas Johnson proposed as the basis for an ideal society that the greatest possible opportunity be provided "for each person in it to realize himself, to develop his potentialities as a human being of dignity." To this must be added that each must accord to every one of his fellows full respect—and be granted that same regard by all others.

Structuring Your Character

You must be responsible too for building your character, deriving from how you act and what you do in reference to others. Some have said cynically that "nice guys finish last." This has been proved wrong many times, and undoubtedly by examples within your personal experience.

Most important, wherever he or she finishes, the "nice guy" is far more likely to esteem himself for his attitudes and conduct. Self-satisfaction from "doing the right thing" can always outweigh gains won by dirty play or putting down the other fellow—which besmirches oneself.

When a person exerts evil on others, it has been noted by a knowledgeable observer, "the spirit is troubled. There is an unrest that has no name, a diffuse dissatisfaction. Humans are moral beings, and can no more ignore the hunger of their consciences than of their stomachs." Such individuals "lie to themselves in order to keep from hating themselves, and will hate themselves because they lie."

The "nice guy" carries no such dragging burden on his conscience. He is free of its stifling weight and oppression on his spirits. The result for the "nice guy" is an uplift of mind and attitude, enabling and helping him to live more cheerfully and at peace within himself as well as outside himself.

"Our characters are the result of our conduct," according to Aristotle. That is only partially true. One's character is structured also by observation, thought, weighing pros and cons—and proceeding accordingly. "Character," it has been emphasized, "is the governing element of life, and is above genius."

How much influence should others have on the shaping of your character and attitudes? (Character-building never stops, regardless of your age.) Generally it is wise to listen to the advice and experience of others who know a good deal about the problems which concern you—whether about your work or loving or living. But you must realize that no one has exactly the same problems and capacities as you have.

Therefore you cannot apply another's experience and advice to your own needs precisely. You probably should and certainly can consider the counsel of knowledgeable persons, friends, family, and others. Nevertheless, only you, drawing from your personal character, experience, and needs, can arrive at your best conclusions and decisions.

In doing so, you alone should take the ultimate credit or blame, no one else. And you must understand that beforehand. If you do, then you can and will honor yourself and grow as a sound, persevering individual who likes himself . . . and others.

What's "Ordinary"? What's "Eminent"?

A lovely but self-belittling schoolteacher, Arline H., met me at a resort. Sending me some information later which I had requested, she noted in her accompanying letter: "I wonder why one as eminent as you bothers with such ordinary people as myself. You know such interesting and sophisticated personages, and are yourself so exceptional and prominent. Why give time to such commonplace persons like me?"

I replied vehemently: "Your letter filled with self-depreciation upset me very much. I wanted to shake you and shout, *'Don't put yourself down!'* I'm afraid that this has become an extremely damaging habit with you, mutilating you severely. I must make you recognize that awful flaw and act to repair it now, at once.

"You have a great potential which you can achieve readily for your enduring benefit—but only if you change your view of yourself drastically. As of now, you demean your worth and diminish your abilities as you subjugate and deny your value as an individual. You should picket yourself, carrying a big sign: 'Unfair to ME.'

"You must pay more attention to pleasing yourself rather than concentrating so totally on pleasing others. Once I asked one of the top mystery book editors of all time, Lee Wright, how she managed to publish so many very successful novels. She explained, 'It's very simple. I buy the mystery manuscripts that interest and please *me*. And it turns out that what pleases me also appeals to many, many others.'

"You, like each living person, are a very special individual. You have a rare ability to teach, and an admirable quality for caring and sharing, a warmth which communicates and helps others. You must recognize your fine

85

attributes, and take pride in your sensitivity, awareness, and wisdom. You have much to give—and you give it. Realize that you have much to gain by honoring your individuality—and enjoying it.

"Who the devil am I anyhow, just because I've achieved some public recognition? I am worthy for what I am as an individual, nothing more, nothing less. No one person is better than another in essence. I have met many famous dignitaries, powerful and wealthy men and women. Many I found were inflated and tiresome, and I walked away fast. Others seized my attention, interest, and homage—but always as worthy, involved individuals, not for their titles, eminence, or riches.

"And it is true of you that we spent time together because we enjoyed and gained from each other as individuals of quality. Please respect your personal totality. Recognize and pride yourself on your character and aptitudes—or else very few others will. Why spend time criticizing yourself when it can be put to much better use improving yourself? Promise that you will stop erasing yourself—as of right now. Vow that no longer will you put yourself down. Then you'll find yourself saying joyously, 'I respect myself. I'm not afraid any more.' Promise, and follow through."

Do You Put Yourself Down?

If yes, please stop. Promise. Faults and flaws are to be recognized and corrected, not exaggerated or dwelled upon. Take pride in your good points, not demanding 100 percent perfection of yourself. Your justified pride will become you and help lead you to greater consciousness and appreciation of your potential for enjoyment of a happier, more rewarding life.

Rating yourself high, no one can keep you down.

Gandhi, the Indian leader, practiced and preached nonviolent, passive resistance against any oppressors. He couldn't arm the impoverished people with guns or munitions of any kind, so he fortified them with the only weapons they had—their bodies, their courage, and their personal, unyielding dedication to their freedom, independence, and improvement. In effect, *they found their weapons within themselves.*

If you cannot find happiness and peace within yourself, then you are not likely to find it anywhere. Emerson stated this eloquently:

> Though we travel the world over
> to find the beautiful,
> We must carry it with us
> or we find it not.

Knowing Yourself

"Knowing oneself" or "finding oneself" is a worthwhile search but not to the extent that it becomes a constant crusade which excludes most other thought and pursuit, as happens in many cases (as touched on earlier). When thus exaggerated, in effect a fixation on one's navel, then the fashionable "search for self" is self-defeating rather than self-expanding.

The blindness of the individual concentrating on self to the exclusion of practically everything else is illustrated by an obtuse, astonishingly egotistical actor. He spoke to an acquaintance interminably about his own exploits in the theater, his habits, fancies, and procedures. Finally he paused and said to his dazed listener, "But enough of talking about myself. Tell me, what do *you* think of me?"

Humorist Jean Kerr, a bright, responsible lady, was one of a panel being interviewed on a television show on the subject of women in today's world. One overbearing young woman went on incessantly about how she was looking for herself, trying to get to know herself, to understand herself, to "get myself all together." She turned to the others, "Isn't everyone looking for themselves?" Jean Kerr burst out, "I'm not looking for myself any more—*enough is enough!*"

I had seen the program and agreed. "Jean, you know who you are and what you are, and you feel reasonably pleased about it. I know who I am and what I am; I respect myself for it, and get along fine with myself. The crux of the matter is that we've 'found ourselves' not so much by probing and examining our innards constantly, but by *doing the things* that lead a person to be on good terms with herself—and with life."

One simile for self-respect might be self-use. Speaking of the hard work of rehearsing a play involving strenuous dedication, Lauren Bacall said, "You get the feeling that you're making good use of yourself, and nothing makes you feel better than that. It's exhilarating. . . . My eyes are open, my ears are open, all my senses are at work. . . . It's called doing-the-best-you-can. That's what you call it."

Doing-the-best-you-can rather than the amount of success attained must lead to self-esteem. Many a day I have worked from early morning until twilight pounding the typewriter. Then I collect the ten or so pages I have written (not counting those crumpled and tossed away). Re-reading the words, I may wind up with only three or four pages worth saving. But I feel great. I worked to my utmost ability. I used myself. I did the best that I could.

Whatever your work or effort, you know yourself best by doing-the-best-you-can, not by lying about and moping and fixing on your self-analysis exclusively. You find your sustaining knowledge of self, of your personal truth, by doing—not by dozing or dazedly dreaming. With the strength of that kind of action and conviction, you can even admit inevitable errors, and go on to rectify them while avoiding similar mistakes in the future.

Some individuals have sought to rely on outside forces—astrology, horoscopes, palmistry, mysticism, mind-reading—or fads and fancies such as special ways of eating, breathing, cogitating, or whatnot. But face it: life is not a bowl of yogurt. Whatever their merits or lacks, you cannot lean on such outside aspects alone. You must count on yourself to form your life and make each day, using your inner resources.

It isn't inevitable that you will or must have a "bad day" or a "good day" due to external forces. To a great degree, you create your happiness or unhappiness in every day by your personal attitudes, involvements, and purposeful thoughts and actions. Basically you must fix on your own star, embodied within your thinking, functioning self.

Meritorious spiritual disciplines such as yoga boil down in essence to a sense of oneness with yourself and others. How can you best achieve this boon which is embodied in conscious happiness? Not by magic or mystic rituals. Not by strange mind or body manipulations. But by building and sustaining respect for yourself and others through all the facets of day-by-day living, as delineated on these pages in all their variety and intricacies.

"The longest journey is the journey inward." It becomes a natural, bolstering part of your attitudes and activities to find and know and fortify the caring individual that you are—when you try, try, try to be your best self, using and applying yourself toward enjoying conscious happiness and spreading it to others.

There is a saying that "Character is what you are in the dark." In your reflections alone in the still of the night, or determining the tough decisions during the day, the ultimate responsibility comes right down to one person: *you.* Not to a swami or a star or a bowl of yogurt. Tell yourself, as Truman did when President: "The buck stops here." If you haven't strong self-respect and reliance on self, you may lose yourself and everything else. But possessing justified self-esteem, you can gain your best possible world.

Yes, know yourself, strengthen yourself. For you are known by what you are, and you are not just what you say but what you *do*.

Once you learn to be yourself, to weigh and accept and honor yourself for what you are, you find yourself more wide open to expand and grow as you learn to respect others for what they are as individuals. Rather than being bound up in self-doubt and lack of self-confidence, you feel free to investigate and accept others.

Some persons are likely to say, "If you are intent on 'being yourself,' then you don't care for others." The opposite is true: Once you stop concentrating on your inadequacies, and accept yourself for what you are, then you are free and willing and more eager to accept others.

It works. Think of yourself trudging along unhappily, bowed down by a great, oppressive weight on your back. You are so burdened and so worried about the weight that you can't think about or care about or even view anyone in sight clearly.

But once you have thrown off that overpowering, weighty burden, you can look up, look around, breathe freely, and *see*. You recognize and appreciate nature's wonders. You perceive and investigate other people. You are free of the distorting weight and encumbrance of self-torture and self-concern. You are yourself, a self-respecting, consciously happy, free individual.

This glorious sense of freedom is each person's right and heritage—and your own. If you find yourself tightening up, constricting yourself, it may help you as it has lifted me at times to reread this little old-country rhyme for skipping rope:

Little rope, little rope, oh my little rope,
Unwind yourself from the round ball:
Twirl round and round and high.
Take me outdoors to the air and the sun.
Out of the room, out of the house, the narrow house;
Nobody can catch us!
Little rope, little rope, oh my little rope,
Unwind yourself from the ball.

* * *

This above all is true in achieving deep, lasting conscious happiness—that you must respect yourself as an individual, and continually strengthen your individuality. As honored poet Charles Baudelaire asserted firmly: "There can be no progress . . . except in the individual and by the individual himself." You will move ahead happily by valuing and always building your self-respect for the individual you are and can be.

Studying these guides and practicing their significance can help you positively and enduringly:

1. Recognize and believe in your supreme worth as an individual.
2. Know that you, the individual, are of utmost importance even in the most crowded, complex society.
3. Achieve the right balance between underrating and overrating yourself.
4. Assess yourself accurately, and do the best you know how—then accept, honor, and live with the results securely.
5. Benefit and build yourself up by utilizing the always present, supportive externals.
6. Exert your personal will and energies to produce unpredictable "miracles."
7. Accept your responsibilities fully: "The buck stops here."

8. *Always be aware that your conduct determines your character: you are what you do.*

9. *Don't put yourself down—realize clearly that as an individual you are essentially as much as any other individual.*

10. *Be yourself—to be a self-respecting, consciously happy, free individual.*

A significant example of the practice of individuality along with essential regard for others is crusading attorney Clarence Darrow. As Robert E. Lee wrote: "He couldn't see people as masses, or fuse personalities into impersonal movements. . . . He never saw a jury; he saw twelve human beings. He never saw a defendant; he saw a man on trial . . . every act of his life showed his reverence for humanity."

Such honoring of others as well as yourself is a vital building block to conscious happiness. In a soul-searching moment, Dwight D. Eisenhower summed it up: "After all, the most important thing is one's self-respect." Realize, and never forget it, that you as an individual are as good as any other individual in the world, regardless of his or her eminence. And, as instructed by the Queen in Lewis Carroll's Alice in Wonderland, *always honor and "remember who you are."*

7

Self-Quiz:
Seeking and Finding Your
Personal Truth

TRUTH IS WITHIN yourself—but frequently it is clouded or twisted by other motivations and inner subterfuges, so that you have to sight and dig deep inside you in order to find your clear personal truth. That means truth without self-delusions, no hiding any actuality from yourself or anyone else.

Finding, examining, and accepting your basic, simple truth—simple because all shadings and pretexts have been removed—can be one of the most satisfying feelings in living. "Truth is truest poesy."

You must acknowledge this: If you lie to yourself or deceive yourself, inevitably you know it. From that point, you may doubt your ability to recognize and tell the truth to yourself, to anyone. It's essential to keep digging. Removing all self-deception is like ripping away a distorting veil which clouds your vision and irritates you so that you can't function happily. Suddenly you *see*, and in seeing honestly and accurately, you throw off a loathsome burden—of which you may never have been fully aware.

Then—when you have unloaded the weight of self-deceit (even though perhaps you never realized it existed) —you achieve a new, liberating understanding of yourself and others. Feeling this energizing freedom makes you wonder, "How is it that I never enjoyed such clarity and exhilaration before?" Carlyle said it with a smile: "Make yourself an honest man, and then you may be sure that there is one less rascal in the world."

Knowing your personal truth—what you are, what you really want of life—without self-concealment, opens you up to reach a much higher level of effective living. No longer do you delude yourself or others. You see truth. You speak truth. You feel emancipating truth throughout your being. No more constricting your honesty or expressiveness.

A theatrical coach scolded a young actress who didn't express well the words she was saying. "Stop!" he admonished. "You're not speaking from your gut. You're 'phoning in the part.'" In similar vein, actress Ina Claire, rehearsing a new play, told playwright S. N. Behrman: "Don't put it all in the stage direction. You fool yourself doing that but you don't fool me. Get it in the *dialogue*."

Go to the core, don't fool yourself. Solzhenitsyn declared in his Nobel Award Lecture: "One word of truth shall outweigh the whole world." By seeking and finding the truth in yourself, you make wonderfully clear, supportive discoveries about yourself and the world around you. Others recognize a refreshing and appealing new candor and openness about you. They are attracted to you, for "you cannot lead if you mislead."

Finding and establishing your full personal truth is not a mysterious search. You can do-it-yourself readily. Supplying your own honest answers to the questions that follow can help you advance your rewarding quest for the self-truth that liberates:

1. Do You Face the Truth Fully Without Fooling Yourself?

Have you ever (or often) concealed the truth from yourself, pretending to yourself that you took the wrong action out of conviction or necessity rather than falsely? Yet, upon frank analysis, you realize that you actually did it by concealing the facts from yourself and others? This can be deeply self-damaging as it whittles away at your self-esteem day after day.

A very simple, clear example: An attractive, formerly heavy woman, Alice T., confessed, "I told everyone that I hated being overweight—when I was chubby—but that I couldn't help it. I contended that I simply couldn't reduce because whenever I tried to diet, it would make me feel weak and ill—so I'd have to eat a lot again. I also insisted that I was a very small eater. I even tried to convince myself while I gobbled oversize portions and gorged on rich snacks.

"One night I made all those same old tired excuses to a knowledgeable doctor who sat next to me at a dinner party. He looked me in the eye, shook his head slowly, then said gently with a slight smile, 'But, dear, please tell the truth to me—and mostly to yourself. You really *love to eat*, don't you?' I turned bright red with embarrassment as I nodded agreement reluctantly. . . .

"So, finally, I made myself face the plain truth: According to my past habits, eating too much and stuffing in the most fattening foods had become more important to me than being slim, healthier, and with a better chance to live longer. Having admitted that blunt truth to myself, I went on an effective diet and stayed on it until I slimmed down. I've never put on overweight since—once I faced the fact honestly that nobody but myself was to blame for my former chubbiness."

That's just one slight example of how revealing and beneficial it can be to face the truth within yourself, and then act on it forthrightly. Losing weight may seem trivial to some in relation to all of living. But this particular instance of cause and effect serves to illustrate specifically how seeking and finding your personal truth can comprise a giant step toward attaining greater peace of mind and conscious happiness. It applies to every aspect of living.

2. Do You Tend to Blame Others for Your Own Flaws?

It's a valuable release when you finally admit—in all phases of thought and action—that you have no one to blame but yourself for many things that go wrong. Such candid self-examination makes it easier to correct a situation straightforwardly and accurately. A truthful outlook becomes a precious, most helpful part of your character, and contributes enormously to your improved well-being.

From the negative viewpoint, evading your personal truth and shifting blame to others weakens your character and tends to make you uneasy and unhappy. Journalist Lincoln Steffens insisted, "Men do not seek the truth. It is the truth that pursues men who run away and will not look around." Running away is an unsettling evasion that tears you down. Facing and living with the truth of yourself builds you up and bolsters your self-confidence and self-liking. You live with yourself boldly instead of avoiding productive confrontation with yourself and life.

Part of shedding hypocrisy and self-delusion is the willingness to admit personal faults, flaws, and mistakes. Refusing to concede that you were wrong is a heavy burden to carry—and to impose on those close to you. This results in a loss of trust—trust of self, along with forfeiting the esteem of others. Lack of trust is disastrous for everyone, from the lowliest individual to a head of state.

But when you finally refuse to delude yourself any longer, you find your inner truth. This doesn't mean that you then weep and wail and kick yourself around because of your failings, if they exist. Assessing yourself results inevitably in lifting yourself, not putting yourself down. You make corrections and adjustments. You recognize your personal truth, and live accordingly, in greater peace with yourself.

A highly successful individual asserted, "The ability to look at yourself hard and honestly—admitting both the good and the bad—*is the most powerful untapped source of human energy.*" Remember, "the truth shall make you free."

3. Do You Know and Acknowledge Your Limitations?

In finding your inner truth, you must weigh your limitations as well as recognize and take pride in your abilities and assets. Even Tolstoy, rated by many as one of the very greatest novelists of all time, realized that he could go just so far and no further—in spite of his genius. His daughter noted that he would rewrite the chapter of a book a dozen times or more, but "when he felt that he could not do any better, he was through."

This gifted master didn't demand more of himself than he had the capacity to create and give. Nor should you. Enough is better than a feast, and healthier in every way. You must learn never to be overdemanding and accordingly overwhelmed, instead of full and contented with your efforts and yourself. That's common sense—which is often the most uncommon sense because too many people are let down by their personal realities if their abilities don't live up to their most wishful fantasies.

You should make the most of what you are, shunning the temptation to be what you definitely are not. If you try to be too much, you may wind up being very little, less than you actually are. "Look not too high . . . lest a chip fall in your eye."

It's just as true that if you set your sights too low, you may never reach the full extent of your capacities. The basic truth about yourself is what you must seek and find. This can be accomplished by full, weighted self-assessment. It isn't easy, but the honest effort is well worth the ultimate result—bringing you rewards for a lifetime.

Facing your personal limitations, as you uncover and confront them, may be very hurtful at first. Once you recognize them, however, that truth becomes highly sustaining. You see yourself and life with self-relieving clarity, for then you can cope with whatever comes, operating within your most effective capacity. "You needn't fear to handle the truth roughly; she is no invalid." And you will be stronger for the handling.

4. Do You Condone Damaging Self-Delusion?

"Failures in self-honesty are at the root of almost every emotional and mental disturbance." That's the judgment of a psychiatrist who has dealt with many thousands of individuals professionally and intimately. Leaders in all phases of activity affirm this reason why many people fail: They delude themselves about their abilities and attitudes.

How can you know if you deceive yourself? Look in the mirror. Look into your mind. Take the time to examine yourself. Ask your husband or wife, or a trusted friend, to level with you. But mostly ask yourself, using as a checklist all the points covered in this book: Your sense of awareness . . . Being fully alive . . . Appreciating your individuality . . . Finding and pursuing your best personal goals . . . Assessing your joys from work and effort . . . and on and on.

Another aid to accurate self-analysis, to help eliminate self-deception, is to write out the problem. Some time back when I was about to ask for a position in my firm in a different department—for which I thought I was better qualified—I found myself confused about the desirability of the move. Finally I sat down and wrote a long letter to a friend in the same type of business. I listed the pros and cons of each job, then asked him a series of probing questions.

As I assessed the problem on paper, I found myself answering the questions. I never mailed the letter because by the time I finished it, I knew the best ultimate solution for me: I stayed in my job, having realized that my personal qualifications fitted it best—and vice versa.

I mentioned this self-confrontation to a woman executive, Eleanor H., over lunch. She nodded and confided, "I often do the same thing, but somewhat differently. I turn on my little tape recorder and tell the mike what my problem is, what all the twists and blockades are, as well as the good points. Then I play it all back. By the time I've listened through to my own voice listing the positives and negatives candidly, I see the solution clearly. In effect, I've consulted and analyzed myself."

You might try this question-and-answer method to combat deluding yourself about any number of matters: write out or tape the details, or whatever suits you, such as talking to husband, wife, or a friend. The results of frank self-analysis and discovery can lift you and help you not only to cope, but to soar . . . as in the prayer that "I may soar as high as I can now discern with this clear eye."

5. Do You Deceive Others to Some Extent?

If you deceive another, aren't you really despising and undervaluing the other, and her ability to know what is the truth? Primarily, however, and even more corrosive, you undermine and weaken your self-respect to a point where you don't mind engaging in further deception. This crumbles away one's inner foundations gradually to the point of possible collapse.

You demean yourself further if you act the hypocrite, pretending to have beliefs or virtues that you don't actually hold. Why bother? You simply shred yourself away, as though you were a cloth clown-horse at the circus with the front part and the rear pulling in two different directions and ripping you apart.

Please keep in mind always that self-trust is an essential in attaining and enjoying conscious happiness. But you can't trust yourself fully, or perhaps even partially, if you permit yourself to indulge in deceiving others. It may work with the savage animal but not with the human, not with you. It builds your inner strength to give candor—and to demand it from others.

6. Do You Seek Too-Easy, Illusionary Solutions?

You also limit your personal scope if you narrow your capacity for living fully by settling for some temporary and faddish "life style" as an instant solution to the problems of living. This rarely achieves enduring gratification or even satisfaction. Examples of "easy solutions" to life problems include the way you eat or dress or adopt an intriguing fad. Nor can one find all the answers in the stars or in the palm of the hand, or in any such diversions.

Years ago there was a hit song: "Life is just a bowl of cherries." But it's clear to any thinking person that life is not a bowl of cherries which can be lived happily simply by eating and spitting out the pits. Nor is life a dish of "health food" or a handful of multiple vitamins, or wearing faded blue jeans or triple-high heels—or whatever the current rage may be. Nor are life solutions truly available in any of the multitudes of advertising slogans and promises, no matter how extravagant and perhaps convincing.

Fads as fun? Yes. As a passing phase? Sure. But regardless of the seeming merits in such illusionary, shallow solutions, getting the most out of your life isn't that obvious. Going for such expedients 100 percent, to the extent of making what you eat, as one example, a substitute for how you think and act is ultimately self-defeating. It usually winds up as a jolting letdown, or worse.

Organic foods or kooky clothes or high-fashion or low-fashion hair styles, anything so shallow in the full spectrum of living, cannot and will not solve basic problems of existence. Because neither fads nor fripperies, but rather the self-esteem arising from gaining your personal truth, is an essential base for conscious happiness. Conviction growing from your strong, well-rooted inner character can save you from foolishness and vanity.

So—gulp your vitamins and wear whatever attire you prefer, but you can't ever consider such slight material elements a substitute for the sound, proved actuality of developing personal responsibility, understanding, and integrity. The value and importance of building your inner strength is timeless. Back in the sixth century B.C., Chinese philosopher Lao-tse observed: "He is strong who conquers others; he who conquers himself is mighty."

7. Do You Ask Yourself: "Is It Right?"

When you have established your personal integrity firmly, you can ask and depend on the validity of the answer when you question yourself about any matter, *"Is it right?"* If your answer is anything but a reasoned, sure affirmative, then your strong, sustaining personal truth will operate to warn you and turn you away from the wrong action. When you respect yourself, and are mentally faithful to yourself, you are likely to come up with the right answer.

A high government employee, Egil Krogh, became involved in serious trouble by knowingly carrying through the illegal directives of his superiors. After his actions were revealed, and he was punished by the law, he warned everyone in any type of endeavor: "When contemplating a course of action (no matter who ordered it), I hope that you will never fail to ask, 'Is it right?' "

Your truth should be mightier than any directive. If you ignore or subvert your own clear inner answer, you risk failure or worse, for the ultimate responsibility for every action you take is yours alone. If you don't accept that truth beforehand, then you may suffer the consequences later.

No matter where the command comes from to take a wrongful step, or how forcefully stated, if you follow directions exactly and the results are disastrous nevertheless, you will be held to account. You will be blamed, nobody else—*you*. Carrying this to an extreme, if someone were to order you to murder another, and you did it, you would be and should be punished as being the murderer. Your pointing finger points back only to you.

Every benefit you receive, such as the boon of freedom of personal volition and action, which each of us demands as an individual right, carries with it the burden of personal responsibility. Before taking any step, you must ask yourself, "Is it right, morally and sensibly?" Your answer must be your own truth, not self-delusion or evasion. What you think of yourself is probably basically sounder than what others think of you.

That, in essence, is the foundation of honesty and reality in practically anything you undertake. Consider this statement by a leader in the art of writing, Willa Cather:

"Artistic growth is, more than anything else, a refining of the sense of truthfulness." The great artist seeks his or her own essence, his own viewpoint, his own truth—to paint or sculpt or create his personal vision in any work.

That applies to anyone, artist or not. You, too, can refine your own thinking and seeking by asking first always: "Is it right?" Thus you arrive at your personal truth in what you do and say—leading to greater enjoyment of your personal vision and attainment of happy living. Based on your clear, not clouded, truth, you make that vision into your day-to-day living reality. And you achieve and live with conscious happiness.

8. Do You Convey Your Personal Truth Clearly?

Here's an essential part of arriving at your personal truth, and conveying that inner integrity to others—for their benefit and yours: Make it a point not only to think and reason clearly, but also to transmit your conclusions most simply, accurately, and thus effectively. Thinking truth and telling truth to yourself and others is a great aid to clarity in speaking out. No confusion, no cover-up . . . for "Oh what a tangled web we weave when first we practice to deceive."

Noted speechmaker Chancey Depew contended that the best advice for public speakers could be summed up in six one-syllable words: "Stand up. Speak up. Shut up."

Deceitful thinking and deceptive or evasive talk, on the other hand, involves ineffectual camouflage as you try to drown others in a flood of fumbling words. The truthful individual who has no answer can say simply, clearly, and with great personal relief, "I don't know." The conniver, one who lies or practices sleight-of-mind even on himself, might mumble grudgingly, "It would be utterly and manifestly inappropriate for me to comment." Translation to every listener, "I haven't the guts to speak out; I'm hiding the truth."

A friend, Joe Fitzmorris, told the true story of a blustering army colonel who covered up his lack of confidence in himself, along with a deficiency in ability, by shouting and garbling his words. Late for breakfast one morning while staying over at a hotel in Japan, he rushed into the restaurant and yelled to the waiter, "I won't tolerate any pettifogging procrastination, bring me eggs in a hurry! Y'hear? Eggs in a hurry!"

He waited, kept waiting, waited some more—then rapped loudly on his plate. The headwaiter burst from the kitchen and rushed over, book in hand. "So sorry, sir," he apologized. "We regret the unavoidable delay, sir. Not our fault. In our cookbook we find 'Eggs Benedictine' and 'Eggs Florentine' and 'Eggs Hollandaise' and multitudes of esteemed egg dishes, but we cannot find a recipe for 'Eggs Inahurry.'"

As a writer of nonfiction books primarily, one of the finest compliments I've ever been given by a reader was this: "*You teach, not preach.*" When you clarify your thinking and expression in a spirit of truth with yourself and others, you don't preach, you teach—yourself as well as others. You profit from one of the prime benefits of conscious happiness—you find that every day is an enriching learning experience.

When you are confident of your personal truth, you tend to speak out when you have something to say, for you have nothing to conceal. And you say it straightforwardly, clearly. A wit noted, "Procrastination is the thief of time . . . and so are a lot of other big words." You speak simply and clearly from an unconfused spirit, but if you don't know, you keep silent—unlike the blabbermouth who would rather be wrong than be quiet.

Always you may be guided basically, as I am in daily

living, facing challenges, and making decisions, by the ever-echoing words of Thoreau: "Simplify! Simplify!"

9. Have You the Courage to Analyze Your Personal Truth?

"Courage consists in equality to the problem before us," Emerson asserted. Is your courage equal to the searching scrutiny of genuine, uncompromising self-analysis? I believe that every woman and man has the capacity to search, analyze, and discover her or his own truth—if the understanding and the will exist. You can if you will.

A courageous man, confessing his misdeeds in court, said he had to speak out because "Nothing is more imprisoning than being locked into a wrong idea. My concept . . . had been wrong. . . . If I had won the case on that defense, I would have been identified with that idea for the rest of my life. I had to expose myself . . . to find real freedom."

Facing and recognizing his clear personal truth head-on gave him confidence, he asserted. Once he made his decision in complete self-honesty, after deep self-analysis, he felt a liberating sense of relief and release. He said that this resulted in a sustaining feeling of growing, within himself and with his family. They all stopped trying to "run away from everything. We've been getting closer and closer."

The paths to rewarding self-analysis are reported throughout this book. As in practically all aspects of attaining conscious happiness, *you* must take the first step—and then keep moving forward to your personal uplifting, supportive conclusion. I promise you, based on positive, experienced knowledge, that the rewards are worth the striving. Emerson stated: "Nothing is at last sacred but the integrity of your own mind."

105

10. Do You Accept and Respect Yourself?

Once you discover and strengthen your personal truth, you inevitably accept yourself more readily—and you reinforce your self-respect. You trust your intuition and your sense of fitness. You speak up without fear of inadequacy, for, as Henry Van Dyke noted: "The woods would be silent if no birds sang except those who sing best." And, being at ease with yourself, you know that those who try to say too much too often wind up registering nothing.

In essence, you achieve personal truth and its wonderful bonuses when you see life as it really is. You accept yourself as you really are—no more, no less, always aware of the exciting, stimulating effort and joy in making the most of yourself.

An observer said of an unhappy man who died after failing in the arts that he had lived "a life of perennial self-analysis in the pursuit of his self-esteem"—of trying to find his intimate self and his basic truth. But he failed. Why?

If you try too single-mindedly to "find" yourself, it is easy to lose yourself. Relax. Work at it, but not at that search exclusively, not centering all your thinking on that one target. Enjoy the pursuit, realizing above all that you find and strengthen your personal truth by what you *do*, how you act, not by peering at your innards endlessly and dreaming and wishing for self-knowledge and self-fulfillment.

Do. Act. Live. Then your insights and understanding of yourself and others—your inner truths, your illuminating, clarifying conclusions—will develop surely and solidly.

A profound book, *A Passion for Truth*, contains the statement: "Love and Truth are the two ways that lead the soul out of the inner jungle. Love offers an answer to the question of how to live. In Truth we find an answer to the question of how to think. . . . Understanding can begin only when man undeceives himself for he cannot survive in deceit."

It comes down to this, as you can tell yourself honestly when you have evolved through your thorough self-analysis: "This is my truth. This, then, is me. I recognize me. I accept me. I will live contentedly with me, with my assets and limitations. Accepting that, knowing me as I am truly, as I must be—I will like me. And I will attain and enjoy my personal conscious happiness from now on."

* * *

Self-analysis, prodded by this self-quiz, and probing the suggested ways to determine your personal truth, requires deep, self-searching thought. It's worth taking the time to think through to your solutions now and in the time ahead.

Noted creative thinker Alex F. Osborn provides a tip in the story of the gnarled New Englander who sat silently each night in a chair on the porch of the general store. Asked what he was doing, he replied, "I just think."

"But—how can you possibly think that long, that much?"

He explained, "Thinkin' is like sin. Those who don't do it are scared of it. But those who do it enough get to like it."

Please think through all the preceding points, then ask yourself: "What are my personal answers to these self-quiz questions?"

1. *Do you face the truth fully without fooling yourself?*
2. *Do you tend to blame others for your own flaws?*
3. *Do you know and acknowledge your limitations?*
4. *Do you condone damaging self-delusion?*
5. *Do you deceive others to some extent?*
6. *Do you seek too-easy, illusionary solutions?*

7. Do you ask yourself: "Is it right?"
8. Do you convey your personal truth clearly?
9. Have you the courage to analyze your personal truth?
10. Do you accept and respect yourself?

Finally, ask yourself: "Are these the best possible answers toward building my conscious happiness?" If not, I urge you to work toward the desired goal which will be most rewarding for you.

When high school science teacher John T. Scopes was tried for discussing Charles Darwin's theories of evolution with his class, Judge John Raulston summed up: "It sometimes takes courage to search diligently for a truth that may destroy our preconceived notions and ideas . . . to declare a truth or stand for an act . . . [but] a man who is big enough to search for the truth and find it and declare it in the face of all opposition is a big man"—or woman.

Such courage, like truth itself, cannot help but fortify one's pride and pleasure in each day's living. Your personal truth can be your best personal friend—if you will remain true and dedicated to it. That works for me; it can and will work for you, a certainty that will uplift you always.

As for the value of telling the truth, Mark Twain had the final word: "If you tell the truth, you don't have to remember anything."

8

Doing What You
Want to Do

"I WANT TO live my life energetically and productively. I enjoy working hard and long, using myself. But one thing I insist upon: I'm going to make my living by doing the work that I want to do."

That's the statement of an earnest, self-respecting young man who had successive careers, each lasting for several years. As a high school student he had been told by a caring instructor: "Don't become set firmly on any one career because of what someone else urges. You will be a success in anything you choose. So be sure of this one fact—that you will be happy in what you do. Achieving that, all other good will follow."

But success eluded him, perhaps because he didn't know what he really wanted, what would satisfy him fully. First, he was a retail worker. He moved on to demanding labor and long hours as a medical field man in a remote, primitive country. Next he became a published writer (author of a book about the faraway land and customs), then an editor, and finally a book publishing executive.

Always he maintained a sense of searching. He often recalled what his grandfather had told him as a very young child: "Always look into and study the petals of a rose. For the beauty doesn't lie in the rose—it's in the person who sees the rose."

The young man received encouragement from his father who wrote: "It is my conviction that you are pursuing exactly the right course in seeking determinedly the way of life you want most. That's far preferable to settling apathetically into the usual first convenient groove. You are trying, working at it, not just lying around and 'thinking about it.' I'm confident, as you are, that you will eventually arrive at what is most fulfilling for you."

The maturing man immersed himself in each of the successive phases of endeavor. He gained a great deal of varied knowledge as he went along. He had always been interested in psychology, so he undertook further investigation in that field. As a result, a decade after leaving college, he enrolled again at a university. He studied and worked double time to support himself for the necessary years in school.

Now he is successfully, deeply involved in psychology, happier than ever before in his life, because "I'm doing what I like to do."

That man is our son, Jeff. He told me, "When we talked at one point and I said I wanted to be a writer, you smiled ruefully and said, 'Nobody becomes a writer by wanting to write; to write you gotta write.' I say, 'To learn to live, you gotta *live*.' And only through living can one gain the conscious happiness you pointed out to me."

Facing Your Alternatives

One hot Friday evening in early summer, I was working hunched over a writing pad at the picnic table in our backyard. A voice hailed me. I looked up and saw our perspiring, weary neighbor, Frost Walker, still in his business suit, wilted shirt, knotted tie. Obviously he had just returned from his office. "Busy?" he asked.

He accepted my invitation to join me under the big tree and relax with a long, cold drink before dinner. He loosened his tie, dropped his jacket and hat on the grass, and came over. After taking a deep swallow of his drink, he shook his head haplessly. Then he half-grinned without humor and murmured, "Mmmm . . . almost makes me feel as though I'm alive."

"Cheer up. You're off for vacation tomorrow, aren't you?"

He nodded dispiritedly. "Yeah, and we look forward to two weeks away from the rat race. Man, how I yearn for that. But this is what gets me down: Isn't it crazy to spend fifty weeks a year slaving away at a job in order to earn two short weeks of relaxation and real enjoyment? Fifty to two are terrible odds." He sighed. "Ought to be the other way around." Silence. "Got any solutions?"

After a pause, "I don't know about solutions, but I can suggest two alternatives: Make it a point to get some real enjoyment out of your work every day, one way or another, so you stay up instead of being beaten down. Or, if that isn't possible, your other option is to change your work." He looked shocked. "No, you don't quit overnight. But you start thinking, planning, and ultimately make your move." About a year later, Frost made his move, using his skills for a more satisfying, more rewarding way of life for him and his family.

It's essential to *like* what you're doing. Not every minute perhaps, but much of the time—*enjoy* your work. Otherwise it's difficult or impossible to be truly, fully, consciously happy—as you, as every human being, has the right to be, and should be.

That one factor, getting some pleasure from your daily work or other way of life, whatever it may be, can make a

111

pivotal difference in how much true gratification you get out of each day. Personal fulfillment is the key element, not money as such, or other material rewards alone. Deep self-satisfaction is a solid, ever-present source of personal strength and sustenance—which benefits all about you as well as yourself.

A brilliant woman, a scientist, Doctor of Philosophy in Molecular Biology, Dr. Joan S. was paid less than a laboratory technician and many manual laborers. Her low salary was standard in the department where she conducted her complicated and important experiments. In spite of her many published and highly praised scientific papers, and decades of intensive and continuing study, her pay in money remained minimal.

She was offered positions as a scientist with giant conglomerates in the pharmaceutical world at salaries many times more than she was getting. Asked why she put up with the gross inequities and continued with her demanding, low-paying laboratory research, she said simply, "I'm doing the work I want most to do . . . in the independent way that I like to do it."

A civil service worker expressed the attitude of countless others involved in jobs that are far from glamorous or remunerative, yet highly rewarding in the way that counts: "Long ago I had enough brains to know I would not get rich in city service. But it has provided something better in job satisfaction. I have always had the feeling of being needed. Is there any better feeling in the world?"

"You Are Certain to Get It"

According to a wit's definition, "An individualist is a person who dares to be different . . . but he's an oddball if he's different from you." Nevertheless, if you have a firm conviction about what you want to do, consider daring to work toward that ideal, no matter how "different" it may be.

It tends to become disheartening, if Thoreau's words are true, that "the mass of men lead lives of quiet desperation." He undoubtedly meant this pessimistic view to apply to women also. If you fit this category, living in quiet desperation, shouldn't you at least give serious thought to effecting a change?

A big part of arriving at productive change is building a solid sense of conscious happiness—along with reflection on a switch to doing what you want to do instead of being trapped by an unsatisfying way of living. One thing is sure—you'll never know what you can do until you try it, or at least think about it.

A successful man said that his sense of achievement boiled down to two words: *I will.* George Bernard Shaw asserted, "People are always blaming their circumstances for what they are. I don't believe in circumstances. The people who get on in this world are the people who get up and look for the circumstances they want and, if they can't find them, make them."

Set your sights, work toward your desired goal, and nothing can keep you from the joys of striving—as just one gain. It has been reported that the sensationally successful Beatle, John Lennon, was brought up by an aunt who had very specific ideas. After he scored so astonishingly in the world of popular music, he gave her a house. Then he hung on the wall a plaque commemorating what she told him repeatedly, all through his growing up: "The guitar's all right, but you'll never earn your living with it."

There is a qualification to pursuing your own course in spite of opposing forces: You must take great care and finally be sure about what course you set, that you determine exactly what you want to do most. For, as someone warned, "Once you set your mind and actions on a specific personal goal, you are certain to get it." The decisive factor must be primarily not what others think you should do, but what you think—and, even more to the point, what you *do*.

Steps to Your Decision

How can you manage to do what you want to do in life, to use yourself most effectively and enjoy the days most thoroughly? It's a great help to analyze yourself, decide what you want most, set your sights . . . then plan and work to achieve your individual objective. There's provocative challenge in Dr. Jung's observation: "Man invented rulers out of sheer laziness."

You can decide to rule yourself, to guide your destiny instead of yielding to whatever comes along; then you work toward the wanted goal. If you want to pursue your most gratifying individual course, instead of being "ruled" by others or oppressed by a job or environment that you abhor, you must exert strong personal effort. Then you never let down until you succeed in finding your own best way to gain the greatest gratification from each day's living.

A hard-working young novelist, Shane Stevens, who had received some recognition but little money said, "I find my brave new world not ideal but very real. I don't write for money. If there was no such thing as money, I would still write my novels because I am driven that way. I need to do that. As with all creative writers, I have my own vision of the world, and the compulsion to present it to others . . . to bring creative order out of the chaos of my life. I write to find out what I have to say. That's my drive."

In determining and setting your goal, you must realize this always: No matter how you organize and change your way of life for the better, you usually won't achieve what you want unless you mold and change *yourself* continually for the better. Otherwise you may find yourself in the dilemma of a man who complained, "My new job is far more desirable than my work used to be. But the trouble is that *I'm* still what I used to be—unsure of myself and depressed about it."

That partial application to your thrust is as faulty as the unthinking act of "a surgeon who sews up the incision without removing the tumor." In setting your sights on the career or future way of life that appeals to you, the first requisite is that you must want it with your entire being, so much that nothing else could possibly do. Generally, pursuing so determined a course embodies unsparing application and some self-sacrifice.

Advising his daughter, Clara, about her desire to be a physician, a friend and realistic father, Walter S., pointed out, "You must understand, since you want marriage and children eventually, that such a career involves a great many difficulties and extra hard work for a woman. You want to raise a family the way you think best—and, in addition, study and practice as a doctor. That's tough—"

The young woman protested, "But I want to be a doctor more than anything in the world—"

"I know, I know. In any case, you'll do what you want to do so much that you're imbued with it, and that is what is best for you. I agree beyond question that one of the most important things in life is to work in the way that one wants most. And to hell with seemingly gigantic obstacles. You're very lucky that there *is* a career you want so much. I'm with you."

"How come, Dad?" young Clara asked. "You seem so sure."

"I learned," he smiled wryly. "I kept it to myself, but for much of my working life I was despondent deep inside because I wasn't doing what I wanted to do. I kept making headway in a business that was profitable but unsatisfying to my spirit. And I felt a pervading sense of gloom because I could see only nothingness ahead. . . ."

He shrugged. "Finally I concluded that it was either change or give up my dream of a better way of living for me—not for anyone else, but for me. With an enormous effort, I changed my outlook and my work from business to what had always been my prime interest—education— my present work, as you know."

"I'm so glad you made the move."

"Me, too, so glad." He grinned. "Now I know that each day offers much in itself. I live for the day and for the most I can make of it for others, and thus for myself. You know, I exult in whatever slight or huge portion of enjoyment I can derive from every day. It's possible because I work at it, and pursue the individual course I set."

"I feel that about you," she said, "and so do others."

"Thanks. Above all, I know—and I can tell you positively because of my experience: I could not have gained this pervading, constant uplift of conscious happiness if I had not set my course on doing what I wanted most to do." He added, "And I believe that if I hadn't spent years of drudgery at work that didn't fulfill me, I wouldn't appreciate as much my good fortune in doing my own thing. So, it's never too late—or too early—to begin."

Beware the Wrong Analysis

It's vital that you don't misdirect your thinking so that you come up with the wrong answer, due to reacting against something rather than going toward a better way. An acquaintance who seemed to be enjoying his work and way of life told me one day, "Everything has gone sour. I'm thinking of leaving here, getting into something else, some other line, moving my family for a fresh start."

I suggested that he ought to dig deeper, that he consider whether his relatively new dissatisfaction might be due to problems other than his work.

In this instance, he discussed his oppressive problems with his longtime family doctor. The physician said that the basic troubles might stem not from him, but from his wife's discontentment with her way of life. He arranged to examine the bright but listless woman. After a series of medical treatments for depression, she took a part-time job which appealed to her.

As a result of being stimulated by doing something challenging that she liked and which employed her inherent abilities (in this case, hospital administration), she shed her lethargy and gloom. The home atmosphere became pleasant and inviting. Her husband tackled his own work with new vigor and his daily living with renewed zest and optimism.

Sometimes just adding a new interest can make your daily work more pleasing and rewarding to your psyche. In this instance, Stella H., a young woman with several very small children, who loved her family, felt irritated, unhappy—"stifled," as she put it. "I know that I have creative abilities outside the home, but no chance to express them. This household routine is driving me out of my skull—yet it has to be done, and it's my responsibility. . . ."

Her caring husband investigated and suggested that she take several art courses available evenings in the local high school. That did it for her. Soon she joined the area art society, participated in meetings, exhibits, other activities. Her creative desires now activated, she had more fun daily —and so did her family.

Self-fulfillment is always an important element in attaining conscious happiness. Not talking about what you yearn for and need, but doing something constructive about it. You can make it happen. Only you. And you are the prime beneficiary.

Fundamentally you must decide, at any age or stage of life, in choosing your course, that you will be doing what you want, not what someone else decides is best for himself or everyone—and therefore best for you. You may even elect, if your situation permits it, to enjoy your days freely and graciously without a job or set routines. In any case, you must do "your own thing," not anybody else's, not what others say is "the thing to do," not the vogue or the "in" thing, but your own thing.

If you decided to choose, as an example, between a career in industry or in art, you would have to ask yourself: "What is my prime objective? Is it to achieve rich rewards in industry, or will I gain more personal fulfillment as an artist or through a career in the arts . . . or via some other endeavor or way of living?"

Not any one way of life is better or worse than another in general or in total. What counts is what will be most gratifying for you in particular. If you seek material success, popularity, and applause, then what offers that result is the right way for you. Any way is your better selection —as long as you do it consciously and don't deny to yourself or others that this is your personal choice.

And this is absolutely essential for your well-being: You must be willing to accept the responsibility for bad as well as good results. Personal choice embodies personal responsibility. Otherwise a letdown or failure can cause you to fall apart and be unhappier than ever. You will have built your edifice on shifting ground.

Your Obligation

It's an inescapable and sometimes brutal fact of living that if you aim to fulfill yourself through pursuit of your own concept of the best life for you, then you must bear the obligation of handling difficulties and even failures.

You may succeed in every way. Or you may fail totally— as far as outside recognition and approval are concerned —without failing within. That's possible only if you accept responsibility right at the start and throughout. Otherwise you may strike out irrationally at others—to evade your own responsibility and flaws.

Real freedom, I have found, as have many other consciously happy and secure individuals, comes not from escaping or evading responsibilities but in facing up to them. When you assess your lot, if you decide that your abilities or circumstances won't permit a successful change right now, then you probably proceed as before for the time being. But you keep planning for a possible switch in the future. Your spirit is bolstered by having faced the issue squarely and reached your reasoned decision responsibly.

Thereupon you choose your personal course, for now and looking ahead, willing to live by what develops, good or bad. Former president of Harvard University, James Bryant Conant, suggested: "Behold the turtle: He makes progress only when he sticks his neck out." You can always change at any time if you wish.

Then you go on to the next step—courageously, steadfastly, eagerly. I can assure you that there is great conscious happiness which you feel instantly in setting your way and following through to wherever it may lead—*for you are leading yourself, assuming all obligations honestly*. You can then find your personal way of living more joyous and fulfilling than you ever dreamed possible.

Using Time? Or Time Using You?

A friend and former business associate, Donald W., president of a sizable corporation, was dumped practically overnight by the Board of Directors in one of those take-over political maneuvers that occur too often in volatile enterprises. He was stunned by the sudden blow, didn't know how to plan his future. I considered him a decent, sensitive individual, out of place in a cutthroat environment.

I wrote to him: "The happiest years of your life can be beginning now. I tell you so as one who has enjoyed my best, most rewarding years since quitting my successful business career—to do what I wanted to do. What has caused this to happen for me and so many others? It's this simple . . .

"The great step forward—which I hope you will take, whatever your future activities may be—is this: Make sure in your new endeavor that *you will use time as you want to most, rather than having time use you.* The one most precious thing that you and yours possess now is your time—to cherish, to make the most of, to enjoy to the full.

"Please realize, in your thinking, that all other considerations are minor—money, accomplishment, prestige—compared with attaining a deep, fulfilling sense of happiness. In my years of working with you, I found you a most intelligent, warm, able man . . . but I never had the feeling that you were really happy and at peace. Always you appeared under tension, beset by unrelenting problems. . . .

"My suggestion and hope is simply this: You will be receiving many remunerative offers based on your proved ability and record in the field. Before you grab one, especially now when your ego is bruised, please stop to analyze what you want—as you are clearly capable of doing. Then make your decision to use time in the future the way that will fulfill you most, you personally, nobody else. And that must eventually please also those who love you most.

"In instance after instance, I have watched competent

women and men who finally seized or made the opportunity to do the thing that each was most interested in doing. As they worked at it, diligently and intelligently, seemingly insuperable obstacles faded, somehow almost taking care of themselves. The gains they made in joy and self-esteem were far more precious than any monetary rewards—but usually those came along too.

"What is of utmost importance to me, and please consider how it may apply to you, is the freedom to pursue life along the course I prefer, and the freedom that results from doing so. I recall Maugham's words: 'If a nation values anything more than freedom, it will lose its freedom; and the irony of it is that if it is comfort or money that it values more, it will lose that too.' I'm convinced that the same applies to each of us as individuals, and I live accordingly—happily, zestfully. How about you?"

This intelligent gentleman refused a number of pressing and promising offers as he elected to think things through first. He and his family went off for a brief vacation. Upon his return, he said he had arrived at the realization that he couldn't be truly content in the hurly-burly of giant corporate pressure and big city life. "For many others, yes. For us, no. And, after all, we live primarily with us."

He moved back to his country origins where he soon became involved in a small, thriving enterprise. He reported a year later that he and his family were all glowingly happy, with snapshots to prove it. Simultaneously a small package arrived from him. Opening it, I found a gift, a magnificent wristwatch. Attached to it was a card: "Here's a gift of time which you called our most precious possession. Now I'm using time my way . . . with enduring gratitude."

The Courage of Your Convictions

Doctors are often in the position of telling patients who feel tired, dragged out, without energy or volition: "There's nothing wrong with you physically. Vitamins, tonics, other medications can't help . . . " As a result of the physician's extended questioning, it turns out with surprising frequency that the person is imprisoned in his own mind by lack of interest in his work or way of life.

This destructive plight can come about among young and old, poor and rich, regardless of sex, race, religion, or other such aspects. The result: mental and physical fatigue stemming largely from dissatisfaction and disinterest, often expressed as "Nothing seems to work, there doesn't seem much point in going on . . . "

Some women, for example, thrive on the hard work of raising a family, keeping up their spirits and energy in spite of exhausting demands from morning to bedtime and beyond. Others, with fewer demands and responsibilities, feel listless because "Something is lacking, my life is empty." The same happens to men.

If you feel caught in a work trap or lost in a vacuum, or crushed by unrelenting pressures, a change toward what appeals to you may be the essential happiness-saving tonic for you and yours. Certainly you must face the issue—at the very least—and strive determinedly for the right resolution. *Each of us was born to live not resignedly, but exultantly.*

You can't very well do what you want to do unless you know what you want and have convictions about it, believe in it intensely. Strong beliefs, in turn, make you stronger. Do you lack the conviction that you can succeed in your personal best direction, to express yourself, perhaps to start a new enterprise or a new course and make it come out right?

"It has all been done before," an acquaintance complained. "So how can I expect to make my own ideas and desires pay out?" I urge you not to feel blocked or defeated by the old saw that there's nothing new under the sun. You will discover that *everything* is new under the sun, every day—if you believe in that, and work at it hard and long enough.

The obvious fact—though few think about it clearly— is that everything you do under the sun is new because you, the individual, are endowing it with your unique, special individuality. Nobody else in the world, in the long history of mankind, ever has, ever will, ever can do anything precisely your way. You are an original—exclusive, exceptional. Nobody else is you.

The perceptive writer Flannery O'Connor affirmed that basic truth: "There may never be anything new to say, but there is always a new way to say it. And since, in art, the way of saying a thing becomes a part of what is said, every work of art is unique and requires fresh attention." I assure you from my varied experience, that the same is true in every kind of endeavor; writing is only one example.

"I Believe . . ."

When I met Dr. Irwin M. Stillman, a superb, knowledgeable internist, we conferred in detail about the pervading problems of overweight. Our views meshed, we liked each other (an essential in any joint endeavor), and we decided to write a diet book together. After months of concentrated work, we finally had a detailed outline of the book and the opening chapter.

I mentioned this at lunch to a close friend, a leading magazine editor. Her face fell. "Oh, poor Samm," she sighed. "Save your time and energy, drop the whole project. No diet book such as you describe will ever make it. There's a book coming out next month which gives the details of every possible kind of reducing diet—the diet book to end all diet books. I tell you from my vast professional experience not to waste your time riding a losing horse."

I thanked her but insisted, "I believe in this book."

Our agent, canny Josephine Rogers of Collins-Knowlton-Wing, Inc., started presenting the diet book material to publishers—she too had faith in it. But soon it began to appear that my friend had been absolutely right. The first publisher stated, "Well written, but it hasn't a chance. Too many diet books. It's all been done before." Sixteen publishers turned down our manuscript.

But we knew the effectiveness of the dieting method, and our ability to help overweights reduce—in essence, in the doctor's knowledge and our very personal approach. We kept working, kept writing, finished the book in spite of the repeated rejections and failures. We believed, and we'd learned from experience that "half the failures in life arise from pulling in one's horse when he is leaping."

The seventeenth publisher accepted the manuscript. We learned later that the editorial board had turned down our book, like their predecessors. But a determined editor, brilliant Ann Pinchot, who had followed the manuscript instructions and lost weight rapidly on the diet, had faced the president of the publishing house and asserted, "I have faith in this book. If you don't accept it, then you have no faith in my judgment—and I'll resign." He yielded reluctantly.

One individual working with other individuals can move the world. The book was published as *The Doctor's Quick Weight Loss Diet*. The rest is publishing history—the volume became the best-selling diet book of all time. Clearly, faith can move mountains (even of fat). Never underestimate the value and power of doing it your own way, of following your personal star.

"No Sitting Back!"

This is certain: If you haven't strong personal convictions, and the courage to pursue them—if you haven't enough faith in yourself—then you can't expect others to have belief in you. Faith and courage and effort are three essentials; wishing won't make your desire for independence come true.

Daphne D., who had worked her way up to a well-paying executive position in a sizable business, still didn't feel fulfilled. "I'm sick of group action, endless conferences. That's great for many others, but for me a conference is a meeting of the bored." Her consuming hobby was gardening, and she determined to make it pay off economically through individual initiative. Studying nights, weekends, every spare minute, she attained the qualifications of a professional landscape engineer and gardener.

Taking a deep breath, and with fingers crossed ("It's hard to use a trowel that way," she murmured), she resigned from her position and started a small nursery. After two years of seeming failure, barely getting by, almost literally working her fingers and split fingernails to the bone, the little enterprise took hold and produced a small profit. She smiled and said, "For me, happiness is doing what I like best to do—" she examined her calloused hands ruefully "—and working hard at it."

Live? Or be lived? The choice is yours.

A contented man in his mid-fifties explained, "I discovered long ago that all man really has is himself. It is his God-given responsibility to expand his life and spirit, to constantly fight boredom and mediocrity and cheapness." More than that, you must endeavor to make the most of your individuality—to get the greatest good out of every day's living. The result inevitably is conscious happiness. But it won't come about if you keep waiting instead of taking the first step toward self-liberation.

James Cagney was asked whether he'd ever played a gentleman of leisure (in the movies). He laughed, "No, but if I had, there wouldn't have been anything leisurely about him. . . . I always had that vaudeville feeling: When you're on, you're on! You've got fifteen or twenty minutes to make it in . . . No sitting back!"

Whether your personal yearning is for leisure or for a specific career or other goal, sitting back is utterly self-defeating. It's up to you to use your time best toward your desired goal—*get on with it.*

Some Day . . . Or Now?

Talk about it—or do it? That difference between wanting and getting applies to every phase of work and living. For example, many creative people in advertising complain, "Some day I'm going to write a best-selling book— but now I just haven't the time." Very few, hardly any, ever write any kind of a book. (Incidentally, you must set your priorities straight whatever your goal; in this case, for instance, first you must write the book—and then you *hope* it becomes a best-seller. Only one in tens of thousands makes it. But you still gain the joy of having written a book, best-seller or not.)

During the years that I labored early to late on Madison Avenue, I managed to write ten books and scores of stories and articles. Asked how I could possibly handle combining a busy executive's life with a career as an author, I explained simply, "I write books—instead of wasting time talking about writing books." I answered repeated accusations that I must be goofing off with this letter in an advertising magazine, *Madison Avenue:*

"In behalf of other advertising people who write books, as well as myself, I'm answering the barbed query of Philip H. in your last 'Letters' column. My explanation applies to everyone who engages in productive activities outside of his daily work. He wrote: 'When do men like this find the time to write books?' His implication is that while we're pounding typewriters at home, he's sweating incessantly over business problems. We suggest the following to him and others [and to you]:

"During a typical week, at the end of each day, jot down how many hours you spent on bridge, golf, watching TV, theater, movies, sports events, gardening, tennis, sailing, skiing, bowling, at social gatherings, dreaming, gazing out a train window, just plain moping, doing absolutely nothing, and so on and on. Finish your list? Did you sweat incessantly over business or other daily routine demands to the exclusion of all else? Your list provides the answer. Of course you didn't!

"Now I don't think it's any more commendable to write a book than to enjoy golf, play cards, watch TV, or whatever you personally prefer. You do what you want to do—and God bless you. I do suggest that Mr. H. and his ilk stop claiming that 'I'd write a book too if I had the time.' You have the time to write a book or for other off-hour accomplishments—it's up to you how you use your time. Always it's your choice, as it should be. Just don't make fake excuses.

"By the way, I wrote this letter while on my commuting train, scrawling on a pad instead of dozing over my newspaper. But we book-writers don't claim to spend every out-of-office minute writing books either. Sometimes we even look at girls. . . ."

Keeping a close eye on the slippage of time, and making use of time best—that means the way you want to most, you, not anyone else—is neither a new nor original thought, but a sound one to observe. Way back about A.D. 50, Seneca noted: "Part of our time is snatched from us, part is gently subtracted, and part slides insensibly away."

Does time control you mostly—or do you control your use of time substantially, consciously, instead of letting it slide away interminably? Even if you use time dreaming or dozing—realize it, appreciate it, enjoy it.

No Crying Over Spilt Milk

Are you held back from doing with your life what you want to do because you moan, "It's too late"? Or do you spend so much time lamenting "I've wasted my life" or "There's no way out of my bind" that you have no volition left to make a change if it's wanted and needed urgently? Browning suggested that instead of crying over spilt milk, do something about it: "Since milk, though spilt and spoilt, does marble good/ Better be down on knees and scrub the floor."

There is a special positive aspect to making a change even after many years of pursuing a demanding but unsatisfying course. A friend, Ralph S., who had endured terribly grueling pressure in a dog-eat-dog business for many years, finally gave it up. Since he loved sailing, he took a job in a small boatyard. He told me at lunch months later, "I'm so damned happy, I should have made this move way back."

"Whoa!" I exclaimed. "Don't expend energy uselessly by crying over having delayed your move in the past. Think of this: Would you be enjoying and appreciating your new career as much if you hadn't been in the pressure cooker for so long?"

Surprised, he thought about it. Then he burst out laughing, "That benefit escaped my attention. Like the old saw that it's worth wearing tight shoes because you feel so good when you take them off." Another way of considering this is to think about wise man Marcus Aurelius' statement: "Everything that exists is the seed of that which shall come out of it."

As part of doing what he wanted to do, Ralph and his family had included in their plan the fact that they'd have to sell a lavish home on many wooded acres. In turn, for much less, they bought a small house on an inlet. When his brother visited them, Ralph's wife pointed to their little dock and peaceful water view, "We love it, this really feeds our souls . . ."

"Sure," the man interrupted, "that's fine for now. But you'll soon become indifferent to that. When you've seen one view of water or trees or whatever, you've seen them all—and it's no longer much help."

"Not a chance," she replied. "What you don't understand is that it isn't the dock or the water view that makes us happy. It's living the way we like, doing the simple things that we enjoy most—finally being *ourselves* as we want most to be."

The people who fail themselves and everyone else are those who constantly complain about "the way things are"—but don't do anything about making them better. Are you in this category at all? Too often we tend to use trite, defeatist phrases such as "I can't" . . . "No way" . . . "Too late." Instead, I recommend considering the inspiring, effective approach: "*I will.*"

Change for What Reasons?

Another vital point to mull over: Change for the purpose of pleasing yourself and getting more out of each day is constructive. Change principally for the sake of change, precipitate and unsure, can be seriously destructive. If you approach the desire for change in bitterness and anger, you are likely to make the wrong move.

On the other hand, if you should assess possibilities from a basis of clear thought, and to attain fulfillment and conscious happiness—then, regardless of what the end result may be, your chances for success are heightened enormously. You, your attitudes, your spirit, your strong sense of well-being and self-reliance are the key essentials. For, whatever changes come about, *you* remain.

Your attitude must be to *move forward* to something better, rather than to make a switch *away from*, because of discontentment with your lot and yourself. The results of a rash, unthinking move may cause you to suffer disillusionment as warned in Frenchman Alphonse Karr's proverb: *Plus ça change, plus c'est la même chose*—the more it changes, the more it's the same thing. Instead, you plan your change—if any—carefully, sensibly, optimistically, and the result must inevitably be better for you.

You are extremely fortunate if there is something you are especially enthusiastic about, that you want to do more than anything else. Whatever it may be—to raise a family, teach, be involved in business, mechanics, science, any of the arts, building, merchandising—you name it, and *only* you can name it.

Whatever it is, it must be something that excites, impels, and pleases you deeply as an individual. Then you make your move to become engaged in that endeavor for greater personal fulfillment.

Charles R. Brown commented, "We have too many people living without working, and altogether too many working without living." Not shirking, but working at what inspires or at least satisfies you is a fundamental ingredient in living fully, exultantly. Each of us has that as a birthright, and can and should attain it.

I don't agree with the poet who wrote that "Somewhere above us, in elusive ether/ Lies the fulfillment of our dearest dreams." Dreaming can be fun but it can't be counted on for lasting fulfillment. To strengthen and expand your rich conscious happiness, *doing* is far more dependable than dreaming. Chaucer is more realistic: "Thou shalt make castles then in Spain/ And dream of joy but all in vain."

If you are not doing what you want to do most, please consider the rewards of planning and working toward that better goal now. When you are sure of where you want to go, even if you aim for the number one spot but have to settle for number two or even three, you will have made gains nevertheless. And even minor progress will uplift and sustain you.

The wonderful gains in doing what you want to do have rarely been described more feelingly and effectively than in this statement by the renowned musician Pablo Casals:

"I am thankful to think that at my age I can work on things that are worthwhile. I am almost ninety, perhaps I will die tomorrow. But I try not to think about death. You would have to say that I am an optimist. . . . I refuse, as I always have, to do anything without honor, or without feeling that it is something I really want to do. Never in my life have I done anything I didn't want to do.

"Imagine! At my age I can still do exactly as I did when I was young. What a privilege it is that I can still do everything—still play, conduct, compose, travel, work up a real sweat from time to time. I get tired, of course, but young men get tired too. It's a great thing to be able to work as I do, and I attribute it all to my love of life. I know that I am a happy man. *Alors*, that helps me get along. . . ."

Few of us can say that we have never done anything we didn't want to do—I can't. But, more to the practicable point, can you, do you say that you are a happy individual? If yes, then you are lucky, privileged—and you know it,

131

you appreciate it, you work constantly at keeping it so. If not, appraising how you can turn to doing what you want to do—as indicated here—can help lead you to enduring conscious happiness.

* * *

Checkpoints to Ponder for Possible Personal Action:

1. *Facing your alternatives clearly and squarely.*
2. *Setting your sights accurately.*
3. *Avoiding the wrong analysis.*
4. *Considering your obligations carefully.*
5. *Building the courage of your convictions.*
6. *Strengthening your determination.*
7. *Timing your move . . . if any.*
8. *Rechecking your reasoning, pro and con.*

9

Setting and Reaching Your Most Fulfilling Goal

"A MAN [or woman] must make his opportunity, as oft as find it," advised statesman and philosopher Francis Bacon. You *can* make things better for yourself and for others you care about. But it's very chancy to count on stumbling over it. You can't very well set out on a trip to a known destination where you've never been before without a road map (it's different, of course, if you don't care where you're going).

In addition to most other things, that applies to attaining the goal of conscious happiness to uplift you for the rest of your life. Plan, follow through—as noted here—and you have a good chance of succeeding, at least partially. Then you keep pressing on toward further attainment of what you seek.

A gag sign states: "No amount of planning will ever replace dumb luck." For me it has always been true that no amount of dumb luck (I've had more than my deserved share) can ever replace planning—and doing. What appears to be dumb luck is often the result of that planning and exerting element.

Ask yourself: "Am I counting too much on a stroke of luck—or complaining about lack of it?" An acute observer asserts that "One half of life is luck; the other half is discipline"—and the latter is probably the more important half, for without discipline and volition you wouldn't know what to do with your luck.

For instance, my success in writing diet books with Dr. Stillman might seem to be based on the dumb luck of meeting his daughter-in-law accidentally at a dinner party, and her insistence that he and I get together. We did, and then coauthored five extraordinarily successful books. But we probably would never have joined if it weren't for two other factors:

First: I had been planning to write a diet book for more than ten years; I had studied, researched, collected material toward that goal. Second: When the dumb-luck encounter occurred, I was ready to recognize and seize the opportunity instead of putting it off on the basis that I was busy (which I was). Strokes of fortune pass you by if you're not alert and ready for them. "When good luck comes to thee, take it in," Cervantes urged.

But if you sit around aimlessly, hoping for the lightning of good fortune to strike, probably nothing will develop except an aching back from sitting too much. I planned continually and worked whenever possible for over twenty years on the book you're reading; no dumb luck about it. And it occurs invariably that the rewards from gaining what you seek are all the sweeter for having planned and worked for them.

Furthermore, life is far more interesting and fulfilling when you commit yourself to something, whatever it is—career, avocation, business, or even getting the utmost enjoyment from your use of leisure. A bright lady wrote to "Dear Abby": "I would rather go through life wanting and working for something I don't have—than having and griping about something I don't want."

An expert in the field of mental health divided people into three categories: Sane . . . Insane . . . Unsane. He stated that most people, although "sane," were not fully using their abilities and gaining available goals. Accordingly he labeled them "unsane." Regardless of the groupings, have you asked yourself recently, "How much of my potential am I utilizing?"

Planning or Drifting?

Of course, if your planning makes you reach for too many goals, that fragmented targeting can be self-defeating, as is just drifting about aimlessly. Unless you aim right at the main target, you may be beset by a totally fuzzy view and distorted thinking, fooling yourself and getting nowhere.

With her experienced wisdom, Eleanor Roosevelt warned that many individuals proceed "on the sea of life without any chart or compass, or any special port in view. They are drifting they don't know where. They will never enter the harbor of success. The person who has no definite purpose in view, who aims at nothing in particular, is almost sure to accomplish nothing."

That "success," it must be emphasized, need not be measured in terms of money or position or applause. The greatest accomplishment may be in achieving peace of mind, perhaps rewarding leisure. Ultimately your goal is to gain the sense of pervading happiness and enjoyment of living that is this book's objective for you and justification for me. Whatever your purpose, you are not likely to score a bull's-eye if you don't set up a clear, visible target to shoot at.

You know that if you aim at a number of targets at the same time, your chances are reduced of hitting any one of them in the center. The quickest and most effective way to accomplish anything usually is not to tackle many things at once, but to handle and follow through to one end at a time. On this point, consider the wise commentary in the Bible:

"For which of you, desiring to build a tower, does not first sit down and count the cost, whether he has enough to complete it? Otherwise, when he has laid a foundation, and is not able to finish, all who see it begin to mock him, saying, 'This man began to build, and was not able to finish.' "

Concentrating on your objective is valuable in all kinds of activities. O. J. Simpson, the football superstar, explained why, during a break in a game, he went to the end of the bench, away from all other players, and sat there alone: "I wasn't playing well. . . . I just wanted to get away from everybody and just think about the game. Just concentrate. I hadn't been concentrating and I hadn't been running well. And after that, I got going. Concentration. You've got to concentrate."

He explained further why he refuses all public appearances such as banquets and speaking engagements in the days before a game: "If you don't, you find you can't concentrate." And, the star emphasized, if you don't concentrate, you can't win.

Another too-common mistake made by concerned individuals is that they may concentrate on the problem itself so doggedly and exclusively that they never get around to a solution. Thus they remain at a standstill because they're overly involved in unraveling details or dwelling on negative aspects of the problem. Happily you will find that it's surprisingly simple to analyze the problem by sighting correctly and directly, and then going on to work toward the solution.

Problem . . . Target . . . Solution

A frustrating situation may at times be resolved as readily as in the following case: An attractive young woman, Paula E., complained to me over a period of months, every time we ran into each other, that she wanted to meet "the right man" and get married. "But there just doesn't seem to be any opportunity to meet men naturally, and I'm not going out to hunt them down at singles parties and bars and such."

Here, both her problem and the target were clear. How resolve the issue? Not by complaining and concentrating ineffectually on the problem and target—as she was doing. I asked the obvious question, "Don't you meet any men in your daily work?" She explained that she was the secretary and only employee of a lawyer . . . "And he's married but solidly."

"Ever think of switching to a large law office, with a greater opportunity to meet men, and other women your age who might introduce you to men they know?"

She brightened, "But, of course—why didn't I think of that? Go fishing where the fish are . . ."

When I saw Paula some months later, she told me that she'd landed a good job in a huge legal department, with many men around. She grinned and pointed to her engagement ring, "The plan worked, right?" She added thoughtfully, "But I've talked to a lot of the other girls and, you know, it doesn't always work."

Nothing always works. But when you analyze a problem, set the target, and plan and proceed on a hopeful, practical course, your chances to reach your objective are certainly far better than if you simply brooded over the-sorrow-of-it-all. Whining, self-pity, hopeless acceptance of an undesirable situation—they are all dead ends. Think of what you want to do most of all, then consider actually doing it instead of just thinking about it.

Bellyaching about an unsatisfying condition won't lead you to a gratifying solution. When Katharine Hepburn discussed acting one day, she pointed out that there was too much theorizing going on about it and not enough doing. She said bluntly, "A lot of hogwash is talked about acting. It's not all that fancy! Talk, talk, talk, talk, *talk!* Spencer Tracy always said acting was 'Learn your lines and get on with it,' so does Larry Olivier, so does John Gielgud, all the great ones."

After careful thought, she went on slowly, "*Life's* what's important. Walking, houses, family. Birth and pain and joy—and then death. Acting's just waiting for a custard pie. That's all . . ." In short, get to it, do it, don't ponder too much.

Make a start. The next step is to aim at the right target, and then follow through to successful completion, as delineated on these pages. Keep in mind the instructions that a captain in a lifeboat would give to his oarsmen: "Don't miss anything new on the horizon. Look for an unexpected ship or other help. *But keep on rowing straight to the shore!*"

Analyzing Your Problem

Before you begin, you must realize that you cannot set your true target or find your right solution unless you have first analyzed your problem correctly. "Oh, come on," you may be thinking, "I'm not a simpleton—I know what my problem is, naturally." Do you—really? You can't start successfully in the middle of a plan; you must begin at the beginning to achieve the best ending. Please consider the point carefully, in thorough detail, before you set any personal conclusion firmly in mental cement.

In step two of the Six-Step Creative Thinking Method in my Bantam book, *Your Key to Creative Thinking*, I delineate how to analyze each problem in order to focus on the wanted solution or target. The fallacy of analyzing a problem incorrectly is illustrated by the old story of the red-faced man who told his doctor, "My problem is high blood pressure causing my headaches." After examination, the physician advised, "Nothing wrong with your blood pressure. Your problem is tight collars bringing on headaches."

You can't very well come up with the right answers unless you start with the right questions to lead to your true objective. You have to analyze and understand exactly where you stand and what your goal is before you decide in what direction you should make your moves.

Samuel Johnson put it this way: "That fellow seems to me to possess but one idea, and that is the wrong one." You cannot very well decide what is right and what is wrong until you have a pretty clear determination about what is right or wrong for *you*. Nor should you settle for the obvious. It pays to look around, behind, beyond. Take that second look—and more.

An analysis of your problem made too quickly, right off the top of your head, can aim you in the *wrong* direction. You could miss your mark just as surely and devastatingly as a football player running with the ball to the opposing team's goal line. Beware the swift, stubborn answer. "A closed mind, like a closed room, can be awfully stuffy." (However, it's reassuring to me that if you didn't have an open, searching mind, you wouldn't be venturing into this book.)

It's not only foolish but wasteful to press a trigger before you've taken careful aim. You must sight mindfully, question what you really want of life—not just fix on the first glib, emerging answer or so-called solution because it's easier that way. For instance, if a student analyzing the situation for her higher education asks, "What's the best college?" she is asking the wrong question. The right approach is, "What's the best college *for me?*"

Your thinking must be right on target for best results—thinking that is going places, not just being dissipated in many directions on vague generalities. That "Think" sign on the wall can lead to great waste of time if you let your mind grope aimlessly instead of directly and purposefully. You should learn to think *creatively*—as covered in the next chapter.

Try Self-Analysis

One excellent way to sight your personal problems clearly is through self-analysis, as discussed earlier. Take your time (your entire lifetime is ahead of you) to be influenced productively by your correct analysis now. Talk it over with yourself, concentrate for yourself (or, as an additional approach, discuss the matter with your husband, wife, close friend, or others). Ask penetrating questions such as these to elicit the revealing, clarifying answers you need:

1. What is the basic problem I must resolve for my happier future?
2. Why is that my fundamental, pivotal problem?
3. Are there other problems that may be more important?
4. Think deeper, consider other aspects . . . am I sure that this is the one biggest issue influencing my way of life?
5. Don't decide yet, keep digging . . . can't I list some other possibilities?
6. Would any of these alternatives be a better answer for me?

7. Okay, I've double-checked all my answers . . . but hadn't I better delineate my problem *in detail?*

Try the write-it-out system of self-analysis too. Instead of just pondering the answers in your mind or in conversation, write them down. You don't have to be "a writer." Don't be concerned about grammar or syntax or style. Just clarify and utter truth to yourself, then write out your answers. Set it down clearly, you can reexamine, dissect, revise your answers again and again.

When too many thoughts start tumbling around in my mind, I make a list. Then I attend to each thought in turn, crossing each one out as I analyze it, one after the other, both on the list and in my mind. That helps clear the brain and arrive at the final correct solution which I then set down and recheck.

After that thorough kind of forthright, probing self-questioning and analysis, you are a lot more likely to know and understand your many problems (if any) accurately. Then you move ahead to set up your target goal, and work toward your resolution. On the other hand, a so-called solution or answer without enough thought often is the wrong answer and can mislead you in your quest for a happier way of life.

Avoid complicating matters, however, by looking for meanings within meanings endlessly. When I was in the business of writing advertisements, working late one night, I was surprised to see one of the mailroom boys, Henry, at my office door. I called out, "Anything I can do for you?"

He flushed, hesitated, then blurted, "I'd like to write ads. But I don't know how to start. I guess you have to check those five basic points, huh—getting attention, focusing buying interest . . ."

"Whoa! Don't complicate it and get all tangled up. Simplify. It's this easy: Pretend you're the salesperson be-

141

hind a retail counter, facing a customer on the other side. What you tell her in person is what you write to sell her through an ad. Ever sell anything to anyone?"

"Sure. I sold storm windows during college vacations."

"Fine. What did you talk about first? Five basic points? The factory? The manufacturing process?"

"No. I said, 'You can cut your heating costs ten percent next winter . . .'"

"Great. No complications. That's your headline. Then you go and write your ad."

"Gosh," he grinned, "writing ads is easy." He left, very chipper.

I turned back to the typewriter and pecked out, "You can cut your heating costs ten percent next winter." Only trouble was, I was writing an ad about brassieres . . .

Once you are sure what your fundamental problem is, then your goal and your target for improvement become clear. It may be that you want to get out of a working or living-style rut . . . expand your mind . . . add new, more challenging activities. Whatever the problem may be, how can you best achieve your objective?

Ways to Get There

Instead of taking a quick and possibly disastrous leap into uncertainty, isn't it much wiser to *make haste deliberately and intelligently*? That's entirely different from putting things off, and never getting to your goal. In a reasoned way, you can move ahead carefully, surely, confidently. The astronauts' "one giant leap for mankind," landing on the moon, as pronounced by Neil Armstrong, was no sudden spring or somersault. It took decades of effort and slow advances to reach and score the final stunning achievement.

The tastiest dishes are usually cooked in small batches. Long practice sessions produce the most proficient musicians—but, if necessary, you can learn to play an instrument well by practicing in small snatches of time whenever you can. Many authors like myself, when required, have written books by using a few minutes or longer whenever available to add some more lines and paragraphs, growing into pages. You can make great headway toward your goal in short, cautious steps; at least you are less likely to trip and fall on your face.

At one time in business I asked my secretary, Mary Chiat, to compile a list of two hundred sources for specific kinds of information. "Two hundred?" she echoed, horrified. "That'll take the rest of my life!"

"Try it this way: First, aim at collecting twenty-five names. Then twenty-five more. At that point you'll be a quarter finished already. After one hundred, you're more than halfway there and heading down the home stretch to the end. Now that isn't so tough, is it?"

She went at it that way and completed the list in a few days.

It's disastrous to your digestion as well as to your success plan to try to eat a whole portion of food or to consume almost anything in one huge, all-encompassing bite. Or to use up all your energy and drive in one gigantic jump forward. Metropolitan Opera star Robert Merrill said that one of the best pieces of advice he'd ever received was from voice teacher Giuseppe De Luca: "Don't draw all your voice out of the bank. Leave some on deposit."

But that doesn't condone endless delay—"I'll think about it tomorrow." Sure, think about it tomorrow, but you'll never make the headway you want until you transform those tomorrows into today and decide: now, this is it, time to act. Time is stolen from you primarily when you let it slip by.

What Do You Know?

It's revitalizing to learn more about the subject that interests you most and that you find most fulfilling—to make your future better. Dig into what excites you personally and gives you the greatest lift. Ability based on know-how is a tremendous asset.

There are many ways to gain valuable information that can help you move forward as you wish. Search out illuminating books and other publications at libraries and bookstores. Look into educational opportunities usually available in adult programs in schools and universities in your area, special training schools, even courses by mail. "Learning is the eye of the mind."

You can wake up and expand your mind further by investigating in every possible way whatever interests you most, in or out of your chosen field of activity. Any such delving improves your thinking processes, brings greater enjoyment of life through learning. And it makes you more able and productive in whatever you do.

Learning helps to equip you with the tools you need for any endeavor, including daily living—you are better prepared. The renowned pianist Artur Rubinstein was stopped after a concert by a young man who held out an autograph book and asked for a signature. Rubinstein agreed, "Give me a pencil or pen." "I'm sorry, I haven't any." Rubinstein thrust the book back and snapped, "I'm a pianist so I bring a piano. You want an autograph—bring a pencil!"

I have taught and lectured at a number of universities through the years, yet I take some kind of educational course one night a week at a university twenty-five miles away. I've been doing this for many years with an educator, a friend who heads a sizable preparatory school. Why do we use a precious evening each week this way? Because we dig into something fresh and outside our daily work, reaching toward new horizons, new challenges that prod, open, excite the mind.

Such mental exercise can make you more able and effective at whatever you undertake. The stimulation inspires and elicits ever more rewarding conscious happiness within you.

Education, whether in organized classes or self-education, develops and improves all your capacities, including your appreciation of all about you. It augments and boosts your ability to look, to see—and to want to. You'll find that in many ways you can do things that you never could do before. Joseph Addison stated: "What sculpture is to a block of marble, education is to the soul." How about digging into available knowledge, and taking one or more courses to excite your mind and enhance your living?

Making Dreams Come True

Aimless dreaming won't work. However, it can happen that a person dreams that something he's involved with will come true—and then he acts to *make it come true*. Otherwise it might never have come to fruition. And that sequence of dreaming-plus-action can be effective at times.

An example is a man, Richard G., who had an interview during the day for a new job that he wanted very much. The interviewer finished by saying, "We'll call you and let you know." That night Dick dreamed that he'd received the call, went in for a second interview, and got the job at a big increase in salary.

Waking up, he realized that it had all been a dream. He hoped the resolution would come true. Furthermore, he was now convinced that he wanted the job more than ever—so he went into action. Instead of waiting for the phone call, as he had intended, he sat down and wrote out in detail how he would handle the position. He set down some of his ideas which might work well for the employer. Then he delivered his presentation in person.

The following day, just as had happened in his dream, he was called and granted a follow-up interview. He was complimented highly on his presentation—and was hired. Joyously Dick told me, "See, dreams *do* come true." His wife, Betty, interrupted dryly, "Sure—especially when you knock yourself out to make them come true."

One of the greatest gains from setting a plan and moving forward is that you become imbued with a surprising sense of thrilling new adventure. It's as though you've elected to try, and then find yourself climbing, advancing to a towering mountain peak, a new higher plateau. You have a sense of a beckoning new phase of life opening up, with the very special feeling of exultation that *you have made it happen*. Not chance or fate—*you* did it.

For you are seeking, learning, gaining in exposing yourself to something new. And that is not the end, but rather is the beginning—always another beginning. You increase your ability to judge, to plan, to move forward, constantly searching, venturing, not pressing too hard but wide open and eager. Always you are ready for more happiness as you open yourself wide to experience, saying in effect, "Here I am, life. I'm ready, willing, eager"—and then you act.

Making the Most of Skills

Another way to a solution is to make the most of skills and inclinations that you possess but haven't used fully. In one case, William T., sales manager of a greeting card concern, had his income cut drastically when the company was taken over by new owners. Distressed and disgusted, he told his wife, Marjorie, that he didn't want to be in that kind of insecure situation again. He yearned to be his own boss.

She came up with an idea: "We've both always loved playing parlor games and, let's face it, we're darned good at it. Boxed games are in the same general field as greeting cards in some aspects. Why don't we create some new games and have them manufactured. I have time on my hands with the kids off at school, I can run the office while you do the selling."

Thus, the problem was analyzed and defined. They set their target and proceeded with a detailed plan. After early hard times, as provided for in their long-range prospectus, the business took off and grew way beyond their calculations. Best of all, they were exhilarated by doing what they wanted, based on what they'd always liked.

Think about it: Is there something you're doing right now, or something you enjoy very much—an avocation, a special interest, a unique ability, an exceptional possibility —that you could expand to add to your happiness? Would it enable you to use more of your time in the most fulfilling way for yourself?

In another instance within my personal experience, a food merchandiser who had become fed up with his daily grind griped to me about it. He also talked a lot about his love for gardening. After many probing discussions, he decided to look into the commercial possibilities. He tracked down some promising gardening products, and eventually left his job to package and sell his own items. He is having a ball in a field that gives pleasure to so many, as well as himself. He finds it profitable in every way.

These individuals, like many others, women as well as men, are doing what they want, based on what they'd always liked to do. Can you apply similar angles for yourself perhaps: problem . . . target . . . solution? Have you special talents and abilities? Never stop trying. There are great rewards even in the trying itself.

Combining your abilities with another's, or perhaps with several people, often leads to achieving a goal. A gifted and very successful fabric designer, Boris Kroll, who creates breathtaking, intricate patterns, had a tough time originally. He told me, "I couldn't get going in the early years because all the millmen I encountered looked at my designs for reproduction on motorized looms and said, 'Impossible to weave them.'

"Finally I met one enterprising expert—yes, your father —who studied my painted patterns carefully. He became enthusiastic and said, 'They're beautiful. Let's see how we can solve the manufacturing problem. I have an idea . . .' Combining our abilities, optimism and energy, we succeeded—the impossible became actual." A possibility for you to make the impossible come true by joining your abilities with others?

Always keep in mind that advances can be made without overpressuring yourself by aiming to overachieve beyond your energies and capacities. You don't have to accomplish everything "today." By leaving something over, you reserve a challenge that you can look forward to for interesting possibilities tomorrow and tomorrow and tomorrow. "The impossible takes a little longer . . ."

Do Something . . .
Lead, Follow . . .
Or Get Out of the Way!

Those words are on a sign I saw framed on an office wall. You can analyze your problem, sight your target, and plan on getting there. But all that isn't conclusive and fully productive unless you *"do something"* about it—even if what you do is to decide that your best move is to "get out of the way" by staying put and making the most of your situation in living as it stands and develops. That's true whether your objective is to achieve conscious happiness or, in addition, success in some new endeavor or enterprise.

Daring to consider something new takes volition, courage, and time. Improving yourself always involves some risks. But, as Frederick B. Wilson noted: "You can't steal second base and keep your foot on first." At least make a beginning. You'll gain stimulating rewards even from just thinking thoroughly about possible moves forward toward greater happiness.

You must work unceasingly to reach your goal. Author MacKinley Kantor defined this in respect to a would-be writer's essential drive: "He will write, and continue writing, and continue learning from his own mistakes—he will write in the face of poverty or illness or physical suffering, or the misery of lost love; he will write, you can't stop him; he will write in his mind and soul and heart—write while he is washing dishes or digging ditches or driving a taxi or flying an airplane or helping to lay out a corpse; he is a writer, he knows it, and he wants the world to know it; he will keep trying to convince the world, no matter how the sweat pours off, or how the blood flows."

Plotting a Better Future

If you don't make a determination as to your future course, confusion and discontent will continue to burden you. Don't let ingrained timidity or negativism hold you back: "Inhibitions are tied up in *nots*." If you don't think it through and come to a conclusion about where you are going or want to go, then you'll never even know it when you arrive. In spite of the old saying, all roads *don't* lead to Rome.

And, of course, you must plot your itinerary to your goal clearly and as precisely as possible, taking your time in sighting it correctly. Get involved, go right to the nub, don't waltz around the edges of your objective. When I write a book, I strive not to just write *about* something but, rather, the book must be completely involved with *the something itself*.

Get excited about what you're doing, even if it's continuing on your past course—but with fresh, new insights. Your enthusiastic approach when you begin or even continue something, in effect getting your second wind, can influence the outcome greatly. William James asserted, "Human beings can alter their lives by altering their attitudes of mind." Look for, find, and then use the extra possibilities, pluses you didn't see before because you weren't looking. The extras are invariably there—all you have to do is discover them.

As a case in point: I attended a meeting about an improved little product at a manufacturer's office. "What's special about this item?" I asked the gloomy sales manager. He kept staring at it without enthusiasm. "Well," he mumbled, "we're improved it but nothing that really shows, nothing we can hook a sales story to. It's not different enough."

I examined the item carefully, then proposed, "Let's really look at it, see if there's something to get excited about. Why is this reinforced band set here? Why this opening here? Isn't this material a lot stronger than the other?" More questions—why? what? how? The group caught fire.

By the time I had all the answers, jotting as they talked, I was able to say, "Look at this list—nine new or improved features—this item is nine ways better than before!" The others became aroused about the "nine ways better" product. The dramatic, informative advertising interested women. Sales were nine times better than before.

Get excited, simplify, make your move—"Short steps are better than no steps at all." Remember that by doing, you make your own luck—for good luck is usually being able to seize opportunities that develop when you have planned and prepared to benefit from them before they occur.

A child asked, "Where does the world start?" And a wise teacher answered, "At your fingertips." But you must reach out for it and clutch it. And you must never let go, but keep reaching always; your arm can be as long as you will make it be.

"But I'm No Einstein . . ."

Some people tend to grumble, "Well, getting places is a cinch for others with more ability. Take Einstein, for instance. It was easy for him to accomplish miracles. As a scientific genius, solutions came readily for him. But I'm no Einstein . . ."

The truth is quite the opposite. Einstein had trouble getting even passing grades during some of his schooling. He admitted, "I cannot do mathematical calculations easily. I do them not willingly and not readily." He had to work at it incessantly and even painfully.

A teacher who had known Professor Einstein at Princeton told me that, as a student, he delivered some papers to the scientist at home, and was asked to stay for tea. The young man plunged into the possibilities of a new scientific approach he had in mind. Swiftly he drew some graphs on paper and was presenting his ideas pell-mell when Einstein held up his hand and stopped him. "Please," he asked, "go slowly. Please. I don't learn things very fast."

151

That tremendous brain, like many others not nearly so bright, learned the tough way that working hard on a project or problem, and overcoming obstacles, often produced the best results. And, equally important, brought the deepest satisfaction.

It should be obvious too that it's wasteful and counterproductive to indulge in negative thinking, to sigh, "I just haven't the talent or prowess." Consider a test involving athletes who felt they had reached their peak performance. Under hypnosis, in a group experiment, many of them improved their performances by as much as 25 percent over their previous records.

Realize that it wasn't the hypnosis which caused them to do so much better. It was the fact that they were released from inhibitions and limitations *they had imposed on themselves.* You can't know how well you can do until you try. But you'll never get to that starting point of trying if you downgrade yourself and thus hold yourself back.

Please don't sell yourself short. If you believe in what you're aiming for, keep trying, keep pushing. Possibly the most famous children's books are those by Dr. Seuss (Theodore Geisel). His first book was rejected by twenty-seven publishers on the grounds that verse and fantasy don't sell, that his stories were too unusual and not instructive. The author persisted. The twenty-eighth publisher issued the book just because he liked it. Millions of Dr. Seuss books have been sold. Next time you think of giving up, ask yourself, "Have I tried twenty-eight times worth?"

". . . the Time Is Now . . ."

Perhaps you will find exceptional inspiration, as I do, in a letter reprinted in part from my book, *Samm Baker's Clear & Simple Gardening Handbook.* The communication came from a gracious lady in her seventies, Mercedes Boyle, whom I knew only through correspondence after she wrote me a fan letter. Her words always provide a lift for me, and I hope for you:

"Mr. Baker, I'm a gardener in a hurry. Forty years ago my husband and I bought land and built a house. For forty years I planned to garden but never planted a flower. With children and then grandchildren and other matters, it was always 'perhaps next year.' Finally the time is now. I started and my plants are flourishing and my lawn is green.

"My husband who is eighty-three years young asks me not to work so hard when planting my glads, for instance. He said, 'Just take a broomstick, roll it around and drop the bulb in—it will grow.' But your instructions were carried out to the letter, and every gladiolus planted is flourishing, every one of them.

"Now from across the street an elderly lady tells me how much she enjoys seeing my grass and gardens from her window. Persons passing admire how my garden grows, and are particularly interested in my blueberries and tell me how they picked them in the wild. Soon I'll pick them from my yard.

"I'm a person with a plan long cherished and at last accomplished. *My aching back vanishes and my garden grows!*"

There is motivating force for action—perhaps the time is now—in Shakespeare's evocative words:

> There is a tide in the affairs of men,
> Which, taken at the flood,
> leads on to fortune.

When is the tide "at the flood" for you, as it comes repeatedly for each individual? Right now, this minute, today, tomorrow—whenever you elect to ride with the impetus. "Every delay that postpones our joy is long." There are no charges, no tolls for setting out on the road to conscious happiness. You merely assert your will . . .

Will you?

* * *

Think about the statement of Oliver Wendell Holmes in relation to your future: "I find that the great thing in the world is not only where we stand, but also in what direction we are moving." Please check again these guideposts toward setting and reaching your most fulfilling goal:

1. *Don't just drift and dream . . . plan.*
2. *Analyze your problems thoroughly.*
3. *Fix the target clearly.*
4. *Work toward your best solution.*
5. *Use your skills to the utmost for most wanted results.*
6. *The time to start is: now.*

Realize that making a start to your better future is as simple as stated by actor Spencer Tracy: "I took a part and did it—the best I could—not bothering to analyze the why's and wherefore's. I DID IT—and that was that."

Do it!

10

Recognizing and Developing Your Creativity

REGARDLESS OF WHAT has happened with you before, from now on you will be a more creative person. That's important to you, for alert, searching creativity is a vital asset in achieving, maintaining, and enjoying to the utmost a surging sense of conscious happiness.

What do I mean by creativity here? And what does it mean to you? As noted earlier, I devoted an entire book to the subject (*Your Key to Creative Thinking*). But right now I want to help you and urge you to recognize, develop, and use your inborn creativity, in order to gain the most from life for your fullest appreciation of inner satisfaction.

You, along with every other individual, possess creativity—to greater or lesser degrees. That doesn't necessarily require special ability in the arts—painting, sculpting, music, writing, and so on. As you will note, creativity is involved in every aspect of living. Your mind, whatever your interest, is all the power plant your creativity requires. What you have to do is operate it consciously for greatest benefit.

What is creativity? Others have defined the quality...
"Involving new and beneficial ideas put into action" ...
"A process of planning, experiencing, acting, and interacting" ... "Thinking which results in a solution not
previously known to us." Here's my definition of creativity
with its integral link to conscious happiness:

> Creativity is alert thinking, involvement, and activity
> each day—aimed to see and use and improve upon
> everything possible—for most satisfying, fulfilling, and
> enjoyable living.

To repeat purposefully, everyone possesses some
creativity. Certainly you do, or you wouldn't be acting
to help improve your future by reading this book. But
are you aware of your full capacity? Are you using it to
make every day the best it can be for yourself, and for
others? If you doubt that you are at all creative, please
accept my assurance, and that of many authorities. Creative thinking is constructive thinking that becomes action
—your personal action and interaction from first to last.

A psychologist stated that the capacity to be creative
"is not limited to the highly gifted person, but is the
birthright of every person." Another affirmed: "Creativity
is in every one of us." An educator throws this challenge
at you: "Virtually every person has more creative ability
than he is putting to use."

A research specialist in the field concluded: "In children, creativity is universal; creativity was in each one of
us as a small child." He stressed that the use of inborn
creativity diminished in many adults. . . . "What has happened to this enormous and universal human resource?"

What has happened is that creativity lies latent and ineffectual without conscious attention and use. But it is
there within you, a lode of precious gold to be mined by

you actively always—and certainly from now on as you become more aware of its presence and value.

Granted that everyone, that you, possesses creativity. Now please ask yourself, "Am I using my creative abilities and capacities to the utmost—to make my life happier, more fulfilling, for myself and others?" Whatever your answer—realizing that the only answer worthwhile is an honest one—your greater attentiveness to your creativity is sure to make your future more rewarding.

Expanding your creativity cannot help but make things better, as you concentrate consciously on using your innate and gradually augmented capacities. As with everything else worth gaining, you must work at it. President Woodrow Wilson admitted, "I use not only all the brains I have, but all I can borrow."

Your enlivened, more assertive creativity can help you to overcome many obstacles and problems which have beset you in the past. Nobel Prize winner Dr. Glenn T. Seaborg said: "I believe that one of the characteristics of the human race—possibly the one that is primarily responsible for its course of evolution—is that it has grown by creatively responding to failure."

And you respond with increasing gains to success as well. For creativity can capitalize on and speed your movement forward, mentally, emotionally, in all aspects. But you must apply the effort. Henry Ford said bitterly, "Thinking is the hardest work there is, which is the probable reason why so few engage in it."

I believe that thinking is easy, and thinking is fun. The primary reason why people don't exert their creative thinking power more is that they are not aware of the possibilities, and therefore don't take advantage consciously of their thinking potential. But now that you know, you will in the future make advances powered by your known and utilized capacity.

157

Improving Your Creativity

One way to expand your creativity is to open yourself to new knowledge and subsequent thought by attending classes, lectures, exposing yourself to stimulation by other minds in every way, wherever and whenever possible. Returning from a lecture which dwelt with the background, growth, and ideas of Professor Einstein, I sat down at once and wrote in a letter to my son:

"In the lecture series I'm attending, tonight's choice of great figures that influenced history was Einstein. It was an exciting session, probing the man as a human being, his theories, dramatic example of how genius can change the world. Always I leave the classroom with a real high of intellectual elation. Learning about creative people strengthens my own creativity. It affirms the challenging line of Holmes: 'A man's mind, stretched by a new idea, can never go back to its original dimension.'"

You exercise and strengthen your "mental muscles" by becoming involved, participating in stimulating activities —town meetings, school committees and special events, library presentations, engaging in thought-provoking conversations. Why not set out to take part in more such opportunities?

Such availabilities exist but you must look for them, and then exert the volition to participate. Discuss, argue, ask questions. You'll be thrilled at how your mental activity and resultant creativity—prodded by the thoughts and ideas of others—tend to expand as you become more mentally alive than before.

You'll find yourself hugely enjoying "the adventure of the human mind" as you venture into new realms of mental growth through an increased flow of ideas, yours and those with whom you come in contact. Yes—originality and inventiveness can grow just from a fresh look at things. You will find that "thinking is the most satisfying experience in life" (as Socrates stated)—well, at least one of the most satisfying experiences in life.

Do you hesitate because you feel an age barrier, whatever your age? Forget that. There is no reason why that should be true. Usually it's just an excuse for holding back through shyness, lassitude, laziness, lack of confidence, or for whatever other reason. The ability to be more creative, to your fullest capacity, isn't restricted by being too young, too old, or too in between. And the more you use your creativity, at any age, the more you uncover. The supply is limitless, confined only by disinterest, by yourself.

New Yorker magazine's Brendan Gill, at almost sixty, found himself in an unprecedented surge of activity, based on his lifelong experience. Working twelve hours a day, as never before, he had produced—aside from his regular work—three books in two years, along with a stream of short stories. Two more books he outlined were contracted for the following year. Asked how he managed it after about six decades of living at a slower pace, he explained:

"I've had a burst of creativity due to coming of age, my two youngsters off on their own, my wife occupied with her own work and activities, so now—I could let myself go." He grinned with fierce enthusiasm. "I'm just bulling everything through. It's crazy, but it's my kind of craziness. I find I have much more energy in these years— I'm at the typewriter from 7:30 to 7:30. . . . Every day something good comes along."

Meeting this ardent gentleman, I found sheer enjoyment of living—conscious happiness—radiating from him. He was interested in everything, and consequently interesting about anything. He affirmed that whatever he does, he approaches it with the anticipation that "something wonderful will happen." And you will find, with a similar creative approach, that something wonderful, or at least stimulating, does happen. New ideas are certainly more likely to enter and be absorbed by an open mind.

This constant sense of alertness and anticipation provides ever-fresh stimuli to spark your creativity so that fresh ideas erupt. You must continually bring in new thoughts, facts, details that you gather from exposure to provocative events and people. Then it becomes easier, in fact irresistible, to get the ideas out and in use.

As an example that you must be constantly alert: a creative scientist doesn't come upon his innovative theories or inventions by brooding alone and then suddenly shrieking, "Eureka, I've got it!" He or she has invariably put in years of studying, of painstaking and persistent research, of exposing herself to all kinds of thoughts and possibilities before arriving at the trend-setting productive conclusion. The same is true for each of us, in applying and gaining from our creativity in daily living.

Benefit from an Avocation

Every hobby, avocation, additional productive activity of any kind adds to your creativity—and uses it for your immediate and lasting benefit. It can be in the arts but doesn't have to be at all—the scope is unlimited. Gregor Piatigorsky, world-famous cellist, provides assurance: "Everyone who strives for and achieves excellence (in any endeavor) is an artist. I have not yet met a person without a talent for something."

Yours may be a talent for collecting, making things with your hands or with machines, designing, sewing: pratically any productive activity is a possibility. Yours may simply be a valuable, very helpful talent (if you will use it fully) for giving and sharing friendship. It may be sheer enjoyment of living, appreciation of beauty—taking walks, gardening, birdwatching—you name it, you know yourself.

A charming acquaintance, Diane F., told me that she was concerned about her creativity being stifled to the point of being practically nonexistent. She complained, "My family chores, humdrum but demanding daily duties, keep me from expressing myself." Usually this means, upon analysis, that the person is simply accepting what goes on and not making any positive attempt to "express herself" or himself.

I'd heard that this lady was rated as an exceptional cook and hostess. I suggested that she consider exerting her creativity consciously in those directions. "Why not take specialty cooking lessons through classes or books? Since you're so great at decorating your own home, how about taking a flower-arranging course at the local women's club, or learning more about the business of home decoration?" She looked surprised, "I never thought of that. . . ."

When we visited her at home for dinner several months later, she said enthusiastically that she had become absorbed in flower arranging, as exemplified by the beautiful creative displays in the living room and on the dining table. "I won a prize last week," she exclaimed, "and I'm going to prepare a really artistic entry for the annual area Flower Show next month. I enjoy handling flowers so much, selecting unusual containers, decorating with little stones and shells—it's all so creative!" "Careful, Diane," her husband laughed proudly. "Soon you'll be a pro."

A man in his fifties, Ted M., decided to express his creativity finally by becoming a ham radio operator. A friend mocked him, "That's for kids. It's too late for you." But he refused to be discouraged. Visiting him recently, he took me to his "radio shack," a little room in the eaves of his old house.

His eyes lit up with adventure as he turned on the

many-dialed equipment. Tubes glowed. "I put that set together from a kit," he explained joyously. "Me, who used to have ten thumbs. And it works! After a tough day's work, instead of being shot I feel all charged up when I come up here." A strangely accented voice emerged from the loudspeaker, repeating his call letters, "XXXX, Brazil, calling KKKK . . . are you there, KKKK?" My friend turned to me, his face animated, "That's me—I've got friends all over the world!"

Your creative activity can be practically anything with a positive aspect, helpful in adding to your personal gain in conscious happiness from what you do, along with your wholehearted participation in what goes on about you. Gain from what *you cause to happen*—that's creativity. You benefit in expansion of yourself, by yourself.

Just decide what "other" activity, aside and in addition to your regular way of living, would interest you most— and go to it. The idea of travel excites you? Make it a hobby, for whatever length of time you can give it—investigate, plan, dig into the literature, scan maps—enjoy! Whatever you choose, you profit in many ways that will keep you keyed up creatively and in other ways beyond your expectations. Each chooses for himself or herself, often going very far afield from the past norm. Coin collecting? Stock market analysis? Social work? Volunteer efforts? Do it!

Creative Self-Discovery

Popular singer Tony Bennett took up amateur painting, and expressed his delight at the rewards: "Painting encloses me in a bubble of warmth. When I'm on the road, I take a sketchbook, and it's a relief, between cities, to sketch everything you see. Later, a lot of those sketches turn into paintings."

"Warmth" . . . "relief." Those are only two of the beneficial feelings you get from the creative act, whether it's painting or puttering that's enlivened with your personal touches—anything that especially pleases *you*. Tony Bennett found that his extra creative activity made him a happier person in the deepest sense, and a better husband, father, friend as well. Expand your creative individuality and you can't help but become a livelier, better individual—for yourself and others.

Using your creativity, you will find, spurs your greater self-discovery. Pulitzer Prize–winning novelist Joyce Carol Oates said, "The average person is deeper, more talented, and more intelligent than he or she probably believes." Famed English painter John Constable stressed this aspect: "Painting is with me but another word for *feeling*."

The same bonus accrues from any creative activity. You will find that using your latent creativity opens your pores wider to living. The pursuit itself enhances your increased enjoyment of every possible moment of living.

Again, don't think that your special interest must be something exalted and perhaps out of reach for you, primarily because you have convinced yourself that it is so. It doesn't have to be in the arts, it must be emphasized. But if you've always had a hidden yen to try painting, sculpting, ceramics, anything like that, go ahead—*try it*.

As a sometime artist, married to a professional painter and art teacher, I assure you that you don't need special talent to enjoy the exhilaration that comes from painting a picture, or molding a figure from clay. Great art requires extraordinary talent and dedication. But the thrill of producing art of whatever caliber is available to everyone, to you. The time is now. No extravagantly far leap required. You begin, then you expand if you like. And you move ahead step by step in creative pursuit at whatever pace you desire.

Einstein's out-of-laboratory avocation was collecting

mathematical puzzles and games, including the simplest, childlike riddles. That simple involvement tickled him and, he claimed, activated and enlarged his thinking when he concentrated in his daily work on trying to solve the puzzles of the universe. An outside interest can be that helpful for an acknowledged intellectual wizard—and for you.

Look Beyond the Obvious

At one time I was involved in creating advertising for a well-known liniment which had proved its effectiveness for years in relieving aching muscles. Discussing the search for a fresh theme, a weary copy writer in our group moaned, "No use, it's impossible to come up with anything new. We've done so many campaigns over the years, we've exhausted the possibilities . . . "

I persisted, "There must be a way of taking a new look." "No," the discouraged writer shook her head. "We've examined every which way what happens on the skin. We've analyzed the product all over again. Sniffed it. Patted it on. Rubbed it on. Sprayed it heavily, lightly. We've tested every possibility that might reveal itself on the skin—"

"Wait a minute! We haven't looked into what happens *under* the skin. . . ." A laboratory was hired to work with patients, using recently developed infrared photography. They checked in detail what occurs under the skin. The pictures showed vividly how application of the liniment expanded veins under the surface, bringing fresh supplies of blood fast. Those photos were used in dramatic, new, informative ads, which proved exceptionally successful.

What's the point? The creative view is unlimited. Creatively you look beyond the obvious—above, below, behind, within, sideways, every possible and almost impossible way. You seek the *inside story* as well as what meets the eye and the mind at first sight. You always, whatever the view and the viewpoint, try to see "beyond the range of sight."

Groups of assorted people look at the same thing—but how much they derive from the viewing varies. Philosopher Thomas Traherne pointed out: "All men see the same objects, but do not equally understand them. Intelligence is the tongue that discerns them and tastes them." To intelligence must be added *conscious creativity*—the desire and the act.

Being creative means looking a little harder, deciding that average isn't good enough. So you keep trying for that little extra—caring, seeking, exerting yourself and your intelligence and abilities a little more.

Realize always, and be inspired by the fact that there are no set boundaries to energetic, searching creative thinking. Don't fence yourself in. Being aware of and using your alert creativity can help you make every moment new, inviting, and more satisfying.

A vital part of creativity is using your imagination—to which you know there are no limits. A radio newsman, Philip G., told about visiting a wonderful Italian lady, Marie M., aged seventy-one, who is blind. She supports herself by sewing clothes creatively and beautifully for others. There was a huge color TV in her sparsely furnished room. She said that the TV gave her great enjoyment.

He asked, "But why did you spend a lot of money on a color TV set? You must know that a black-and-white TV set is much cheaper." She made a grimace of distaste and explained, "Oh, I don't enjoy black-and-white TV at all. This way I can imagine the colors better—costumes, backgrounds, everything."

165

Don't be afraid to use your imagination, whatever others may say. It's all yours, there's no charge for employing and enjoying it. Someone remarked that he couldn't become interested in eating artichokes—until in imagination he started thinking of the leaves as petticoats. Then he became curious as to what was under them. . . .

Patience!

After a discussion in this vein, a woman complained to me a couple of days later, "I don't feel any more creative than I did when we talked, and I've been trying . . ." It turned out that she had only been thinking about trying rather than setting out for a specific goal as suggested.

In any case, I urged, "Patience!" Each day that you consciously exert your creativity toward a decided target strengthens that quality and your ability. It is a muscle that is exercised—the muscle doesn't expand and firm immediately. Keep at it, and there is notable improvement week by week—and similarly with your creative ability. You must flex it purposefully to make it grow.

And you must not be concerned about the possibility of not succeeding to your highest expectations. You will improve, you can't help it. Even the trying itself produces the gratifying rewards of attempting something innovative, and alerting your senses as you exert effort. The act of attempted creativity alone is unfailingly exhilarating.

The inventor of the Polaroid camera, Dr. Land, has noted that any scientist trying to create something new is permitted to fail repeatedly. He or she keeps trying until he finally gets the result he visualized—or tries another tack. Dr. Land stressed, "*An essential aspect of creativity is not being afraid to fail.*"

You Own a Treasure Chest

Since it has been affirmed by so many authorities (and I agree with them completely), you can believe it: the mind of practically every human being, from the earliest years until the end, is a treasure chest of ideas. But you must open the treasure chest to benefit from the contents. You must lift the lid, open the box, reach in, use the treasure. And then repeat the process non-stop, day after day.

T. S. Eliot, speaking of just one of the numberless forms of creativity, said that writing poetry is "turning blood into ink." Although I'm no expert on poetry, the same is true of any creative endeavor. You must exert and use your brains and blood and emotions to express yourself—it will therefore be much more rewarding.

You reach to make the most of yourself this minute and the next—not in a frenzy, but with an awareness of what goes on within you and about you. You push to the fullest extent of the possibilities and potentialities. You will gain the ever-increasing joy of using yourself, of tapping and revealing your true inner personal "express-ability."

A highly creative individual, Professor Erik Barnouw wrote: "Eskimo artists, when they carve ivory, we are told, do not begin by deciding what to carve. They say, 'I wonder what is inside.' As they carve, they finally find it. It was there, waiting for discovery and release."

Realize, if you doubt your creativity, that this is a basic, all-important lesson to be learned from primitive people, not highly renowned for "sophisticated" intelligence. Creativity begins as soon as you approach anything, everything, with the open, questing attitude: *I wonder what is inside.*

167

What's the next step? You look until you find the answer. And even if you never achieve the ultimate, hoped-for result, you gain from the multitude of answers you encounter in the seeking. Yes, whatever your age, you can change, grow, recharge your creativity, knowing that it will accumulate and grow in power as you use it.

You, like everyone else, have a talent for something, often for many things. You simply look within yourself for what you like to do most. Track it down, apply it, develop it, improve it constantly. You will gain greater peace of mind and contentment in everyday living.

The power of creativity to make your living more enjoyable is as certain and dependable as it is incalculable. As Albert Schweitzer explained: "We see no power in a drop of water. But let it get into a crack in the rock and be turned to ice, and it splits the rock. Turned into steam, it drives the pistons of the most powerful engines. Something has happened to it which makes active and effective the power that is latent in it."

Somewhat the same thing happens when you unleash the power that is dormant and undeveloped in your creativity. It is moribund only if you let it lie unused. Unleash it by activating it. Every kind of creative effort you apply, you will find, helps to keep your creativity rolling at top speed—snowballing, expanding—a free gift to enjoy and employ for your entire, better, future.

* * *

As you review the specific tips here, realize definitely that your inherent creativity provides a special personal opportunity to do more, enjoy more, gain more each day. Even in this computer age, Dr. A. Whitney Griswold, former president of Yale, emphasized: "Creative ideas spring from individuals"—not from computers, not from machines, but from you. It is your clear, individual birthright. Please give this deep thought, unlike the querulous woman in an E. M. Forster novel who complained, "How can I know what I think till I hear what I say?"

When you respect, develop, and use your creativity—not necessarily in the arts, remember—it becomes a most valuable asset. Note an illustrative example: Picasso and a few other modern masters were asked to write brief statements about art for a forthcoming book reproducing some of their work. They agreed. All supplied their observations promptly, but Picasso kept delaying.

Finally, facing a deadline, the desperate publisher pressured Picasso to send his words. Soon after, a large envelope arrived. On sheets inside, Picasso had drawn the alphabet in huge letters, with a brief comment, "Here's the alphabet—make up your own words." The publisher printed Picasso's alphabet, noting that Picasso had become so imbued with supreme creativity that even when he drew the ABC's the result was strikingly artistic.

Similarly, as you practice and use your creativity in anything—cooking, ideas for your business or other pursuits, whatever—it deepens in your blood, becomes as indicative a part of you as your fingerprints. Poet James Oppenheim asserted: "We are what we create." J. G. Saxe added: "'Tis wise to learn; 'tis godlike to create!"

Will you take the steps here toward greater creativity? Pamela Bowlin warned: "Most of us live our lives the way we watch television. Even though the program isn't as good as we would like it to be, we are too lazy to get up and change it." I count on you to reject that negative course in your drive for conscious happiness. Using your certain, innate creativity will help you make the most of yourself, your days, your life.

11

The Joys of Work
and Achievement

A LIVELY AND successful woman, imbued with conscious happiness, was asked whether she had given thought to what was the basic ingredient producing her very fruitful life to date. She said that her "secret" could be summed up in three little words that always kept her bright and eager: "*Make an effort.*" Justice Holmes made a similar point in five words: "*To live is to function.*" And to function is to live—more rewardingly.

Making an effort has helped many to get an especially gratifying zest out of living. It's an essential for building and maintaining a sense of self-respect and self-fulfillment. A woman told her housekeeper after several years together, "Mary, you're really wonderful at your work. You seem to get the same feeling of satisfaction as I do in keeping this house beautiful." Mary smiled gently, "Thank you. But, you see, it's *my* house, too."

A close friend, Dr. James W. Smith, plastic surgeon and coauthor of our book, *Doctor, Make Me Beautiful!*, wrote to me for some information on a subject I knew a good deal about. He asked me to phone the answers the next day: "I'll be in my office from 8 A.M." I called him with the needed data a few minutes after eight the following morning. When he learned that I'd already been working for an hour, he said in mock seriousness, "Samm, I think you ought to see a psychiatrist and ask him what causes your work compulsion."

I retorted, "Hell, you're exactly like that too. You're usually involved with your patients from about dawn until midnight and later."

He laughed. "Sure. I want you to ask a psychiatrist so you can tell *me* why we knock ourselves out like this. . . ."

Later that day, another friend, playwright-novelist Henry Denker, phoned. During our conversation, he told me that he had finished his latest novel the week before. "I then decided to take a few months for rest and goofing off. But," he complained, "after three days of doing nothing, I find myself back pounding out another book." I started to tell him about my earlier discussion with Jim—

He interrupted, "Well, I *did* ask that question of a leading psychiatrist about a year ago. He replied, 'What do you care why? With a work compulsion that absorbs you, fills you, excites you—don't question *why*. Just be very grateful that you're one of the lucky people who has it—it's like discovering uranium. Use it. Enjoy it. That work compulsion helps keep you mentally and emotionally healthy.' "

Sir John Gielgud, stellar actor, affirmed at age seventy, "I only get bored and depressed when I'm not working."

To work at something you want to do can be happiness enough for many people—even if that were all. But it certainly need not and should not be. Alert, involved individuals are generally interested in lots of things rather than just the one dimension of work.

Executives have asserted repeatedly that it's more fun to be overworked than underworked. But you must manage to *like* your work, for the benefit of your total health as well as emotional well-being. Work is fun when you apply yourself to it eagerly, intensively. In one of my co-author books, *Vigor for Men Over Thirty,* Dr. Warren R. Guild of the President's Council on Physical Fitness stated: "If you really dislike your work, you become restless, all churned up inside. You find it hard to live with yourself and others. Your health is affected not so much by the number of hours a day you work, but whether you enjoy or hate your work. . . . All other factors being equal, there is less danger of a heart attack for the man who works twelve hours a day and loves it, than for the one who works six hours a day and hates it." He added the proviso that at no time should you exhaust yourself, physically or mentally.

Dr. Hans Selye asserted repeatedly that "stress is the spice of life"—referring, I'm sure, to stress that you *enjoy.* Composer Duke Ellington observed, "People who make a living doing work they don't enjoy wouldn't even be happy with a one-day week."

How much effort should you, can you, apply? Dr. Howard Rusk summed it up for us: "Stress is really an integral part of life. We set our whole pattern of life by our stress end-point. If we hit it exactly, we live dynamic, purposeful, useful, happy lives. If we go over, we break. If we stay too far under, we vegetate."

It's worth asking yourself: "Am I going over my personal correct stress point? Or am I too far under?" Your thoughtful consideration of this query, your honest answer, and subsequent readjustment, if necessary, can be a productive step toward attaining your utmost measure of conscious happiness.

The crucial difference is not the kind of work you do, whether it's running a home or any type of endeavor—but the spirit in which you approach it. In many cases it's up to you to come to the realization that you *must* regard and handle the work as an inviting challenge rather than as an imponderable burden. Then you get set and make the most of it rather than griping and demeaning the work and yourself—and piling on misery for others.

One realist in a book by Gavin Black emphasized, "If you are really set on a certain job—due to choice or whatever—you do that job. And if you don't manage to do it really well right up until the day you die, at least you are among the tryers. The real division between people, the fundamental one, is that some try and some don't. And the ones who don't think that the ones who do—particularly when it isn't necessary—are psychiatrists' fodder."

You make the decision for yourself about trying or not trying. And you gain or lose within yourself accordingly. A sociological study conducted by Judson T. Landis affirmed: "People tend to be happiest when they are busiest." A friend who visited Picasso when he was nearing ninety reported, "He's in splendid form, younger and more cheerful than ever: he is working, therefore all is right for him." Is that true for you?

Which Are You?

There is no conclusive answer that fits everyone, which will serve specifically for you as an individual. You must ask yourself: "Which am I? One who tries? Or one who doesn't?" If your honest answer is negative, isn't it time to start trying, really trying? In that way, you reach for conscious happiness positively, and usually productively. You advance toward making your work better for you, and you move in definite strides toward what fulfills you most.

Just whining, complaining, feeling hopeless—all that accomplishes nothing desirable. But there is great reward in the trying alone. You will be surprised and delighted at

173

how often you succeed, even if only fractionally. Do it *your way*; as Goethe stated: "Let everyone sweep in front of his own door, and the whole world will be clean."

One man remarked, "All I hope to do in my work is to *survive*." Another, prize-winning television producer Fred Freed, observed thoughtfully, "If that's all there is to it— the mere surviving—to what I've been doing these twenty-three years, I think I have paid an extravagant price in my personal life. I always had a sense that I was doing what I wanted to be doing." His friends considered him a fulfilled individual.

Like his, your goal must be to gain self-satisfaction, self-fulfillment. You must strive to make what you're doing— even though it may not be your ultimate desire—the thing you want to be doing then, until you can make a change for the better. Just surviving shouldn't be good enough for anyone, certainly not for you—for you are striving toward a better way or you wouldn't be reading this book.

Practically any kind of endeavor—housework or any other type of effort—offers personal rewards or seemingly insurmountable barriers, depending on your attitude. A story tells of one acquaintance asking another:

"How long have you been working for your present employer?"

"Ever since he threatened to fire me."

Industrialist Henry Kaiser firmly believed in his succinct formula for sure-fire achievement: "First decide what you want to do. Then have the courage to start toward the goal, no matter how impossible it looks." He added the clincher: "If you want to get there badly enough, nothing can stop you." In short, again . . . you must keep working at it.

Discussing his difficult, demanding work, sculptor Chaim Gross said simply, "It gives me great happiness, and when I'm not working I'm miserable. . . . I tell my students, 'Don't wait until the muse wakes you up at night and says do this and that. Make a point of working all the time.' " He emphasized that too many would-be artists and sculptors want to become artists through some heaven-sent magic, rather than by working for it: "They don't want to study; with them everything is philosophy, and they depend on miracles. . . ." They never make it.

A youthful woman in her early forties, a close friend, Ellie H., felt exhausted after working for more than twenty years at grueling jobs. After talking about the situation for some time with her husband and us, she was persuaded to resign from her well-paying position to devote herself to more leisurely enjoyment of living.

She has worked at doing just that by setting a pattern of daily living for herself, doing the things she wanted to do: Reading a list of books she had missed . . . working one day a week for a retired lawyer . . . going to theater and ballet, which always had enormous appeal for her . . . playing tennis after a layoff for years . . . being involved in volunteer, political, and social activities . . . and taking college courses in subjects that appealed to her.

I consider her a great success at this "work," for she had planned the use of time—including taking advantage of random opportunities—as suits her best personally. "If I hadn't made such a plan," she admits, "I'd have gone off my rocker in a hurry. As it is, I enjoy my use of time, using it the way I like—consciously, even exultantly. Sure, in a very specific way, I 'work at it'—at making the most of my custom-fitted design for living."

Whatever you are working at, there is joy in achieving by giving a little extra push at any point where you feel that you may be failing. When I was teaching our small daughter, Wendy, how to ride a two-wheeled bicycle, she'd get going, start wobbling, and I'd have to catch her as she was falling. Tearful, "Dad, I can't get going. I have to give up. I'll never make it. . . ."

"No, you just about have it licked," I assured her. "It's

my fault up to now because I didn't point out to you that when the pedal comes to the top, you have to give it *a little extra push*." Reluctantly, she tried again. The bike wobbled . . . and then just as she was about to fall, she gave the rising pedal that little extra push. The bike straightened. She cried exultantly, "I'm riding! I'm riding! I can ride!"

Whatever your goal, you must apply yourself in order to reach it. You can't cause it to come about by philosophizing or wishing. I've never known anyone to fail in achieving some satisfying measure of success and conscious happiness—if she or he pursued it hard enough and long enough. These individuals, in every field of endeavor, agree on one thing: *it's worth the work*. You struggle. You grow. You gain.

Use Yourself to Like Yourself

One of the greatest joys of working hard and exerting every possible effort you have to give is not in finding a pot of gold but in finding yourself. The one who sits or lies around doing nothing much of the time tends to feel useless to himself or to anyone else. Usually that individual doesn't realize that he or she is beginning to dislike himself.

In such a case involving yourself, growing lack of self-esteem makes you feel increasingly irritable with yourself. In turn it leads to impatience with others, especially those close to you. Thereupon you strike out at them, trying to hurt them. You convince yourself that you dislike or even despise them, and that they dislike you. Ultimately you tend to convince yourself that you don't respect them or their way of life. But actually it is yourself that you dislike and despise.

If the individual in such an instance faces up to the

fact that this may be his condition, he can do something about it. Primarily the solution is to use oneself, to exert effort toward a productive course. Then one is likely to feel of use and of value. You like yourself because you respect yourself for being effective in striving—at the very least.

And, liking and respecting yourself, you not only get optimistically involved in striving to gain your goal, but become more pleasant to others, like and respect them, and get along amicably with them. You have been relieved, you should realize, of the deep anger, irritability and hostility that had developed within you because you felt useless, inadequate, worthless to yourself and to anyone else.

Is laziness—for that is what shirking and non-involvement add up to, whatever the cause—ever worth such self-degradation and resultant deep misery?

"Usefulness is Everything"

Of course working hard doesn't mean non-stop effort. Everyone needs a break—a day in the country, change-of-scene weekends, vacations. No matter how much you enjoy a demanding work challenge, letting up can bring you back refreshed, more eager and effective than before.

There is such joy in using yourself productively that you can't help but like yourself better and enjoy life more. Schweitzer said: "Usefulness is everything." Conrad asserted: "A man is a worker. If he is not that he is nothing." "Let me wear out, not rust out," was Theodore Roosevelt's view.

When you are unused, you tend to feel useless. You are likely to become more tired, more listless from not doing anything than from keeping occupied. It needn't necessarily be at a pressing job. Looking, seeing, touching, keeping yourself involved—that's keeping occupied and therefore more contented with yourself.

I have never concerned myself that I might be working too hard, because exerting maximum effort, short of exhaustion, keeps me stimulated, on my mental toes, biting into life. If I ever felt that I wanted to give up applying myself, and instead sit in a corner and mope—then I'd worry. The human being—you, me—was made to *function*, that's the very essence of one's being.

Interestingly, a dictionary defines function as "to perform, to serve." If you don't function, you fail. Most disastrously, you fail yourself. You perform a disservice to yourself, and to all whom your life touches.

If you wait around for something to happen, time dribbles out, and so do the chances for self-fulfillment—as the days themselves waste away. Early in his career, John Wayne was feeling upset with the way his career was going, being typed as a cowboy instead of expanding into other roles. He thought of giving up. Then, as he told it:

"Suddenly I bumped into Will Rogers. 'What's the matter, Duke?' he asked. I said things weren't going so well.

" 'You working?'

"I said, 'Yep.'

" '*Keep working, Duke,*' he said, and smiled and walked on."

Wayne kept working. And it worked out. Sound advice: While you're concentrating on finding your own best direction, or solving your paramount problem, don't let down, don't let go. "*Keep working.*" It has been said that "if the power to do hard work is not talent, it is the best possible substitute for it."

A favorite story about persistence is that of a very popular itinerant preacher in the deep countryside who was asked the secret of his success as an inspirational spiritual leader. "I just keep poundin' my message across no matter what," he explained. "One push ain't enough. First I tell the congregation what I'm *gonna* tell them. Then I *tell* them. And then I tell them what I *told* them."

George Bernard Shaw made the point powerfully: "This is the true joy of life—the being used for a purpose recognized by yourself as a mighty one, the being thoroughly worn out before you are thrown to the scrap-heap; the being a force of nature instead of a feverish, selfish clod of ailments and grievances."

And if you can't find "a mighty purpose," then you keep trying to find your one best goal—and you keep working at what you're doing meanwhile. If you can't handle both endeavors at the same time, then you're not trying hard enough—which usually means that you really don't care enough. Like everyone else, you have the capacity— if you will use it and yourself.

What Values: Wealth? Fame?

A young woman who held an important but extremely grueling job in government was asked why she put up with all the pressure, why she worked so hard . . . when she was wealthy by inheritance. She explained, "No, I don't have to work in order to exist well-fed and well-clothed. But in order to live fully for myself, I must work. The more I work and use myself, the more personal resources I develop—and the more satisfaction I get."

A *Wall Street Journal* cartoon shows two obviously wealthy, jewelry-bedecked women sitting beside a huge estate swimming pool. One tells the other: "This inflation is terrible. It takes twice as much money to buy the same amount of happiness as two years ago." But everyone learns inevitably that things don't buy happiness . . . only *you* can.

It should hardly need saying that money itself can't buy

happiness. (A comedian insists, "Happiness can't buy money.") Jean Paul Getty, one of the wealthiest men of all time, affirmed: "Money doesn't have any connection with happiness. Maybe unhappiness." On another occasion, he growled, "Actually I've never seen the day when I could say that I felt rich. Generally, you worry about paying your bills." The greater the wealth, the bigger the bills. Samuel Johnson advised: "It is better to live rich than die rich."

It has been said that "Money can't buy life." Similarly, Thoreau wrote: "The only wealth is life. If a life of luxury, the only fruit is luxury." That is true unless you seek and strive for the other deeper values as well.

When he was fifteen, our son Jeff learned this vital lesson: Being a licensed ham radio operator, he was asked by a classmate to help him obtain a beginner's permit. As the first step, ability to tap out the alphabet had to be checked and affirmed in writing by a licensed operator. Jeff told young Arthur to work at the code until he had learned it thoroughly. Then he'd be happy to pass him.

As Jeff related this, he told us enviously, "Gee, Arthur said that his parents are worth millions. They've already equipped a fifteen-thousand-dollar radio shack for him—and he hasn't even got his permit, let alone his license." Jeff had built his own equipment with money earned as a stock boy in the local supermarket evenings and Saturdays.

Two weeks later, Arthur showed up for his test. When the boy left, Jeff was unhappy, "He couldn't get past 'C'—imagine that. No matter how I tried to help, I couldn't pass him. I told him he'd have to study a lot more, but he said that's too much work. . . ." A thought struck him, "Imagine that . . . with that super shack, and the millions of dollars, he can't be a ham radio operator unless he's willing to work hard for it. . . ."

Is Wealth Enough?

Are money and public eminence enough? During my years on Madison Avenue, I met a number of multimillionaires, mostly clients. Very few of them were what I consider "happy." Practically all of them concentrated predominantly on making money. They admitted, some even boasted, that they were constantly burdened by enormous responsibilities, the handling of repeated crises, often leading to headaches, ulcers, heart troubles, and worse.

In an extraordinary case, a wealthy sales manager, Joshua G., told me that he had emerged from the hospital recently after a devastating heart attack which had almost killed him. Pale, shaking, he related, "My doctor warned that I'll have to leave my high-pressure position—or die within a few months. When I told this to my boss [a super-rich philanthropist], he laughed and said, 'Look at me—I give millions for heart research, and I kill my executives with heart attacks!'"

Money can buy conveniences, luxuries, many material things that can help one to gain an alluring and pleasant life style. But truly satisfying, enduring happiness—conscious happiness—flows only from one source, the inner qualities you build and possess. These include self-respect, gratifying daily endeavor, peace of mind, giving and getting love and friendship, other facets delineated on these pages. Money or fame alone can't buy them; you can—when you work at it. A wit noted: "Money can't buy love, health, happiness, or what it did last year."

A brilliant friend, Howard Taubman, continued working for years as a newspaper music critic for the *New York Times* although he received lucrative offers of executive positions in concert management, paying double and triple what he was earning. He turned away those opportunities with the explanation, "I'm doing the work I like to do most. There isn't enough money in the world to compensate me for spending time working at something that wouldn't fulfill me. I enjoy my demanding work—so I have it made."

Picasso, whose estate was valued at millions, expressed his feelings about money: "I should like to live like a poor man—with a great deal of money." He dressed and ate simply—a pair of shorts, a broiled fish. He had little use for money, which he felt would clutter up his days. His life force was never money or fame but his work, applying himself energetically early until late to the art he loved, right up to his death at ninety-one.

Like most tennis pros, champion Stan Smith was exposed to many very wealthy people. His comment: "You could probably fill [luxurious tennis clubs] with members who are having problems with their homes and their own lives. . . . I try to realize that this money I'm making isn't everything, that people I know who have done well financially may not be happy, and that some people who haven't done well financially really have fine homes and fine families. There's a meaning in their lives you can really see."

A museum in Deadwood, South Dakota, displays an inscription left by a dead prospector: "I lost my gun. I lost my horse. I am out of food. The Indians are after me. But I've got all the gold I can carry."

An enormously wealthy, obese man sitting next to me at a dinner party wheezed, "Eating is my one big remaining pleasure . . ." he burped ". . . and even that gives me terrible indigestion." Of course, in itself, wealth need not bring trouble, but it often does. On the other hand, writer Sean O'Casey observed, "Money doesn't make you happy but it quiets the nerves."

Poet Charles Kingsley stated that many people "act as if

comfort and luxury were the chief requirements of life, when all that we need to make us happy is something to be enthusiastic about." Food for thought: *rich* is in the head. An anonymous soldier was quoted as saying: "I wished for all things that I might enjoy life, and was granted life that I might enjoy all things."

When I was in the business world, I was told that a close friend, Morgan Ryan, had said, "Samm would be the top man in his field but he lacks one thing: the killer instinct." It is my experienced observation that the one dominating essential to acquire great wealth is *to want money more than anything else in the world.* Then you put family, friends, decency in second place. "Killing" others (not actual murder, of course)—exerting utter ruthlessness in relationships and decisions—that's all part of the game.

To such obsessed individuals, nothing else matters but winning—money, dominance, power, becoming top dog. As a lot, they are the unhappiest people I know. I have lived poor and I have lived well. I have lived with the very poor and the very rich. And my firm conclusion is that possessing a rewarding sense of happiness must come from within the person—from *your* deepest feelings of caring and sharing—not from a giant bank account or lack of one.

Principles for Happy Living

A noted Japanese psychiatrist, Takehisa Kora, set forth his principles for happy living for most individuals; they boil down to this:

1. A person is born to be *active*, to use himself or herself.
2. What you think or feel is less important than *what you do.*
3. You can *function and live well* in spite of emotional

and/or physical distress symptoms, if you carry on an active, purposeful life, day after day—whether the symptoms disappear or not.

4. Even in doing simple, routine manual tasks, *persisting in the act of doing* brings a sense of tangible accomplishment and reward . . . and improves your relations with other people and with yourself.

You don't just think about doing, *you do*. Truman said: "Some of the Presidents were great and some of them weren't. I can say that because I wasn't one of the great Presidents. But I had a good time trying to be one, I can tell you that." Because he tried so hard, doing what had to be done to the best of his ability, many historians consider Truman one of the great Presidents.

The same is true for everyone. You *do*—and whatever you do, you must treat your work with respect—and work hard at it accordingly. Then you can have a good time trying.

And You Keep On Trying . . .

There can even be a certain feeling of reward in rejection—as long as you know that you've worked and tried to your fullest capacity—and didn't stop trying. The superb mystery writer Dashiell Hammett told me that when he was breaking in as an author, he never let a story fade and die if he was convinced that it was good:

"I'd send my manuscript to the top name on my list of editors. If it was rejected by him, I'd send it to each in turn. That took a year or more altogether. Then I'd start over. I'd send the story around again to the same magazines." He grinned, "You'd be surprised how many stories I sold the second time around. I just wouldn't give up. Hell, I believed in those stories!"

At one point I was selling ideas free-lance to department stores, in addition to my advertising agency job. I mailed an idea that I thought had exceptional merit to brilliant Ira A. Hirschmann, then head of the advertising department at Saks Fifth Avenue. He turned it down flatly. But I believed in it as just right for that store. A year later, I retyped and sent the same suggestion again, changing only the date at the top. This time the idea was bought enthusiastically. The resulting promotion won a retailing award.

I learned the hard way in my years in business that a good idea which seemed undesirable at one time might be approved at another date. Timing, feelings, conditions change. One thing that must not change: *Never stop trying*. The thrill is all the sweeter if you finally click after setbacks.

A determined man who was defeated as a candidate for governor of his state acknowledged his opponent's triumph. Then he declared vehemently, "There's going to be another election four years from now. I'm going to work to win next time. And my efforts begin right now."

A woman, Mildred K., who put a lot of effort into her gardening told me that her husband and neighbors were constantly scolding her for working so hard to grow things. She explained why she persisted: "I keep pulling weeds, even though I know that more will pop up inevitably. But, y'know, there are many things wrong in this world, things I don't like. I can't obliterate them with my bare hands. But when I pull out a weed, root and all, it's a goner! I get a kick out of that." Nothing could keep her from her strenuous, rewarding efforts.

Consider how the joys of work, of applying yourself, can sustain you in many ways. When Einstein was getting overwhelming, worldwide applause, he shook off the plaudits with the comment: "The only way to escape the personal corruption of praise is to go on working. . . . Work. There is nothing else." There can be much else, but work is a strong support.

Do you waste yourself by throwing away time? Darwin insisted that anyone "who dares to waste one hour of time has not discovered the value of life." You must often face and endure defeat after defeat, like everyone else. But you won't be defeated so long as you keep trying and refuse to accept final rout.

Included in the wisdom of the ancient Talmud is this profound judgment: "If anyone tells you: 'I achieved something without struggling for it,' do not believe him. If he tells you: 'I struggled and achieved something,' then you may believe him." Nothing really good comes easily, nor would that be desirable, for it would lack the thrill of trying and accomplishing through personal effort.

An individual of strength and character, looking back through the years, said: "I know what pleasure is, for I have done good work." An important part of attaining conscious happiness is to *fill* the hours with what is meaningful to you—rather than letting them slip away empty and unused. Never from now on. You can make the hours productive for yourself, each hour, even if it's through thinking or dreaming or working or just enjoying the flow of time *consciously*.

* * *

To help absorb deeply and most usefully the points made here, ask yourself—and then answer for yourself— these questions:

1. *Are you working at what you really want to do— or merely surviving?*
2. *Have you found the right balance point between overworking and underworking?*
3. *Do you use yourself well so that you respect yourself fully?*

4. Do you feel that wealth and fame are essential for happiness?
5. Is winning what matters most to you?
6. Do you or will you follow the listed "Principles for Happy Living"?
7. Do you waste yourself frequently by throwing time away?
8. Have you gained the thrill of accomplishment in using each day well?

As you answer these questions, please check back over the chapter to determine what answers you will work toward from now on. I hope you will resolve for your inner sustenance that the joys of work and achievement aren't necessarily measured in dollars and fame. A good many individuals who have a talent for material success lack the ability to live fully and joyously—the true measure of achievement.

Even the highest fame is comparative, as illustrated by this true story about Eisenhower: Returning as a triumphant General after World War II, he toured the country to tumultuous ovations. His train stopped at Manhattan, Kansas, where his brother Milton was president of Kansas State College. From the train's rear platform, the General waved at the cheering throng. As they quieted for his speech, a young college student's voice shrilled into the stillness:

"You may be a big general everywhere else—but here you are just Milton's big brother!"

In his novel about an F.-Scott-Fitzgerald type of disillusioned character who had peaked and crashed, Budd Schulberg wrote: "Nothing fails like success." That is true too often if the success isn't founded on solid self-respect and supportive conscious happiness. Possessing these qualities, you become a success in living, regardless of earnings and eminence. True inner achievement can't

187

be measured by an accountant's balance sheet or a press-clipping book.

A wit observed: "No matter how famous you are or how much you have accomplished, the size of your funeral depends on one thing—the weather."

Addressing the Association of Advertising Agencies, advertising innovator Raymond Rubicam emphasized that effort and dedication are more important to achievement than native brilliance. He told of a college professor who had taught many students who later became notable successes. The old professor was asked: "Who was your most brilliant pupil?"

"You never heard of him," the educator sighed. "He wouldn't work."

An Uplifting Example

An inspiring example of true achievement is Madame Marie Curie, who exposed herself to tremendous risks as she and her physicist husband Pierre pioneered the medical use of radium which has helped millions. A poor Polish governess, she struggled for long years to finally become a scientist. After their momentous discovery, she and her husband wouldn't patent their radium-extraction process. He explained their viewpoint: "Radium is not to enrich anyone. It is an element; it is for all the people."

Awarded the Nobel Prize, they worked harder than ever. Stricken when her husband was crushed by a truck in the street, Marie kept striving, rejecting the rewards of fame in favor of pursuing her work. The very radium which they had developed to save lives burned and scarred her hands and arms, and contributed to her death. She pushed on almost to her final day, sustained by her concentrated efforts to achieve more, always more, for the benefit of mankind.

As a beacon for everyone, for you, her daughter Eve Curie wrote beautifully: "I hope that the reader may constantly feel, across the ephemeral movement of one existence, what in Marie Curie was even more rare than her work or her life: the immovable structure of a character; the stubborn effort of an intelligence; the free immolation of a human being that could give all and take nothing, could even receive nothing; and above all the quality of a soul in which neither fame nor adversity could change the exceptional purity."

12

How You Can Gain Increased Optimism, Enthusiasm, Humor

THIS SIGN WITH attractive lettering on a colorful wood plaque hangs on the wall above my desk:

The Natural State of Man Is Joy

Many times, like you, like everyone else, I begin to feel a murky sense of being oppressed and overburdened creeping over me, due to large or small troubles that arise inevitably. In spite of my imbued, reinforced optimism, I find my spirits sinking and my outlook growing gloomy. . . .

At that point, I know I must do something specific in order to counteract the invasion of depression. I must force myself to take some positive action lest I permit myself to become overwhelmed by melancholy and pessimism. I take instant action in this way:

Usually I will look up and read the words on the sign: "The Natural State of Man Is Joy." I make myself restudy the meaning. I let the message seep through me. I agree. I know, at least, that it is true for me. Why then am I giving in to gloom and despair?

I force myself to lift my spirits again. For I must restore myself to my "natural" state of conscious happiness which sustains my sense of living joyously. Otherwise I may slide down deeper . . .

Thereupon I take the most important, essential action for me. I shift into this easy conscious happiness mental/physical exercise which takes no more than a minute or two:

Conscious Happiness
Mental/Physical Exercise

Here's what I do—you can do the same right now, and whenever you want a lift. The brief, simple exercise will help you even more effectively and positively after you have read and reread this book thoroughly—and are imbued with your own personal conviction of conscious happiness. But right now, please try this:

1. Sit in any chair wherever you are—or stand if that is more convenient (as in waiting for a bus, or being outdoors anywhere).

2. Straighten your back . . . lift your shoulders up and back comfortably . . . chest up. Elevate your chin at right angles to your neck, not strained upward. Keep your body tall but relaxed, not sagging, but never stiff or tensed.

3. Close your eyes, keeping the lids relaxed and comfortable, not squeezed together tightly, no squint.

4. Let your face relax into a slight smile, not stretching your lips tight or wide, but simply letting a comfortable Mona Lisa kind of smile take over. At ease?

5. Now . . . with your lips slightly open, breathe in through your mouth slowly and deeply to the fullest expansion of your lungs . . . filling your chest

191

slowly, fully (without straining), as you breathe in . . .

6. *At the same time* as you breathe in . . . speak silently to yourself, and very slowly, saying the words:

conscious happiness

. . . and, as you speak the phrase to yourself slowly, let the two words f-l-o-a-t thoroughly through your mind as the thought permeates your consciousness . . .

7. Your lungs full, eyes closed, concentrating on the silent words . . . let out breath through your nose.

8. Sit for a few seconds in silence, breathing naturally.

9. *Repeat the same mental/physical exercise five times* . . . slowly . . . your mind gradually relaxing completely.

10. If, after five times, you still don't feel thoroughly and comfortably relieved and eased in mind and emotions, the burden of heavy pessimism gone, continue the mental/physical exercise for a total of ten times (but never straining yourself physically).

You should feel quietly exhilarated after that simple little relaxing, deep-breathing session. A rising optimism and hope should be replacing the gloom that had besieged you, and threatened to bog you down. Now your mind should feel eased, your spirits turned upward instead of down—*you are better able to tackle your problems effectively*. Instead of brooding negatively, sinking deeper all the while, you are ready to work toward positive solutions (no, the basic problems haven't evaporated).

That little exercise works constructively for me, and has for years, simply as a general little oxygenating mental/physical lift. It should work for you if—I must state it again, even though stressed repeatedly throughout these pages—*if you will work at it*. Believe me, it is worthwhile—and physicians will tell you that such deep breathing alone helps to promote good health.

The short routine, done five times, or preferably ten times per session, may even ease headache and other temporary minor aches and pains at times. It has helped ease off such physical burdens for me and some others. (But, with strong, continuing pain or other ailments, count on your physician's advice, of course, not on this little mental/physical routine.)

Yes, that little exercise, repeated during the day and evening (as often as you think needed or desirable for you), has for many years helped to strengthen and sustain my conscious happiness. It can do the same for you, performed often, unselfconsciously, devotedly, hopefully. Please try it right now . . . then read on.

The Smile Self-Cure

Adding the even simpler and very pleasant act of smiling can help break a severe mood very often. Whenever I catch myself feeling grim and antagonistic at whatever, usually with expression to match (I am no more saint than you are), I force my face into a sometimes unwilling smile. Not necessarily a great big ear-to-ear grin. A slight smile, more of a relaxing of the tissues and muscles, without even parting the lips, is generally a great help, all that's required.

It's difficult to stay grim when you're smiling. Just changing those drooping or fixed down lines to the little lift upward in a smile tends to loosen your tension. It immediately takes the edge off a sharp, harsh feeling.

Try it in the mirror first thing in the morning even if you feel dopey and low. And repeat it through the day if you find yourself tending toward a foul mood. Look at that soured face reflected in the glass—kind of repulsive, isn't it? You deserve better than that of yourself. That grim, forbidding expression isn't really you, is it?

So loosen up a little and watch your improving mood in the mirror. Relax into a slight Mona Lisa smile, then a little broader than that. It's effective, even though the Mona Lisa's subtle "smile" has been attributed by some cynics as due to a touch of indigestion.

Having just tried the smile "self-cure," doesn't that little action help relax you surprisingly inside? And aren't you definitely more inviting on the outside? Thackeray observed: "The world is a looking glass and gives back to everyone the reflection of his own face." When there is a smile on *your* face, the world tends to reflect it back for you.

The smile self-cure becomes a habit. It's practically automatic with me now. Feeling my facial expression hardening due to the adverse course of a day's events, or for whatever reason, my reflex is to switch hurriedly into a bit of a smile. It's indeed difficult to maintain a gloomy interior when your exterior is relaxed by a pleasant expression.

The mere physical act of smiling can help change your mood from feeling low toward a rising sense of optimism. It may not always shift you from low into high, but you'll be delighted at how often it does work.

The point is illustrated by a favorite "Peanuts" cartoon of fifteen years ago, illuminated by the perceptive genius of Schulz. Charlie Brown stands with face glum, head down, shoulders slumped. He explains to a friend, "This is my 'depressed stance' . . . When you're depressed, it makes a lot of difference how you stand . . . [smiling and standing erect] The worst thing you can do is straighten up and hold your head high because then you'll start to feel better . . . [face and body drooping again] If you're going to get any joy out of being depressed, you've got to stand like this."

An optimistic, erect stance and a true smile work for you two ways—uplifting you on the inside, and others from the outside. But you must feel the sense of smiling all over—and mean it—for it to be effective. A false aspect of geniality fools no one for long, including yourself.

Trust Shakespeare to nail down the benefits: "A smile recures the wounding of a frown." When you frown, you not only wound yourself but others as well. In every way, that grim, forbidding expression that too many people wear habitually is self-destructive. Why wound yourself that way ever? It feels so much better instantly when you switch frowning to smiling. I've read that anatomically it's easier to smile than to frown because you use fewer muscles.

The wonders a simple smile can accomplish! The last poem ever written by Robert Frost appears to be one penned for the private nurse who attended him shortly before he died:

> I met you on a cloudy dark day and
> when you smiled and spoke my room was
> filled with sunshine.
> The way you smiled at me has given
> my heart a change of mood and saved
> some part of a day I had rued.

Building an Optimistic Spirit

Frequently I'm told by others, somewhat enviously, "You really are a lucky s.o.b. You're just a natural-born optimist. I wish I had your inherently happy nature. . . ." My answer goes to the heart of the matter:

"It isn't a case of being 'born lucky.' I developed into

195

a sourball and changed all that myself. Everyone is born with a natural supply of optimism—yes, you too. I wasn't blessed with a greater inherent supply than you or anyone else. You possess a basic if perhaps untapped supply of optimism. It's just that *I use mine*. I've found that those who search hard for the best usually find it."

A young woman, a relative and friend, Edith D., moved across the country. In a letter to her several years ago, I wrote: "You have sounded rather low the last few times on the phone. I hope you're not depressed. I'm so fearful because, in many ways, you're as I was at your age, frighteningly so . . .

"I shudder now over the years I lost being melancholy and constantly feeling *'what's the use?'* But, like me, I think that you strive for efficiency and deplore waste—and each day spent without feeling the joy of living, recognizing and using the opportunities for uplift and happiness, is waste . . .

"Yet I know that you possess a deep capacity for warmth and emotion and laughter. All you have to do is use that ability."

She started "using" it. And for years now, she has been known for her accomplishments in her chosen field, and admired for her air of conscious happiness. You, too—please balance the enormous benefits of optimism against the negatives of pessimism, including being dragged down by the millstones of what's-the-use and waste. "There is such a little time that your life will last . . ."—*make the most of it.*

Consider this elementary situation: Two women, a pessimist and an optimist, start the week on Monday, both involved in a big event scheduled for the following Sunday. The pessimist groans, "It's awful—a whole long, dragging week to wait before Sunday." The optimist grins, "It's wonderful—I have a whole week to look forward to

Sunday." Question: *Which one enjoyed that week more and gained more from each day?*

What's the use of wailing, "What's the use? The world is going to blow up atomically or sink under a swamping wave of pollution . . ."

There's no benefit—only loss for you and those about you! *What's the use?*

There is glory to be seen and experienced right now any time: a child's wondering face, a sparkling mountain lake, a budding tree, a million other miracles, existing to give you pleasure if you will only make the rewarding effort to look and feel. I dare you to say that many marvels don't exist. It's simply that you must be aware, willing, eager to relish them.

Thoreau flings this challenge at all of us, at you: "If we are really dying, let me hear the rattle in our throats . . . if we are alive, let us go about our business."

Optimism as an Affirmation

Certainly you must apply yourself to uncovering and building up a spirit of optimism so that it is integral with you, and an outgoing evidence of your radiant spirit. Optimism is an affirmation that the human force can overcome adversity. If you aren't an optimist now, you'll feel better when you develop yourself into one—and so will everyone around you, especially those closest to you.

I assure you that the easiest and most rewarding mathematics is *counting your blessings*. Do you take the time each day to do so?

Satirist Russell Baker (no relative, worse luck), writing about the "crime" of feeling good, told of a man who greeted his sour wife at breakfast with a brilliant smile and a kiss. She turns on him for feeling good. He apologizes, "Can you ever forgive me, Emma? I didn't mean to feel good. I just woke up this morning and the sunlight was streaming in and there was the smell of wisteria on the exhaust fumes . . ."

Damn the torpedoes, full speed ahead and feel good! We must accept the realistic challenge that you cannot depend on the outside world to lift and carry you always —but more certainly on your inner resources and volition to lift your own spirits. Thus you brighten your hours and days . . . and you are well on your way to possessing the sustaining joys of conscious happiness.

Most of us have to take special care, in avoiding pessimism, not ever to nurture or build a disbelief in self, such as: "Everything I do, anything I say, is bound to turn out wrong." If you keep looking at and concentrating on the negative, things are more likely to droop in that downward direction and go sour.

Just the opposite is true—if you maintain an optimistic attitude, and back it up by *trying* to make things better, they will tend to get better. Robert Browning contended: "Every joy is gain . . . and gain is gain, however small." Think of this, as touched on earlier: You are one of a long line of individuals who—for more than two million years—have survived the assaults of animals, nature, disease, and any number of other horrendous attacks. You have survived. That's cause enough for optimism, isn't it?

Montaigne wrote: "The pleasantest things in the world are pleasant thoughts: and the great art of life is to have as many of them as possible."

"Transmissible by Contact"

When you adopt and maintain a pleasant, optimistic attitude and aspect, you trigger a similar favorable response from others, including those close to you. There is no question that gaiety and humor are contagious, definitely according to the dictionary definition: "Transmissible by contact." An old Chinese proverb warns: "A man without a smiling face must not open a shop."

When he was grown, our son Jeff wrote to me: "Your continued emphasis on optimism, your telling me things which indicated that—after years of living with a sense of despair—your almost unconscious faith that things would become better actually turned out to be true . . . it penetrated . . .

"In spite of my common self-protective rejection of a father's experience some time back, your very repetition and earnestness about optimism as a theme for living registered positively with me. That you could instill in a stubborn son a sense of belief in living—a trust in the enriching promise of adulthood and continued growth—convinced me of the merit and validity of an optimistic outlook."

A few years back I was in Denmark introducing the Danish-language edition of my controversial book, *The Permissible Lie*. Scheduled for a simultaneous television/ radio talk, I told my bright agent, Ib Lauritzen, "But I speak English only. How will the Danes understand me?"

"Many of the viewers and listeners understand English." He added, "But just be enthusiastic, straightforward, and smile genuinely as you do—and they will *all* understand you." It was so. I learned there and in other European countries that an optimistic, friendly approach breaks down even language barriers.

A friend imbued with conscious happiness, Hank S., is an executive in a large business. One night he said, "I enjoyed a special thrill today at my desk. The mail boy dropped a packet in my desk basket, then stood there, swaying nervously. His face red with embarrassment, he blurted out, 'I have to tell you this, sir. I deliver to over a hundred people here all the time, but you're the only one who always *smiles* at me. It's a joy to enter your office. . . .' Then he ran out. I felt terrific, but also a little selfish, because smiling at him and others makes *me* feel good too."

A welcoming smile, an open, respecting, person-to-person attitude that radiates from you, helps you as well as the others whom you face. It provides a mutual lift. Goethe pinned it down: "If you treat an individual as he is, he will stay as he is. But if you treat him as if he were what he ought to be and could be, he will become what he ought to be and could be." A smile lifts more than the corners of your mouth—it can help lift the world about you.

Pessimism Poisoning You?

A dictionary defines pessimism as "a disposition to look on the dark side of things, and to believe that the worst will happen." "A pessimist is a worrywart," said a comedian, "a person who even worries about which side his bread is buttered on. The optimist says, 'What's the difference? I eat both sides anyhow.'"

Sourness spoils milk, including the milk of human kindness. If you ever let pessimism overcome you and poison your days, you dissipate valuable hours of your life. In the comparatively brief time of living a person possesses, can *you* afford to squander a single hour to sullenness, moodiness, a deep funk? It makes sense to squelch any feeling of pessimism—at least until they start loading animals by pairs into the next rocket to the moon.

Certainly great troubles and severe problems erupt. If you consider them so overwhelming that you can't possibly handle them alone, then seek professional counseling help at once. But, in the usual situation, there are two different directions an individual can take: You can handle and move the problems toward a positive solution. Or you can mope about them and gain nothing as you lose precious time wallowing in pessimism.

Ask yourself: "Which way will I take?" Picture how differently two people may confront problems: The optimist smiles, "A big reason why I enjoy life so much is because I never know what's going to happen next." The pessimist bewails, "That's the main reason why I worry so much—I'm apprehensive about what terrible thing is going to happen next."

Realistically, what's so awful about failing—and getting up and going on to try again, and again? "Ah, but a man's reach should exceed his grasp . . . Or what's a heaven for?" asked Robert Browning. Often the difference between a pessimist and an optimist is that, faced with adversity, the pessimist gives up—while the optimist *keeps trying*.

An example is what happened when two frogs fell into a pail of cream. The pessimistic frog moaned, "What's the use?"—gave up, and drowned. The optimistic frog kept right on kicking away, trying to stay afloat and climb the sides of the pail. Suddenly his feet pushed against something solid, and he jumped out. His kicking feet had churned the cream into butter!

You overcome troubles more readily with optimism. Why not treat adversity as a test and challenge of your ability and emotional strength? A cracker-barrel philosopher, Abe Martin, contended, "Being an optimist after you've got everything you want doesn't count." Let's face it, we'll never have everything we want; that would be pretty dull, wouldn't it?

The pessimist complains that he was born unlucky—while the optimist asserts that he's lucky to have been born. Consider the crucial difference in viewpoints based on a snatch of conversation I overhead one morning in an elevator. Two men were apparently heading for the day's work in the same offices. One remarked glumly, "I hope you have a better day than I'm going to have." The other responded, smiling, "I'll try." Which one do you think probably had the better day?

A close friend, an effective optimist, Sue Miller, was concerned as she asked me, "Samm, could I be wrong in my upbeat attitude toward practically everything? I've been called a do-gooder, a Pollyanna, and similar derogatory terms. It's because of my consistently hopeful outlook and eager participation in living. But," she brightened, "I'm not going to change. Let *them* look down, damned if I'll dissipate my life that way."

"You're no Pollyanna," I assured, "since your optimistic attitude isn't contrived or unthinking. You're a realist, a spirited optimist who seeks to get the most and best out of each day for yourself and others. And you succeed in making life more rewarding, even for most of those you touch briefly . . .

"Let them call us Pollyannas. We know that it's not good enough to grope along and lose life in a fog of pervading pessimism. The joys we get from each day, even the tiniest sparks of pleasure, due to living optimistically are reward enough to counteract any negative criticism. I often fortify myself with what Adlai Stevenson said about Eleanor Roosevelt: 'She would rather light candles than curse the darkness, and her glow warmed the world.'"

I was at a large boardroom meeting where others were harshly criticizing the unique ideas being proposed by an eager young woman. Finally the chairman exploded at the hecklers, "Any fool can condemn and downgrade others—and most fools do!"

Of course, empty-headed optimism, giggling mindlessly and continuously at a complicated world, would be self-destructive. A cynic said bitterly, "More than one pessimist got that way from financing an optimist." Certainly optimism must be well seasoned with judgment and a realistic examination of minuses as well as pluses in any situation. A good rule is to do, but not overdo.

Nevertheless, doesn't it make sense to be realistic on the bright side? Why not think of all the good things that have happened to you, instead of concentrating on the bad? When your attitude is, "Let's see how it might be done," rather than the pessimistic, "It can't be done," you are more likely to gain victory. When your mental and physical bearing is defeatist, you invite defeat. Look up. Try saying "Hi!" to others with the same energy as you say "Ouch!"

You can take heart as I do from the children's story of the little engine pulling a long train up a steep grade, repeating stubbornly as it dragged along, "I-think-I-can . . . I-think-I-can . . ." And by chugging along doggedly that way before running out of steam, it made the grade. It must have happened to you, and will repeatedly from now on, that *you can* because you refuse to accept *cannot*.

There's a heartening quote by Arthur Krock of an old, staunch Scotswoman who said, "But let me laugh awhile . . . I've mickle time to grieve."

Easy Tranquilizer

"Laughter is a tranquilizer with no side effects," Arnold Glasow affirmed. I consider any day in which I haven't laughed a lost day. You don't have to look far for a reason for laughter. As comedians will assure you, the funniest things in life are not the devised gags and monologues, but the ordinary things that occur practically every day all around you. But—here's the catch—before you can appreciate them, you have to *look and see* the fun in them.

Again, you gain by developing a wide, optimistic viewpoint. And you must not take yourself too solemnly, or you will miss a lot of the fun in daily living. The philosopher Seneca said centuries ago, "Whenever I wish to enjoy the quips of a clown, I am not compelled to hunt far; I can laugh at myself." Obviously, a sense of humor isn't new—and yet it can brighten each day to make it feel fresh and new.

A gentleman noted for his wit, Arthur C., explained that because "I've always viewed life as a very serious mess, the only way to solve that is to be funny." Laughing at something deadly serious betokens foolishness rather than a sense of humor. You can, however, take yourself and deserving matters seriously without losing your zest in what goes on about you. "It is only when we assume we're perfect that we lose the ability to laugh at ourselves."

A sense of humor is not particularly "telling jokes." It radiates outward from within you in many inviting ways. It breaks down barriers. It helps you and the people you meet to open up and communicate on a more intimate level. It serves as a magnet. The great Helen Keller, blind throughout her lifetime, met Mark Twain and said later, "I could feel the twinkle of his eye in his handshake."

By developing your sense of humor, you gain a new vision of living, with your brighter, less demanding view of things. What may have been a stupid act, making you impatient with yourself or others, may seem rather funny or even silly if you season your understanding with tolerance. Thus you learn not to take yourself and everything else too seriously. Your entrance to this brighter whimsyland is free—no entrance or cover charge as you stay there for the rest of your life, and you live more happily than ever before.

A buoyant attitude alleviates tragedy in many instances. The story is told of a woman whose home was struck by a sizable bomb fragment during the London blitz. Almost giving up on the occupants as destroyed in the rubble, rescuers nevertheless kept digging. Finally, they found and dragged out the woman, pale and unconscious. As she revived, she was asked, "Where is your husband?" She brushed off the brick dust and snapped, "He's fighting on the battlefront, the bloody coward!"

At one time in business, two of my partners planned to retire. I had received a beckoning offer elsewhere so we decided to dissolve the company. I had to break the sad news to a bright young man, Will F., who was a particularly good worker. Only twenty-three, married and with a newborn, I knew he was having a tough time making ends meet. . . .

I was determined to do everything possible to get him a replacement position elsewhere, but I feared that the job loss would break him up. I prepared for wailing and gnashing of teeth, perhaps an angry blowup. As gently as I could, I broke the news. He was silent, then said slowly, "My wife woke up in the night with a heavy cold. I had to handle all the baby's feedings and diaperings. I was so groggy that I fell off the kitchen stool while warming up her 5 A.M. bottle . . . "

He forced a crooked grin, "Some days it doesn't pay to get up in the morning." Leaving the office, he tapped my arm, "Cheer up . . . tomorrow may be worse." I was dumbfounded—*he* was trying to cheer *me* up.

At a dinner party that night I related the incident. A man I'd just met spoke up, "Hey, send that young man around to see me. I can use anyone with that much courage and sense of humor." He got the job, a better one than he'd had with us—it *had* paid him to get up in the morning. Yes, the light touch can pay off unexpectedly—and expectedly in that the least it does is to make you feel better. Have you tried it? Will you?

I was amazed at the favorable response a humorous approach can bring, when our twelve-year-old son bounded into the house carrying a fine new football he'd won in a box-top contest. According to the rules, prizes would be awarded for the best sentences on "Why I like" the product. Apparently the judges had a sense of humor. Jeff's prize-winning contribution: "I like Wheaties because it doesn't snap, crackle or pop—it just lays there quietly and sogs."

Perhaps you will gain inspiration as I have from the cheerful attitude of that unfailing optimist, Duke Ellington. He was asked by an interviewer, "What was your most perfect day?" He thought, then grinned and said, "Any day I wake up and look at."

Survey:
Does Happiness Affect Health?

A psychologist devised a research study to try to track down whether there was a definite link between an optimistic viewpoint, happiness, and health. He questioned five hundred young people in detail, applying his professional expertise to dig for answers and sound conclusions. His results were reported in the *Reader's Digest* as follows:

1. "Happy people tend to be ill less often
2. " . . . they recover from illness more quickly
3. " . . . they even seem to have bones and tissue that heal better [!]
4. " . . . they seem to age more slowly
5. " . . . they have better color, glossier skins
6. " . . . happy people have more erect carriage than their contemporaries who suffer the graying atrophy of depression and anxiety."

Since I wasn't able to obtain the detailed report, I can't vouch personally for the comprehensiveness of the research and the accuracy of the findings. But I agree wholeheartedly with the psychologist's conclusion that *"happiness and health generally go together."*

I've observed, as you undoubtedly have, many optimists

who—even when invalided—exude an air of greater "health" than one would expect normally—and certainly far more than pessimists in a comparable physical condition. I've asked many doctors and found unanimous agreement that cheerfulness is an invaluable aid to health.

Taking a different tack, not concerned with physical health, psychologist John Cohen at Victoria University in England conducted research to help answer the question: "Does a belief in luck influence expected achievement?" Here's his conclusion based on specific study results:

"Yes. In a number of tests, such as running a race, throwing a ball, taking a long jump, we found that an expectation of luck created an improvement of twenty-six per cent over ordinary performance. Expectation of bad luck meant a deterioration in ordinary performance of as much as forty per cent." Obviously it pays to ask for and look for the *best* from yourself—not the worst.

I believe that similar favorable results would tend to accrue in compiling the benefits of an optimistic attitude toward handling and solving daily problems. For one thing, with an upbeat instead of downward motivation and conviction, you tend to try harder—and to keep on trying until you succeed—instead of dropping out and losing any chance of gain in each instance.

As another plus, a beauty editor, Antoinette Donnelly, headlined: "A *Smile Is Cheapest and Best Beauty Aid* . . . Even the plainest face is transformed by a smile . . . Thinking happy thoughts will show on your face. Constantly reviewing the things you don't like in life will cause you to wear a grim, unapproachable expression." It's all yours for the using . . . optimism as a beauty treatment.

A gallant woman, Sybil H., who had retained her cheerfulness through very hard times, inspired me (and now you) by noting in a letter: "Life is like an onion. You peel off one layer at a time, and sometimes you weep. But you don't give in. You wipe your eyes and keep peeling. And

207

after a while you learn that if you peel the onion in water, the tears don't come. And you smile as you continue good-humoredly and persistently until the task is done."

"I'll MAKE Things Better"

Here's another little routine that I suggest you try daily, *a self-call to action,* coupled with the soothing mental/physical exercise at the start of this chapter. This too may seem too simple, but please make the attempt. It forms an integral part of becoming an optimist and attaining conscious happiness. This easy technique has worked beneficially for me and others to whom I've passed it along. . . .

The routine consists of repeating silently to yourself just four words. As you walk, say the short sentence silently in rhythm with your steps. As you sit in a chair or lie abed, repeat it to yourself at least ten times in slow rhythm. Doing this adds power to the mental/physical exercise because now you aren't just thinking about being an optimist, you are doing something more active about it. You are *talking* like an optimist when you say, even though silently to yourself:

"I'll MAKE things better."

You are acting like an optimist by rejecting defeat and depression—by stating specifically over and over:

"I'll MAKE things better."

As the next step, the natural move—impelled by your words and fixation on making things better—is to do something that *will* make things better. The progression to saying that you'll make things better is to actually make them better. If you will try it day after day, coupled with

208

intelligent planning and forthright action, it can work for you as it has worked for me and others.

Please repeat to yourself right now, whether things are good, bad, or indifferent: "I'll MAKE things better . . . I'll MAKE things better . . . I'll MAKE things better" . . . and on and on. You will probably find that you just naturally are moving ahead optimistically toward making things better.

Note the specific importance of speaking those four words exactly as they have been worked out—"I'll MAKE things better." Over the years, I tried dozens and even hundreds of other phrases and sentences. I discarded the other possibilities because they failed in one way or another.

For example: "Things will get better." This sentence isn't effective because it doesn't involve *doing* something, the action of being a forward-moving optimist . . . "I'll MAKE things better."

I ruminated about a line that was popular some years ago. As I recall, it went like this: "Every day in every way I'm getting better and better." Here again, I felt that the sentence fails to help very much in moving one toward action options—because the line is inactive itself.

The big point that has worked for me and others—"I'll MAKE things better"—is that it helps you on the road to action and the desired accomplishment. You are the active focus of this sentence. Your action, *making* things better, impels you toward becoming a productive optimist.

Thus, by acting as an optimist does, you are more likely to grow as a happier individual of increasing strength and substance. And that can pay off for you in many ways for the rest of your better life. Your personal happiness multiplies as you divide it with others.

* * *

Focusing on these high points will build and strengthen your optimistic attitude daily:

1. Practice the Conscious Happiness Mental/Physical Exercise.
2. Try the Smile Self-Cure whenever you're feeling grim or low.
3. Ask yourself pointedly whenever you tend to be gloomy: "What's the use of feeling dreary? Where does it get me?"
4. Never forget that laughter is both a pick-up and "a tranquilizer with no side effects."
5. Realize that an optimistic viewpoint affects your health affirmatively.
6. Remember that a sense of happiness is a prime beauty aid.
7. Repeat again and again, and follow through positively:

"I'll MAKE things better!"

Most of the notable figures in history learned that it helps to maintain a sense of humor, and always will. When Einstein came to the United States to escape Nazi oppression in 1930, a young German commercial artist I knew, Fred Mayer, boarded the docked ship. Wandering, he found himself in a small dining room where Einstein and his wife were having tea alone. Settling quietly at the next table, Fred sketched the scientist. Shyly, he showed the pencil portrait and asked for Einstein's autograph on it.

The professor examined it and laughed. "Certainly . . . and with my signature I'll write a little poem."

Mrs. Einstein protested, "But maybe the young man won't like the poem."

"I'll write it at the bottom," he explained, "so our friend can tear it off if he wishes."

The poem, roughly translated: "This fat little pig (Schwein) . . . is Professor Einstein."

Another noted for his wit, President John F. Kennedy, was asked by a little boy, "How did you become a war hero?"

JFK's eyes twinkled. "It was absolutely involuntary. They sank my boat."

Once he discussed whether a leader should try to win the good will of historians so they'd be kind in compiling the facts. Smiling, he related Winston Churchill's comment: "I'm sure the record will be favorable to me because—I intend to write it myself!"

As an example of retaining a light touch even in the most trying circumstances . . . comedian Danny Kaye referred to the "marvelous humor" which his friend, famed surgeon Charles Mayo, often used to relax patients. Suffering from an inflamed appendix, Kaye required immediate surgery. Wheeled into the operating room, he saw Dr. Mayo scrubbing his hands "just like Dr. Kildare."

The gifted comedian asked anxiously, "Chuck, you have done this operation before, haven't you?"

The surgeon looked up. "Of course, Danny," he said reassuringly . . . "twice."

Smile as you face the future optimistically, and assert always:

"I'll MAKE things better!"

13

Giving Love and Friendship–Helping Others and Yourself

EVER THINK OF the encompassing truth embodied in this statement? "If we learned that the world was coming to an end, and we had only five minutes left to say everything we wanted to say—telephone lines would be jammed by people calling others to stammer out eagerly that they loved them."

Why wait for the world to end before speaking out your love for others? Feel inhibited? Tongue-tied? You can unknot your tongue. Everyone can if he or she really wants to. Speak it out: "I love you." What's so difficult about that? "I love you . . ."

A friend, Irving W., told me one evening, "Today was one of the best days of my life. I'll never forget it. My son came home from college for his eighteenth birthday. When I greeted him at the door, I extended my arm as usual for a handshake. He didn't take my hand. I wondered . . .

"Looking straight at me, his face reddening, he said with difficulty, 'Dad . . . I've grown up enough since I've been away to be able to say right out now, 'I love you.' Coming home from now on, I'd like to kiss you.' We embraced, and I kissed his rough cheek . . .

"Yeah, my eyes were wet. At age twelve, arriving home from camp, he'd ignored my outstretched arms and ordered, 'No more kissing, Dad. I've grown up!' I accepted it . . .

"But now he's really grown up—and so, finally, am I. It took me until now to say to him after a long, long time, 'I love you too.' So our relationship is deeper than it ever was." He reflected, "Y'know, saying 'I love you' can be kind of a miracle, a bridge to greater understanding and communication."

A Supreme Reward

One of the maximum rewards of conscious happiness comes at the end of day, as you close your eyes to sleep, to understand within yourself and to tell yourself, "I feel good—I gave and received love and friendship today. And perhaps I helped somebody, and thus helped myself to get more from this day."

That is conscious happiness indeed . . . *in deed*. There is no more valued gift than the giving of part of yourself. As you give love, it comes back to you in increasing measure.

That sense of deep gratification usually develops when you have given to one or more, and received response in turn—or at least have the satisfaction of having given to someone. That good feeling inevitably rebounds, perhaps helping you most of all. Giving is often joy enough in itself—giving without concern for being misunderstood, and without need for reciprocity.

But those who live selfishly, only within themselves, without caring for others, build a prison about themselves.

One test of a good person, a truly happy person, is how she or he treats people who aren't likely to be able to reciprocate with some favor. The act of giving is severely limited if you require a return.

You gain when you give, give of the glorious love that is within you, the potential of which exists in every human being. But—a big "but"—you must develop and use your potential to love, to befriend, to give and receive, in order to build and maintain your uplifting sense of conscious happiness. How best accomplish it? Let's examine the ways and the benefits . . .

"Love"—not meant here in the specific sexual sense—doesn't reside or grow in just saying the word "love," or limiting its meaning. You cannot, for example, confine it only to a particular segment, like the outmoded contention of some rebellious youths that love and trust must not be extended to anyone over thirty. Love, dictionary love, and in the general context here, is:

". . . the benevolence, kindness, or brotherhood that man should rightfully feel toward others."

". . . affectionate concern for the well-being of others."

Another called love "the overflow of friendship." Love can, of course be much deeper and stronger than limited friendship alone; it can include passion and total devotion. That latter, overwhelming individual-to-individual commitment isn't primarily concerned here.

For those who feel that they do not, cannot love in the broader sense, because of their engulfing pessimism, prejudices, fears, for lack of caring—or for whatever reason—there is great sorrow in store. "For there is only misfortune in not being loved; there is *misery* in not loving."

On the other hand, those who love others, who care, who befriend, gain throughout life. Arthur Wing Pinero wrote: "Those who love deeply never grow old; they may die of old age, but they die young." Loving others, and hopefully but not necessarily being loved, helps to keep you feeling ever alive, and ever enjoying life.

To how many can you extend your friendship and love, momentary or enduring? To all you meet. The capacity for friendship and the impression of love are practically limitless. Pianist Artur Rubinstein spoke often of the life-long "love affair" between him and his listeners, referring also to his love affair with the whole human race. "I can play only for a public I love. If they love me, I am terribly happy."

It has been said that when you make two people happy, one of them is likely to be you. A contrary view was expressed by an enormously fat man, the multimillionaire Gulbenkian, whose main preoccupation was living to overeat. He contended, "The best dinner involves only two people: myself and a head waiter." (He died soon after making the statement.)

Love, even love for others universally rather than love directed at one or a few individuals, is an emotion that must be felt deeply. Love is caring more for another person or persons than about yourself—and giving to others accordingly. When you extend and receive love and friendship, each of the individuals involved is treating the other as a respected equal. In gazing at another, you are in a very specific way looking into a mirror and seeing some reflection of yourself. What you give or withhold is reflected back to you.

William Hazlitt stated: "To be capable of steady friendship and lasting love, are the two greatest proofs, not only of goodness of heart, but of strength of mind." I'm sure that you understand love, momentary or lasting. Then feel love. Use your capacity for love and friendship as sunshine that warms you and others within your periphery. Thus you will enrich your totality of conscious happiness each day.

Realistically, some sourballs just don't want to extend friendship or love to others. One woman, a story goes, told her doctor angrily, "I insist on giving up the tranquilizers you prescribed. They affect me so that I find myself being nice and even liking people that I thoroughly detest!"

The venom of hate such as that poisons the individual expressing it. We must never permit an attitude of such fundamental antipathy to corrode and ruin our lives, not for a single hour. Rather, aiming to like the other person leads to the daily, mounting rewards from friendship and mutual joining for the betterment of all—especially yourself.

Extending Your Hand, Speaking Up

Your capability to receive and enjoy friendship and love is limited only by your adequacy in giving. It is not only what you say but what you do; not what you preach but how you act. When you manifest your good will by an air of openness or a specific gesture, it returns to you eventually if not immediately. Sometimes the reaction to your reaching out appears indifferent, even antagonistic, but it pays to push aside discouragement, and to keep trying.

I walked into an office that I'd never had occasion to visit, and the attractive young receptionist greeted me. I said straight out, "It's a joy to be welcomed with a lovely smile like yours—" Her face turned blank, that "some kind of a nut" wariness. She quickly directed me inside. I was upset that I'd thrown her off key.

On my way out later, I headed right for the exit door, eyes fixed ahead. Then I heard a voice call eagerly, "Goodbye . . . good-bye—" I turned. The same girl was smiling warmly, a hand waving.

I beamed, "Have a good day!"

She responded instantly, "Thank you, I will. You too. You've helped already."

She'd caught the fever; I reminded myself that a smile, even that small expression of "love," is catching. Now that was an *especially* "good day."

It's easy for most people to explode verbally in anger and hate, but not to express love. Why feel repressed or fearful about manifesting and verbalizing friendliness? If there is no response, you haven't lost anything. But you will have gained at least the good inner feeling of extending yourself. You have reached out toward another with good will; the failure to react positively isn't your misfortune, but the other person's.

"Somebody Cared"

There is little or no gain for anyone—as I must stress repeatedly—in merely *talking* about love, friendship, good will. The proof of sincerity and the benefit for both parties is in *doing something about it*. As an example, I noted a little newspaper item about a friend being accorded an honor. I phoned and complimented her, wishing her added good fortune.

She responded, "Your congratulations make me feel so good. Somebody noticed. Somebody cared. You've made my day."

Her reactions made my day better in turn. The call took two minutes.

It means so much to the other person when you make a call, write a note, send a little gift, speak up instead of just saying to yourself, "That's nice for Amy"—and not doing anything about it. Like the tree that falls in the forest, the sound and sight are meaningless if no one hears or sees. It signifies much when you speak up, reach out, touch. Then the contact is felt, benefiting receiver and giver.

A sensitive woman, Barbara T., enjoyed one of my books.

She sent me a small pamphlet of thoughts, along with a letter conveying her pleasure in reading my work. I wrote to her, "Thank you for your kindness in sending the little gift, and mostly for sharing your speculations and sights with me in your letter. It's a wonder of living that we are strangers no more. For this meeting through the writing and reading of words, and then expressing yourself through your response, is the truly heartening touch and feel of life."

It's so easy to transform a stranger into a friend, even if only very briefly. Even for a moment or two, it's worthwhile. Speak up: "What do you do?" "What do you enjoy most?" "Have you a special interest?" You query, you open up each other, you both learn and gain. "Talking is like playing on the harp; there is as much in laying your hands on the strings to feel their vibration as in twanging them to bring out their music."

A little test that helps me is to ask myself (won't you try it?): "*Am I talking to others the way I'd like to be talked to by them?*" That helps to remind me of the value of being a good *listener*, after making the effort to establish an understanding relationship with as many of the people I meet as possible. Listening is an indispensable part of conversing. "We have two ears and one mouth that we may listen the more and talk the less."

Ever Underrate Others?

It's easy to underrate others if you don't keep your mental pores open, not blocked by prejudgment. I had categorized Frank Z., a garage mechanic I dealt with, as a nice guy without much interest in anything except cars. I always limited my talk with him accordingly.

One day I met him in a big music shop. He hailed me

and said excitedly, "I just picked up the great new record-ing of the Brahms Horn Trio . . ." I gulped, hoping that my astonishment didn't show. He goes for great classical music?

He went on to explain to me that he budgets himself for a classical record every week, and that he had accumulated a record library far larger than mine. I kicked myself all the way home, reminded once more not to prejudge, grade, or categorize people casually. And to realize again that each individual can add to his personal conscious happi-ness in some special way, with an outside interest—as this man's was enhanced by the pursuit and enjoyment of fine music. "To belittle is to be little."

I commend to you (and especially to me) the words I heard from a very old man, deep in the mountains of Vir-ginia, who said thoughtfully, "I've never met anyone in my whole long life who couldn't tell me something I didn't know before."

I asked probing questions of a fleshy, forbidding man at a cocktail party—and gained new insights on the financial world when I learned to my surprise during the conversa-tion that he was a financial wizard. A shy woman whom I led into talking turned out to be a leader in college alumni management and learning; she opened a new world of growing educational opportunities to me. By in-vestigating other individuals through a friendly approach, you deepen your perceptions and knowledge. *And you feel good, as does the other person.*

A glowing young woman said to me at a party after a theater opening, "I love being with nice people. And I find them everywhere."

"One reason is that you are 'nice people' yourself," I replied. "I saw that instantly, it radiates from you."

"And now," she beamed, touching my arm lightly, "we're friends."

Now and then you hear the remark about someone, "When she enters a room she lights up the place." Do they say that of you? Why not? You carry the light within you—all you have to do is turn it on—for your own ultimate benefit most of all. "A man wrapped up in himself makes a very small package."

"But," some protest, "you can't *give* to everyone. You must be realistic, ration your energies and spirit." One's "realism" can be a severely restricting limitation. Realism is what you make it. If you strive to live happily, pleasantly—helping others to do the same, going out of your way to make others feel good—then that is your realism. Your energy becomes self-renewing. This makes a far more rewarding realism for yourself, those close to you, and all others whom your kindly, outgoing realism touches.

"Attention Must Be Paid"

You may recall this explosive scene from Arthur Miller's illuminating play, *Death of a Salesman*. A mother tells her grown sons that her father is going downhill rapidly, losing his spirit and sense of reality. She cries out that he feels unloved—"So attention must be paid . . . Attention, attention must finally be paid . . ."

Attention must be paid to other human beings—attention, friendship, love extended. These attentions are paid by giving of your interest, by sharing, reaching out to them—learning to care about others. You can gladden your days by developing an excited interest in the intricacies of human relationships.

You will find it an ever available, stimulating pursuit which can keep you alert and fascinated for life, no age limit. This means sharing with others, not *possessing* them. For me, "touching" another person, opening minds and personalities—if only for a few occasional, passing moments—are among the most rewarding elements that inspire and comprise enjoyment of living.

How does one learn to "touch"? So simple: You discard an attitude of indifference. You reach outward instead of concentrating inward on problems and woes. Look up, and many of your little troubles vanish; often you find yourself wondering if they ever really existed. Some people are perpetually unhappy because they're so sure that they're going to be unhappy at some later date. What a waste of today!

The "how" of giving attention, friendship, and love (a little more of yourself) boils down to an easy formula in a few words: *Pay attention consciously . . . look . . . listen . . . absorb . . . participate . . . express yourself selflessly.*

By paying attention openly, you can cause a transformation within yourself from indifference, even anger and hate, to a permeating feeling of love and joy. Writer James Baldwin said gratefully of such a change in himself, "Now I can receive and enjoy happiness, the light in somebody's eyes. . . . Somebody else's happiness is mine, too."

Unquestionably, the ability to receive and give friendship and love makes you *more alive*, better able to attain and enjoy conscious happiness. A great part of the sublime discovery is to be open to love, willing to love. And to seek love, not indiscriminately, but not permitting interference by your own stiff-necked pride, by self-demeaning excess humility, or by unwarranted fear of consequences.

You keep yourself aware and ready to give and accept friendship and love with an open mind, sound judgment, and an uncluttered, receptive spirit. And you remember always to "use friendship as a drawing account if you wish, but never forget the deposits." I keep being reminded of the right attitude by recalling the best road sign I ever saw, placed by the Texas Department of Highways: "Drive Friendly."

221

"I Love You" Is Not Enough

His mother, Hannah G., anticipated Peter's first home visit during his freshman year at college. Instead of acting pleasantly, he spouted rebellion, slept until midafternoon daily, left his room looking like a disaster area, stayed unkempt and surly, treated her like a decrepit moron. A week later, she drove him to the airport, and was a wreck when she returned home, due to his animosity on the way.

Devastated, she went to the kitchen to brew some coffee as a pickup. Her eye was caught by a torn scrap of yellow paper thumbtacked on the family bulletin board. On it was scrawled: "Dear Mom, I love you. Peter." She burst into tears, berated herself, "Maybe I misjudged him, was too harsh . . . if he could write, 'I love you,' I forgive him."

Peter returned for Christmas vacation. He repeated his earlier horror pattern of temper, tantrums, and downgrading his mother and everyone else. Again the long, quarrelsome ride to the airport—with no thanks for the tiring ordeal of fighting traffic. She returned home, utterly low. On the bulletin board was a pink scrap of paper: "Dear Mom, I love you. Peter."

Hannah sat down and wrote to her son: "I don't believe that you love me. Writing the words 'I love you' is not enough. If you love me or anyone else, *prove it with your actions* . . . by giving and sharing and serving. Without the acts of love, you demean me and yourself and love itself. *Show me*, and I won't be able to hear the loving words from you often enough . . ."

Tolstoy was asked by a student: "What is the aim of man's life on earth?"

The revered writer-theologist-philosopher pondered the question. Then he answered "To serve good—and thereby to build the Kingdom of Heaven on earth."

"But," the young man persisted, "how do I serve good?"

Tolstoy answered emphatically, "Only through *love!* Nothing else. No one will ever discover anything better."

You probably agree, as I do. Unfortunately, however, "love" has come to reflect so many meanings that the essence is unclear in a statement such as that one can serve good only through love. Each individual places her or his own interpretation on this. What is yours?

Does it mean serving love in the romantic sense primarily? By impassioned kissing? Sex acts? Or, as many apparently feel, "one serves good" simply by saying, "I love you." Words then may outweigh actions if just uttering the word "love" becomes sufficient rather than the specific demonstration of serving good through acts of kindness, consideration, and care for others.

Serving good is indeed the crux of love in its true sense. But we know realistically that the word alone can be totally self-serving, thus even destructive, and certainly empty. A dog food advertiser proclaimed, "Love? We package it! Chicken, Beef, Liver and Regular." A soda pop advertiser spent millions reiterating, "X-Brand Ginger Ale tastes like love." How gaseous, how insincere can manifestations of love be?

"Love," in the sense of living most happily with others and thus with and within yourself, is far more than just ping-ponging the word around without forethought and accompanying attentions. It's more than a word printed on a sweatshirt. You nourish and uplift others and yourself when you show and prove love by your acts and deeds. When a person talks about love, without backing it by performance, he or she fails others—but mostly himself.

With true love, there is no limit to caring and proving it. A hard-working, consciously happy mother of six children, Sarah K., managed her house without help. In addition, she somehow participated in PTA committees, and was in the forefront of community and charity endeavors.

Asked how she divided her love and efforts among all her children and many causes, she explained simply, "You don't divide. Somehow you multiply."

There is always enough love to give, if you care enough to give and receive it. Love has the power to move individuals and the world, and to keep it progressing.

But we must realize that even love has its limitations. A six-year-old, Mike, spent the day with us while his mother was in the hospital being operated on for removal of a painful abscess that had swelled out her jaw monstrously. As he sat on my lap, I tried to console little Mike, "You're lucky that you're loved by so many, by your Mommy and Daddy, your grandparents, many relatives and friends, by us—"

Mike nodded, "I love them, too." Then his eyes filled with tears.

I asked, "What's the trouble?"

He cried, "No matter how much love, it can't cure an abscess."

Silence. I held him close. He kissed my cheek, then murmured, "But love helps a lot . . ."

Regardless of all other considerations, whatever the faults or flaws . . . "Love helps a lot."

Test Your Love and Friendliness

If you feel that you give love and friendliness generously, how can you be sure? Here's a little exercise you may wish to try for a week or so: *List your acts of love and friendliness.* At day's end, just before you lie down to sleep, take a little pad and write down what acts of giving you performed that day, no matter how small. Or check them over in your mind . . .

Did you say a kind word to someone, to many?

Did you voice your appreciation for a job well done, for a helping hand?

Did you go out of your way to help another?

Did you lift someone's spirits, touch another with a warming smile, a little compliment ("You look radiant today")—whether a person close to you or a stranger (a waitress? a bank teller? the postman?)?

Listing your little acts of love, of friendliness, kindness, consideration—perhaps involving a little or a lot of effort —will help to make you feel good about each day's living, about yourself. And usually the list will grow a little longer each day—and you a little happier.

You will come to realize more than ever that *live* and *love* are linked even more by meaning than by similarity in spelling. And that when you reach out to other human beings, and are willing to receive love and friendship from others, you are closer to all humanity as well as more at peace with yourself.

"Love Without Its Wings"

Friendship has been called "love without its wings" . . . "a sheltering tree" . . . "the bond of reason" . . . "the most precious boon to men." The spirit of friendship is the cement of human life that binds people together through mutual liking and respect.

If you have one friend, no matter how far away, then you never feel abandoned and alone. Psychiatrist Norman Baur asserted that "if a person is not involved with at least one other human being, he experiences pain akin to that from hunger and thirst." The need for friendship is that basic.

By interaction with friends, acquaintances, even strangers—giving as well as taking from the associations—you

225

come to better understand and appreciate your relationships not only with others, but with *yourself*. You'll find that your self-esteem (discussed in detail in earlier chapters) is a source of constant support in offering others an outgoing and welcoming aspect. Your strength builds from a firm conviction about your personal worth.

To win and hold a friend, you must reach out, offer and give friendliness. And you must be eager to receive the same. If you lack friends, then you are probably not giving enough of yourself—or are not sufficiently welcoming and receptive. The world is filled with people wanting but *waiting* for a friendly gesture. Someone has to be the first to offer a smile, an interested word, an outstretched hand. *Why not you?*

If you want friendship, you must give it and keep on giving—or the friendship won't last. Friendship is understanding and communication between two or more individuals. It is of singular value in an exceptional sense, but can't be sustained in a single individual alone—friendship grows only when divided between two, or more. It gives back to you double, treble, and more—multiplying your own contribution many times over.

If you reach out and touch one person, you open another facet of living fully and most fruitfully. Friendliness is compounded of the difference between merely thinking about contact and *acting* on it with some specific gesture, some reaching, some doing. It cannot thrive within your mind alone. Undoubtedly it has often happened that you've met a person casually, been attracted, and said, "I'll get in touch with you, let's get together." But unless you actually "get in touch," the seed of friendship, unplanted, never grows.

Whose fault was the lost opportunity? Yours. You talked about it—you didn't follow through with *action*. Good intentions are valueless unless fulfilled by good deeds. It's worth thinking about often.

"Why Didn't They Tell Me?"

An executive in a thriving firm, Jerry B., was one of some three hundred employees who received an unexpected extra bonus with the paycheck at midyear. He wrote a warm, grateful note to the president of the company—and was called into the head office a few days later.

The president, Don W., gripped his hand when he came in—"Jerry, the warmth of your note touched me. I'm very grateful for your expression of thanks and your compliment. But I'm somewhat saddened too . . ."

"Why saddened? What did I do wrong?"

"Nothing wrong on your part, quite the opposite. It's what others didn't do that bothers me. Yours was the only thanks or even mention made to me about the bonus. Not a single word from anyone else."

"But everyone is grateful," Jerry insisted. "I know they're delighted. I heard many say so—"

"Then why didn't they tell it to *me*? Hell, I'm only human—I like a kind word, like everyone else." He shrugged, then smiled eagerly, "How about lunching together?" They became close friends as well as business associates. Each had struck a chord in the other.

It pays to reach out; others are usually waiting. Somebody has to make the first move. It doesn't help much to keep your feelings in check, or to know what is the right thing to do—unless you put it into practice.

"Nobody ever talks to me," a pretty girl complained.

I asked gently, "How often do you speak up in a welcoming way to others?"

When you take the initiative and give part of yourself, the gains return manifold. You feel good when you make others feel better—and that inner glow alone is reward enough, isn't it? Shaw said that "the worst sin toward our

227

fellow creatures is not to hate them, but to be *indifferent* to them: that's the essence of inhumanity."

The essence of humanity is to care for others, to reach out, to welcome, to help. By being a friend, you inevitably gain a friend.

One Who Gives Assistance

I don't find dictionary definitions for "friend" very satisfying. One includes the important element, "a person who gives assistance." My definition of friendship is caring about another, and doing something positive about it. Friendship is basically person to person, each friend an individual, with no set limit on the number of friends you can have. Yeats wrote: "Count where man's glory most begins and ends/ And say, my glory was I had such friends."

How much can an individual accomplish in trying to help others effectively? Here's a brief case history from my experience: A very close friend engaged in medical work in a primitive African country, Steven B., wrote to me that certain medications, including penicillin, were needed desperately. They had no money. I phoned many people in the pharmaceutical industry. Finally one huge firm agreed to donate thousands of dollars' worth of the needed medications.

But there was a hitch: I had to arrange to cut the bureaucratic red tape and have a public agency ship the goods. I tracked down the right agency, spoke to one of the heads, was told to fill out forms, and "Perhaps in a few months, permission will come through."

But dying people can't wait a few months. In desperation, I phoned the agency's shipping department, and reached a man who said, "Call me Herb. What's the problem?"

Herb cared enough to listen. Then, cautioning me to keep it quiet, *acting on his own as an individual,* he sent me an official order approving the shipment. He followed through when the goods arrived. I received a letter from Africa: "The drugs have already saved hundreds of lives, checking an epidemic. The people here say, '*Uwashukyru zetu rafiki*'—'Thank our friends.'"

I relayed the fervent thanks to Herb. Grateful but embarrassed, he said simply, "I hate bureaucracy, I like people. I'm glad I could be a *rafiki,* and now have hundreds more *rafiki* . . ."

There is no limit to what one person, *you,* acting as a friend, can accomplish through acts of friendship. Just the opposite, you can't expect others to see eye-to-eye with you if you look down on them, or ignore them.

The rewards of helping others enrich your conscious happiness. A nineteen-year-old Peace Corps worker said after a long stretch in a remote country, "Happiness is the realization that one's efforts and one's work have been worthwhile." Another, a young woman in her twenties, asserted thoughtfully, "My two strongest convictions are that man can attain happiness only through selflessness, and that every man has a profound responsibility to his fellow man."

Isn't it a glorious feeling when you have helped another? The exhilarating sensation that you have shared, given of yourself and thus given joy, is an incomparable uplift. This may be the truest essence of living—the deep gratification when you touch another human being with love, with friendship—when you *give.*

There is an ancient Hindu proverb: "Help thy brother's boat across, and lo! thine has reached the shore." You serve yourself as well as others when you do what you can, day by day, day after day, understanding that you can't possibly correct everything wrong in your world between

229

sunrise and sunset. But you do what you can—and that must be enough.

The Ways of Giving

There are many ways to give of yourself, helping others immeasurably. Many of the luckiest, happiest individuals I know are engaged in caring enterprises: Fighting religious, racial, and other forms of prejudice . . . involved in fostering animal shelters . . . organizations teaching others—newcomers, children and adults with disabilities . . . volunteer work in hospitals, other facilities, day care centers, schools of all kinds . . . and on and on.

The opportunities for helping others are boundless, the rewards enriching for yourself as well as for others. A giving gentleman, Admiral William Raborn, said, "I'm grateful that I'm not one of those people who when he gets up in the morning and pulls on his expensive trousers—thinks that the whole world is well dressed."

The rewards are greatest when you consider the needs of others—and then follow through. This is true specifically when you are giving of yourself, your time, and personal effort—rather than just doling out dollars alone that you can afford. Schweitzer called such self-effort "the career of the spirit . . . your second job."

Have you considered the possibilities for personal participation, perhaps in your community or area? Worth investigating. Live and *help* live is a more fulfilling alternative to "live and let live." When you treat and help others so that they are better for themselves, it's always better for you.

Someone suggested: "Do unto others as though *you* are the others." Another reminder I use for myself is the revealing line in *My Fair Lady*—"The difference between a lady and a flower girl is not how she behaves but how she is treated."

The known rewards of "doing good" are age-old. Back about A.D. 50, Epictetus wrote: "Wouldst thou have men speak good of thee? Speak good of them. And when thou hast learned to speak good of them, try to do good unto them, and thus thou wilt reap in return their speaking good of thee." It cannot fail that when you add to the happiness of those about you, then you add to your own well-being.

Why not take the time to slow down a bit if you are rushing pell-mell through life, so involved and ambitious that you may be unthinking about the problems of others and your responsibilities in that area? Take at least a few moments to consider helping your fellows. A stray fragment of a spiritual lingers in my mind . . . "Slow me down, Lord, I'm going too fast / I can't see my brother when I'm rushing on past . . ."

Here's an intriguing riddle for you: If at the end of a typical day, perhaps today, someone were to pay you ten dollars for every kind, inspiring, or uplifting word you've spoken to others—and also collect ten dollars for every unkind, demeaning, or hurtful word you've directed toward others—*would you be richer or poorer in dollars?*

Again Schweitzer summed it up: "There is only one reason for doing good—the doing of it." And the good it does you in the never-ending pursuit of conscious happiness is a self-enriching bonus—when you give love and friendship, and help others, even just one other. Therein lies the continuous nourishing of your deep, sustaining conscious happiness.

*   *   *

The key to possessing and enjoying friendship and love can be summed up in a few simple words: giving,

231

sharing, caring about the other person, about all people. Examples abound among the most notable individuals . . .

Acknowledged to be one of the outstanding women in American history, Eleanor Roosevelt exhibited more interest in the other fellow than in herself. I learned that personally. For the Annual Awards Dinner of the Mystery Writers of America one year, a special award was designated posthumously for Franklin D. Roosevelt as an avid mystery-book reader. As a committee member, I was to invite Mrs. Roosevelt to accept the award and tell about her husband's reading habits.

Visiting her, awed by her eminence, I stammered, "What will you talk about, Mrs. Roosevelt?"

She smiled and quipped, "I'll talk about ten minutes—" She waved the discussion away with her hand and said, "Now . . . what I'm really interested in is you. Tell me about yourself, your writing, your family, your thoughts . . ."

In minutes, we were friends.

When son Jeff was a cynical nineteen, against religion and much else, he served for a year as a hard-working volunteer with the Albert Schweitzer Flying Doctor Service in Basutoland (now Lesotho) as assistant to Dr. van Aswegen (who once told him, "The serving of others is something I have to do"). On Jeff's way back to the United States, he stayed for several weeks at the Lambarene Medical Compound with Dr. Schweitzer.

When I asked Jeff for his impression of the medical missionary and pioneer, he paused, then said, "He's a godlike man . . ."

He went on, "Once we were walking down a dirt path. I was about to set my foot down when Dr. Schweitzer pulled me aside. He apologized. 'Excuse my roughness, but your foot was about to crush a little beetle.' "

Jeff concluded, "His whole being reflected his reverence for life, even for the tiniest and ugliest living creature."

Schweitzer wrote: "It is not enough merely to exist ... you must do something more. Seek always to do some good, somewhere. ... For remember, you don't live in a world all your own. Your brothers are here too. ... Every man has to seek in his own way to make his own self more noble and to realize his own true worth."

How much friendship and love is one capable of giving? Gracious actress Deborah Kerr tells about her four-year-old Francesca who blurted after a mutual show of affection, "Mummy, I love you ten times."

A pause and then, "I love you twenty times."

Her mother smiled, and the child erupted, "I love you six hundred times."

A hug, a kiss—and then Francesca frowned thoughtfully, and exploded with relief, "Mummy, I love you outside the line of numbers."

Love and friendship have no limits. The more you give and share, the more there is to use, to offer, to absorb.

14

Finding Inner Peace—
Rewards From Beauty
and the Arts

"THE WISE MAN looks inside his heart and finds eternal peace." Peace of mind, a vital ingredient of conscious happiness, must grow from deep within to satisfy and sustain you enduringly. It is not a tranquilizer pill that you swallow, not "a turkish bath in a tablet." You won't find it in any bottle in your medicine cabinet—nor in gulping wheat germ oil or special "miracle" vitamin tablets.

To find peace of mind, you reassess your values along the lines suggested throughout this book. Seeking, uncovering, and then discovering a new dimension of inner peace comes about inevitably as you augment your possession of conscious happiness.

Right now, are you generally at peace with yourself? Or is your mind racing around, juggling a multitude of miscellaneous matters that you feel have to be considered or handled *urgently*? How about taking time from frantic concentration on the "urgent"—in order to comprehend what is really *important* in your daily living? By focusing one-sightedly on the "urgent," we too often overlook and bypass the important. T. H. White counsels you: "Time is not meant to be devoured in an hour or a day, but to be consumed delicately and gradually and without haste."

For a number of years I was part-owner of a demanding business. The necessary attention to detailed work and successive conferences with my fine partners interfered increasingly with what is a most gratifying part of my existence—writing books. Finally I decided to sell my business shares to a partner eager to purchase them.

I called my lawyer and accountant to arrange the sale at what my partner and I set as a fair price. The professionals looked over the record of business growth . . . and at once objected strongly to my proposed action. My attorney, Walter Socolow, warned, "It would be stupid to sell now, Samm. This business is growing so fast that your shares will be worth far more in five years. It doesn't make sense. Why do you want to sell—what will you get out of it?"

My answer was just three short words: "Peace of mind."

He stared at me thoughtfully. . . .

I added, "Peace of mind is far more important to me than any number of dollars."

Walter nodded slowly, "That makes sense—there's no price tag on peace of mind."

A Tip from Outer Space

The Skylab 3 astronauts reported that they attained a new sense of peace of mind during their long stay in space. Col. William Pogue said that watching the panorama of the world, the sun and stars beyond, gave him a more "humanistic view of people" and toward himself. That is, he developed greater thought and concern about other people, and was more caring about his personal relationships with others.

He explained, "I now have a new orientation of almost a spiritual nature. My attitude toward life is going to change, toward my family it's going to change. When I see people I try to see them as operating human beings—and try to fit myself into a human situation instead of operating like a machine."

Lt. Col. Gerald Carr observed that people in technical work tend to "move along with your blinders on. I think this mission is going to increase my awareness of what else is going on besides what I'm doing."

Dr. Edward Gibson, scientist, said that orbiting the earth for days "makes you speculate a little more" about life existing elsewhere in the universe. "Being up here and being able to see the stars and look back at the earth and see your own sun as a star makes you much more conscious of that. You realize that the universe is quite big. And just the number of possible combinations that you can have out there which can create life enters your mind and makes it seem much more likely."

The message seems clear that when you lift your eyes to the stars and let your mind reach into space, you are far less likely to become befuddled about matters which, although irritating perhaps, are relatively trivial in the fundamental, total scheme of your life.

Fortunately you don't have to risk venturing into outer space to achieve greater awareness, perspective, and peace within. You need only care enough to expand the horizons of your mind—realizing always the basic truth, that "nothing can bring you peace but yourself."

I often study the following three tips culled from the reflective astronauts and the lessons they learned in the far, boundless reaches. You too, as I try to do, can profit by applying right here on earth the insights they gained in their forty-eight days in space watching the panorama of the world and the universe:

... I'll "fit myself into a human situation instead of operating like a machine . . ."

... I'll "increase my awareness of what is going on besides what I'm doing . . ."

... I'll "realize the number of possible combinations . . . which can create life . . ." and consider the numberless positives available—instead of dwelling too much on the little nagging negatives of daily living . . .

Please reflect on those three tips derived from the experience of the able, thoughtful individuals in outer space. The lessons can be valuable aids for you in attaining peace of mind. Can be—if you will consider them in depth, and apply them.

More Paths to Inner Peace

Tennis champion Billie Jean King, after winning an important match, tried to explain how she finally won after she seemed to be losing at the start: "Inner peace has come to me. Until about three days ago, I've felt uneasy, not caring about winning and concerned more with other problems. Suddenly, at dinner the other night, a kind of wave passed over me, and I said to Larry, my husband, 'It's O.K., everything's going to be all right.'"

I'm afraid that it's generally ineffective to wait for "a kind of wave" to pass over you. If you simply wait and hope instead of exerting yourself mentally and purposefully, you may remain in comparative turmoil—and never attain inner peace.

But, however you achieve it, the possession will be an invaluable gain for you. All the ways here of achieving conscious happiness have worked for me in acquiring inner peace most of the time (which usually must be enough). I believe that such precepts will work for you if you will accept, think about, absorb, and primarily *use* them. There is further food for thought in these tips from noted figures:

"Peace of mind," explained *famous heart surgeon, Michael DeBakey,* "comes from a sense of contributing to humanity." Would that course work for you?

Congressman Julian Bond: "I find peace of mind in action, rather than in sterile reflection or idle contemplation." Again, stress on the value of *doing things*—instead of accepting inner turmoil aimlessly or complaining ineffectually.

Entertainer Sammy Davis, Jr.: "[For my peace of mind] I try to relate to positive things . . . to look for good in people, in today, in the future . . . through the positive recognition of good." Do you concentrate on the good or the bad in others, in yourself?

Former Vice-President Hubert Humphrey: "How do I find peace of mind? By enjoying what I'm doing, and trying to enjoy the world in which I live . . . determined to do something to make it a better place . . . giving love in order to be worthy of receiving it . . ."

In short, the goal and attainment here repeatedly is gaining peace of mind through striving toward conscious happiness in all the ways delineated on these pages. And the emphasis always is on *doing something*—instead of wandering through life in a vacuum, unthinking, unfulfilled.

Taking Time to Think

Things pile in on us inevitably as we proceed through life. Time after time during one hectic day treading on the heels of another, we may erupt, "I never have time to *think!*" Then, before you realize it, another month, even another year has slipped away, often without enough self-gratification and reward. How can you prevent this from happening in the future?

First and fundamentally, you must give self-recognition to the worth of *thinking productively*, of ordering your thoughts so that you use the passing moments gainfully instead of losing them wastefully. Time to think deeply, time to breathe fully—you *make* such time by seizing the passing moments possessively, and asserting finally, "This time is *mine*—thinking time, meditating time, peace-of-mind time." Thus you can achieve what Saul Bellow called "stillness in the midst of chaos."

Conscious thinking is another valuable element in conscious happiness—consciously, calculatedly keeping the tumbling load of daily events from overwhelming your mind and capacity. Think big, think wide, let your thinking reach as far as it can and will, as long as it is specifically directed by you. Emperor and philosopher Marcus Aurelius suggested: "Live [think] as on a mountain"—thus the entire vista is spread before you, and you choose the direction for your cogitating.

A scholar observed, "When there is no time for quiet, there is no time for the soul to grow. The person who *walks* through a countryside sees much more than the one who *runs*." Again, when you give yourself a purposeful thinking-break, you are using time for stretching your mind, and that is anything but a waste of time.

After I had made several trips to East Africa, each for several weeks among the plains and mountains and stretching sky, a friend, Ed M., asked, "What's your impression of the area—if possible, in one word?"

My answer came naturally, reactively at once: "*Space*."

That's what makes my mind soar most freely and alertly in the great outdoors—space. I suggest that you give yourself a sense of space at some time each day, room to achieve peace of mind through the vehicle of unfettered yet conscious thinking toward a goal. Let your mind explore the unlimited reaches of your consciousness. The result is usually a sense of calm, yet an energizing quality of peace of mind.

And at some time each day, try to be alone, consciously prizing the privilege of aloneness, of silence, of deeply felt peacefulness—even if only for a few moments at a time. It is your right, your privilege, part of self-preservation and self-inspiration, not at all selfishness.

This tiny period of peace is something you owe yourself each day. Use it, savor it, benefit in healing, strengthening fashion from it. "Silence is a necessary preliminary to the ordering of one's thoughts," said General Charles de Gaulle—and to the regeneration of your mental and physical energies.

Your Private Place

It often helps to find a private place which aids you in attaining revivifying serenity. My private place, wherever I travel, is usually by the water—the sea or lake or river—reflecting the sky. I find this notation in my diary: "Gulls fly past my window. In today's super-brilliant sun and light, tops of wings and bodies are bright white, in breathtaking contrast with moving deep grays in the under shadows. It all forms a flickering ballet of tones and movement—infinite joy just for the looking."

For you, your special private place may be under a tree on soft grass . . . or on a bench in a park . . . or in an easy chair in your favorite room, door closed against intrusion. Have *you* a private place, a personal retreat? If not, will you seek to find and settle on one—and use it whenever possible from now on?

In your private place you can escape from what a doctor referred to as "the *bug disease* which may kill people more than any other disease in the world—that is, the infection of letting others *bug you* to distraction." Alone, you can help your mind to ease off deliberately so that no such "bugs" can invade your mental and emotional well-being.

Each period of such productive thinking—whether or not in your private place—is a voyage of discovery. Instead of regretting aloneness, you can make the most of it by using it best. Enjoy the peace of mind fostered by stillness. Apply the healing quiet to refresh your mind and strengthen your spirit. There are sweet rewards when you forsake self-pitying "loneliness" by using the time and transforming it into valuable, productive aloneness.

No regrets—you owe yourself the soul-mending quiet period at least once daily. Use it whenever possible in your busy schedule—early morning, twilight, just before sleep—whenever fits you best.

You can employ time alone for additional pursuits that provide a change and reinvigoration. You don't necessarily have to stray far away from your primary work, as some advisers contend. I found regenerating change in writing stories and books, although a daylong writer of advertising copy and plans; thus I achieved a desirable break in routine. The *personal* writing was my relaxation and mental refreshment, promoting peace of mind. Some find it in golf, which James Reston calls "a torture which reminds all men of their imperfections."

An auto mechanic enjoyed building tiny model cars to help ease after-work tensions. A financier took up oil painting as a flight from daily job pressure—and became an expert in painting dollar bills on canvas! He asserted, "Somehow it's unlike juggling masses of dollars on Wall Street." A canny observer, Brooks Atkinson, has noted that "leisure is a form of private enterprise" in which you can find peace of mind by fulfilling your individual desires.

Writer May Sarton inspired herself and others to spend time alone whenever possible in order to launch oneself into one's own "inner space. . . . Solitude is the salt of personhood. It brings out the authentic flavor of every experience. . . . Alone we can afford to be wholly whatever we are, and feel whatever we feel absolutely. That is a great luxury."

How long since you have explored your own "inner space" eagerly, purposefully? It is worth making the voyage of discovery.

Your personal "retreat" into yourself for a time daily need not be inactive. Quite the opposite. It is often more conducive to enjoy peace of mind through some personal pleasure. There are so many pursuits of this kind available: Reading . . . listening to or making music . . . creative sewing, knitting, weaving . . . drawing, water coloring, oil painting . . . birdwatching . . . walking and looking wherever you are, city or country . . . and infinitely more possibilities.

Only you can know what is best for you. And only you can choose and follow through to attain your own most fulfilling inner tranquility. Thus you will find your personal rewarding *nirvana*—your individual state of bliss.

Peace of Mind Through Religion?

Many people find substance and solace in religion, as in the words of a character in the novel *A Simple Honorable Man* by Conrad Richter, who had spent much of his life as a preacher. He mused: "I think I'm pretty well off, healthy, happy in my job, happier than most people I meet, especially those who don't believe in anything. I think that my belief that God personally supports me, and that His presence and angels go with me, gives me grace to do what I'm called on to do, and peace of mind while I'm doing it."

If you gain similar support from religion, you are fortunate. This can be a lifelong contributing and sustaining element in your possession and enjoyment of conscious happiness. Writer Herman Wouk, a devout man, expressed it sensitively:

". . . I think Judaism [his form of worship] gives you a structure of existence. Instead of life appearing as a random succession of episodes and occurrences, there is a relationship with the rhythm of life, with the turning of the days, with the wheel of the year, with the change of the seasons . . .

"However, I have never taken the position that only religious people are happy, or that the religious life is the only possible life, because I know perfectly well that that is not true. . . . Religion isn't a featherbed. It's a way through the valley of the shadow, and it is my way. For me, it has been, on balance, a way of confidence and hope."

Lovely actress Ingrid Bergman expressed another illuminating view: "I belong to the live-and-let-live group of people. I'm Protestant. Three of my children are Catholic. Some of my best friends are Jewish. I know that faith can move mountains. . . . But, really, I have more faith in the wherewithal of the human being. Joan of Arc said if you help yourself, God will help you. I truly believe that."

I heard a thoughtful individual say, "My father is what I'd call a religious man in the sense that he practices goodness. Recently a friend of his, a pastor, confronted him and said, 'Timothy, in your heart you are one of the most religious men I've ever met. Yet you never come to church. Why not?'

" 'Well,' my dad replied, scratching his jaw, 'I'm afraid that I'd be taking up the seat needed by some real sinner.' "

Isn't the following true? Religion can be in the church, cathedral, temple, or in any or no place of worship. But, whatever else, and above all, it must exist in the goodness within a person, and in decency in all dealings with others —or it doesn't exist at all.

Religion and religious feeling are very individual, entirely personal, in my view. And how or whether one worships is a matter of individual decision. Truly deep religious feeling permits everyone that right without prejudice or persecution of any kind.

My own religious attitude, regardless of creed, boils down to three words that I try to practice every moment of living: *decency toward others*. I often muse over what our daughter, Wendy, said at age eight during a family discussion: "Religion is not where you go after you die . . . it's what people think of you after you are gone."

Graham Greene wrote: "He who seeks God has already found Him." A profoundly religious and totally unprejudiced woman said to me, "God and goodness start with the same two letters, and anyone who pursues goodness has already found godliness."

A scholar wrote that "the belief in God is essentially the belief in the inherent worthwhileness of life." And therein lies a great part of peace of mind.

I suggest for your consideration, whether you are formally religious or not, that you pursue a firm belief in the inherent worthwhileness of life and of your fellow human beings. And, above all, that you advance and believe in the goodness, self-esteem, and worthwhileness of yourself.

Peace of Mind from Beauty Everywhere

"Beauty seen is never lost," wrote Whittier. Rather I commend to you that beauty seen, realized, and *appreciated* is never lost. But beauty that exists in the world doesn't exist for you if you let your eye and mind pass over the opportunities in a relatively unseeing way. Such beauty, existent but unperceived by you, is lost forever. That becomes your loss—so you'd better guard against it always if you seek conscious happiness. Goethe wrote: "The highest to which man can attain is wonder"—including the wonder of nature.

For perception of beauty about you is a vital building element in attaining peace of mind. It should not be a sometime thing—not the occasional walk or vacation viewing—but something that you structure into your integral self by your constant awareness of the beauty about you. In that way, you will make it an ever-present foundation of your conscious happiness, enriching your every hour of daily living.

As just one possibility, consider what the *enjoyment of art* can add to you if you haven't investigated the potentialities up to now. No, you don't have to be able to draw a straight line (or a crooked one). The technique I propose here is not drawing, but *seeing*. All you need is an open intelligence, seeking emotional expansion as well as augmented peace of mind.

A beginning in gaining sustaining pleasure from art can be made in the examination of fine art books—which are as near as a bookshop or your public library. In many superb books, including the large volume I coauthored with my artist/art teacher wife, Natalie—*Introduction to Art* (published by Abrams)—you can investigate hundreds of great paintings and sculptures through colorful reproductions and revealing details about art. The book begins with this invitation to you personally:

> This book opens a door for you into the wonderful world of art. . . . Follow us through that door and let us introduce you to many of the greatest artists, show you how they lived and worked, what they thought and felt.
>
> You will learn some of the secrets of how and why

great art is created by individuals of genius. . . . The artist, by means of his extraordinary talent, can make us see things we never dreamed existed. . . .

May you be inspired to seek out and learn more, always more, about art. Thus will you increase your enjoyment by having a heightened response to all beauty through the rest of your life.

That heightened response to *all beauty* can be yours merely by looking at art wherever it is possible for you. Go to museums, exhibits, books, wherever fine art exists. It is all there waiting for you, to enrich your thinking and feeling, to enhance your sense of peace of mind. It is all yours for the looking and absorbing.

Consider this vital difference for yourself as an example: One unthinking, unobservant person scanning a masterful still life may comment, "So what? It's just a picture of some apples"—and then turn away, unaffected as well as unimpressed. That individual gets no thrill, no quiver of conscious happiness in viewing art or any beauty with that negative attitude.

But if you take the time and make the mental and emotional effort, giving yourself to look deeper, to experience more—you will start to enjoy the rhythm of the spherical shapes, the balancing and pulling of colors, the pleasurable rightness of the light and dark areas within the painting, and much more.

And by opening yourself in that way to a masterpiece or any fine work of art, you will add to your lifelong perceptions and enjoyment hugely—and you will expand your self-renewing, exalting feeling of conscious happiness.

Enduring Inspiration from All Art Forms

You will come upon much enduring inspiration, there to be gained from the entire varied world of art. For instance, reflect on our opening sentences about the gifted French impressionist, Pierre Auguste Renoir:

"On the day he died at 78, Renoir painted some flowers, then said, 'I think I am beginning to understand something about it. . . . Today I learned something.' " You can learn something and more and more, simply by exposing yourself to great art. When you do, you are saying in effect, "Come to me, my mind and heart are wide open for enrichment by all forms of beauty."

As another kind of ready beauty, are you gaining the utmost from "the speech of angels"—*all types of music*—orchestral, ballet, opera, instrumental, classical, popular, and so on? Music is eternal; way back about 50 B.C., Horace referred to music as the "sweet and healing balm of troubles." Through the centuries, and today, music can evoke and strengthen your peace of mind.

Music isn't confined to the concert hall or home. Seek, and you'll hear music in all outdoors, in the whirring wings of a passing bird, the sigh of a breeze through the petals of a flower. Gentle music exists in the tinkling fall of light rain . . . soaring music in the grandeur of a mighty storm.

Addison proclaimed, "Music, the greatest good that mortals know / And all of heaven we have below." Its heavenly balm and uplift can be yours just for the listening.

Many other forms of art are open to you, all imparting a deeper gratification from living, as delineated in the wisdom of Tolstoy: "Art is a human activity consisting of this, that one person consciously by means of certain external signs, hands on to others feelings he has lived through, and that others are infected by these feelings and also experience them."

In essence, art in all its variations, like life itself, is a means of passing feelings from one individual to another. And, in the broadest extent, to all others—*especially to you,* if you will seize and make the most of each opportunity to enjoy the various types of art. Sensitive artist Paul Klee noted: "Art does not reproduce what we see. It makes us see."

A perceptive lady, Eleanor McGovern, wife of the presidential candidate, said in a magazine interview: "I'd like to get up very early some morning again on the plains of South Dakota, and go for a walk with my dog and listen to meadowlarks . . . hearing them is my idea of a religious experience: it moves me to tears. I'd like to spend an afternoon all alone in my living room, drinking tea and listening to Vivaldi. I'd like to live to be 120 to do all the things I'd like to do."

Some might decry such sentiment, "Come now, your emotions are showing." Why not feel fully and forthrightly about beauty and art and emotion? That is what living is all about—to look, listen, know—to *feel* with all pores open. That means being more fully, more consciously alive.

Otherwise, those moments described so fervently might just pass unnoticed, unexperienced, unused—instead of becoming time that is noted and *used* ecstatically.

Finding Peace of Mind in Nature

There is art and music and poetry in all growing things, there if you will look for them, as I urge you to do from now on. It is true wisdom to spend time, to squander time in the contemplation of nature's beauty. It has been said that sight is a physical faculty, but *seeing* is an art.

As an example, please take a flower the next time you can, and look at it close up. Study the details of the miraculous formations—petals, pistils, leaves. There you will find art and music and soaring yet tranquil enjoyment.

If you gain nothing from reading this book and following my suggestions—other than developing the ingrained habit of stopping and looking and *absorbing nature's beauty* each day—you will have improved your life enormously.

"And what is a weed?" Emerson asked, and answered: "A plant whose virtues have not been discovered." Someone noted that if beauty is in the eye of the observer, then so is ugliness. You see what you look for. Do you seek the good, the true, the beautiful in everything? That positive attitude is a big part of possessing and enjoying conscious happiness.

A cornucopia of wonderful personal discoveries awaits you in your fresh, seeking approach to nature's obvious and hidden beauties. You can learn, as I have, from a Chinese proverb: "If you have two coins, buy a bread with one, and a plant with the other. The bread will give you life. The plant will give you a reason for living." The philosopher Spinoza agreed: "It is part of a wise man to feed himself with the beauty of living plants." *That can be true for you.*

"Flowers, plants, trees are like one's neighbors," observed Supreme Court Justice William Douglas. "Get to know them; come on speaking terms with them; introduce them as friends to the children." If you will love plants, tend them well, they will pay back rich, supportive dividends in added serenity. This is simple, true beauty always available for your inner solace.

Much has been said about *speaking* to plants. Well, *Time* magazine printed my conclusions: "About talking to plants, my advice as author of five gardening books is this: Talk, sing, croon to your plants—but also water, fertilize, cultivate, control insects and disease, provide proper light, temperature, humidity. If your plants talk back, then see a psychiatrist."

"The sky is the daily bread of the eyes." Please take some moments each day to gaze up at the sky with interest, wonder, thoughtfulness. Probe its immense, limitless mysteries. Therein lies an added feeling of reach, of peace. But the beauty and sustenance are there only if you will take the time to look and think and feel.

Look: "All nature wears one universal grin." And all of it can add to and multiply your conscious happiness by your act of immersing yourself in observing and partaking of everyday wonders. They are visible only if you seek them and employ them to infuse peace of mind through your whole being.

Art, beauty, nature—all are yours for the slight effort of aiming to enjoy them consciously, fully. And there is no price tag on any of them.

* * *

Checkpoints to Enhance and Solidify Your Peace of Mind:

1. *Reread the three tips from the astronauts toward attaining peace of mind.*
2. *Strive toward conscious happiness to help achieve full inner peace.*
3. *Exert conscious thinking to gain "stillness in the midst of chaos."*
4. *Develop an easing sense of "space."*
5. *Seek and find your "private place."*
6. *Strengthen the "religion" that exists in goodness within and decency to others.*
7. *Discover the beauty in all things, an indispensable element in conscious happiness.*
8. *Immerse yourself more in art and music to enjoy augmented peace of mind.*
9. *Keep your pores open to the balm of nature's beauty.*

Thomas Paine summed up his profound feelings this way: "I believe that religious duties consist in doing justice, loving mercy, and endeavoring to make one's fellow creatures happy."

The emotional artist Marc Chagall expressed his own devotion by linking it to art. He stated as he worked on an etching with a religious theme: "It must sing, it must cry—it is the Bible." Famed for his stained-glass windows in a synagogue in Jerusalem, he asserted as he planned them: "Color is everything, color is vibration like music" . . . on earth as in heaven.

A pertinent story told by presidential contender Adlai Stevenson concerned a little girl intent on drawing with her crayons. Her mother asked, "What is your subject?"

"I'm drawing God."

"But," the mother protested, "nobody knows what God looks like."

The child kept drawing determinedly as she stated firmly, "They'll know when I'm finished."

Deep feelings, the arts, appreciation of beauty—all are available to you, all about you. French modern artist Fernand Leger painted in what some have called "a mechanistic way," relating many of his subjects to machines. He explained: "The age I live in surrounds me with manufactured objects. . . . Beauty is everywhere, in the arrangement of your pots and pans on the white kitchen wall" . . . everywhere.

A message to inspire us always is Isaiah's prophecy: "The mountains and the hills shall break forth before you into singing, and all the trees of the fields shall clap their hands!" This kind of sustaining ecstasy from appreciation of beauty everywhere can be yours positively, daily, repeatedly—if you will actively seek and open yourself to it.

15

Unworthy, Wasteful Emotions: "You Make Most of Your Unhappiness Yourself"

THROUGHOUT THE CREATING of this book for you, I have gained immeasurably in depth of feeling, understanding, and character—by the act of writing what I have researched and noted over the past decades, and learned by living and then proposing vital considerations for you on these pages.

Not the least of my gains has come from examining and consciously casting out of my own daily living unworthy, wasteful emotions—as much as possible and increasingly so. The same benefit can be yours if you will probe and absorb, and then apply your personal ultimate conclusions from now on.

Some years back, before I decided to concentrate on writing nonfiction, I worked for some time on creating a serious novel. I never completed it because I couldn't feel and grasp the theme and the motivations of the characters fully. Why? I discover upon rereading the partial manuscript now that fundamentally it involved the analysis and dissection of a deeply unhappy man (which I was at that time) . . .

One passage from the unfinished novel strikes me as particularly pertinent in our understanding and pursuit of conscious happiness. The words reverberate for me as spotlighting a key cause driving too many persons, perhaps yourself, to live mostly in a state of conscious *unhappiness*. During a heated conversation in the novel, the intelligent, straight-speaking wife tells her morose, confused husband:

> There is something you must realize: *You make most of your unhappiness yourself*. Perhaps I have failed you, and I know you consider that life has failed you. But you fail yourself too. Mostly you fail yourself. . . .
>
> You have become so swamped with ineffectual, wasteful emotions that you aren't capable any longer of sustaining self-respect, or of accepting true love or sincere friendship from anybody. That's why you are such a mess of melancholy attitudes and desperate frustrations. You don't believe in anyone. Most of all you don't esteem and believe in yourself. . . .
>
> You will never be whole and happy until you can and do believe in yourself as a worthy individual— until you unburden yourself of negative, weakening emotions: self-pity, anger, jealousy, worry, fear, and all the rest . . .

"All the Gods Are Not on Your Side"

A sensitive friend, Wallace R., who was troubled and confused, arranged a series of visits with a skilled, understanding psychologist, Dr. C. What she told her patient is a wise, specific reminder that has helped me to handle and overcome adversity many times when I was troubled by forces pressing against me. The blunt advice may assist you immensely also.

Wallace was complaining bitterly to Dr. C. about a situation in which he felt he was being treated unfairly. When he finished his passionate protestations, she said to him gently but firmly, "You must keep this in mind, as must every human being: *All the gods are not on your side.*"

No, none of us can have it all our way. We must face, accept, handle reality. Situations that seem unfair arise inevitably. As instances: A girl or boy attending an excellent school gripes continuously about "one lousy teacher." A woman is extremely upset and complains endlessly because a few members of a committee voted against her proposals. The actions of others unfair? hurtful? Perhaps. But "all the gods are not on your side."

I called a superb novelist, George O., to congratulate him on the many reviews I'd read praising his latest book lavishly. I was surprised to find his response petulant, even angry: "That damned addlebrained critic on that one dimwitted morning newspaper didn't like my book!"

"Hey, George," I asked him, "must you demand and get unanimous approval? Must all the gods be on your side?"

After a long pause, he burst out laughing, his balance and good humor restored. It pays to ask yourself in situations where you might be overwhelmed by distorted self-concern: "Must all the gods be on my side?"

The obvious, rational answer can help to restore your sense of proportion and reasonable well-being when beset by such feelings.

Checklist of Unworthy Emotions

You will probably find it extremely interesting, and it can be helpful, to check the following listing of "character defects" and "assets" provided by an organization known as Neurotics Anonymous, with headquarters in Washington, D.C. (Not that you or I are necessarily neurotic, but we certainly are human, with some emotional weaknesses or failings as well as strengths.) Which of these listed characteristics do you possess, undesirable or valuable?

CHARACTER TRAITS THAT CREATE ILLNESS OR HEALTH
— NEUROTICS ANONYMOUS® —

These Character Defects = Illness		*These Character Assets = Health*	
Self-pity	Depression	Self-forgetfulness	Happiness
Resentment	Anxiety	Love	Rich, full life
Anger	Guilt	Understanding	
Defiance	Remorse	Acceptance of reality	Joy in living
Intolerance			Energy
False Pride	Psychosomatic illness	Tolerance	Lack of emotional pain
Selfishness		Humility	
Greed	Insomnia	Service	Laughter
Blaming others	Irritability	Generosity	Responsiveness
Indifference	Tension	Honesty	Warmth
Dissatisfaction	Suicidal Homicidal tendencies	Compassion	
Impatience		Satisfaction	Love
Fear		Patience	Peace of mind
Self-hate	Abuse of loved ones	Faith	Optimism
		Not judging	Usefulness
Envy	Loneliness	Concern for others	Adjustment
Disdain	Withdrawal	Gratitude	Purpose

© Neurotics Anonymous International Liaison, Inc. 1967

The basic precept of the organization which compiled these traits is also worth considering: "God grant me the serenity / to accept the things I cannot change / courage to change the things I can / and wisdom to know the difference."

The difference between being *neurotic* and *normal* frequently is determined by whether you are aware of and take action to control and overcome destructive emotions—

or whether you just ignore or simply resent them, or give in to them. Isn't it much wiser and more to your advantage to try to handle unwanted and undesirable emotions such as self-pity and anger—instead of letting them overwhelm you?

If you make the constructive moves every time, you are much more likely to build and reflect conscious happiness which makes living so much more pleasant for you and everyone about you. You'll ride the crest instead of sliding into the dumps. You'll accept too that being "normal" certainly doesn't mean being 100 percent free of fear, worry, and other negative emotions. You'll accept your humanness.

Everyone, including you, is *entitled* to upsets now and then. Danger arises and grows when there is too much *now* rather than *then*. However, while not ignoring your faults, you certainly shouldn't exaggerate them. You are justifiably an individual, proud of your individuality. The points offered here are aimed to help you get along with yourself and others best—for the best possible life for yourself and those near you.

Swamped In SELF-PITY?

Self-pity is in effect a disease that swamps the sufferer in damp despair. It plunges and traps the individual in a morass of unhappiness, futility, and resultant impotence in productive thought and action.

If you find yourself experiencing or yielding to the false comfort of self-pity, race from it as from a virulent plague. It is one of the deadliest emotions one can experience. Self-pity destroys the possibility of gaining and enjoying conscious happiness. For self-pity always acts to put you down, never to lift you up. You become so occupied with bemoaning what you lack that you can't concentrate on or even see what you have, the good in you.

Warning: Self-pity is a trickster. Often the weakening emotion disguises itself as a sense of depression, failure, the obsession that "the whole world is against me." How can you recognize it? Ask yourself some key questions:

"Do I accuse myself of being a failure, a dud?" Do you wail to yourself and others, "Everything I touch turns sour"? That's a sure signal of burgeoning self-pity. Such a dark viewpoint drains self-confidence, corrodes self-esteem and self-reliance, weakens your will and ability to succeed in the future.

Let's face it: None of us likes to fail, but we can't get away without having some failures in our lives. We must determine not to be overcome by failure. Truman had the right slant, that crying over spilt milk is "a damn waste of time." Instead, use setbacks as lessons. Employ the newly gained knowledge of what does not work as stepping stones toward devising a better plan that will flourish.

Taking such steps, chasing self-pity through the will to act, picks you up. You replace destructive pessimism with productive optimism. For example, when teaching aspiring writers who despair of ever achieving publication, I point to the *thousands* of rejection slips I received in my striving to become a successful author. I was tempted to give in to self-pity, to blame bias and poor judgment on the part of editors.

But I blamed myself, and determined to do better— instead of yielding to self-deceiving excuses. I kept learning from failure, kept trying, improving, finally attained acceptance. Often I'm reminded of a well-known author's response to my earlier complaints: "Babe Ruth struck out 1,330 times." I've never known anyone who didn't attain eventual success in writing if he or she tried hard enough and long enough, and *wrote enough* in spite of rejections.

I'm asked, "How much is enough?" My answer: "Enough is writing until you make it." And you make it in any endeavor if you replace self-pity with self-responsibility, assertion, effort: "Better light one candle than curse the dark."

"Do I repeatedly blame others when things go wrong?" Blaming others is another way of absolving yourself instead of acknowledging your own errors. It's saying, "Poor me, I'm the victim of the incompetence of others, not of my own failings." Such self-delusion is a dead-end street because you ignore the possibilities of corrective measures through positive action. Your unconscious mind knows that you are lying to yourself—and your conscious self becomes troubled, irritated, fearful.

The weight of blaming others becomes too heavy a burden. Why carry it? If at first you don't succeed, don't blame anyone else! There is a sense of total relief and freedom when you accept the blame for yesterday's mishaps, then set a course forcefully and determinedly to make tomorrow better. The past is the sun gone down; each day brings new light, new opportunities, new hope— but not if your vision is blinded by blaming others, by self-delusion.

After a disastrous love affair, a young woman, Wilma H., was embittered. She blamed the man completely. After we had talked for quite a while, Wilma suddenly acknowledged that she had contributed to the breakup. She breathed deeply, "What a relief to climb out of the swamp of venom and blame and self-pity. I realize now that I learned something, I've gained valuable experience." She laughed, "I've heard that *experience* is what you have left after you've forgotten his name."

You can profit from her experience, and your own.

Finally recognizing your personal responsibility after you've blamed someone or something else can be one of the best things that ever happened to you. It's the sun bursting through a black, turbulent sky, a signal of release, exultation, and reparative action.

"Do I often cry crocodile tears?" The phrase comes from a common belief that crocodiles weep after consuming their victims. In the case of self-pity, you weep because things didn't go as you'd like them to; the victim being consumed is yourself *by yourself*. Your pain is increased by further self-inflicted wounds. The hurt and grieving are clues to self-pity.

"Woe is me, I'm the unluckiest bum on earth. . . ." How often have you said something like that to yourself? Years back I was complaining about a series of spiraling misfortunes, not realizing that I was pitying myself horribly. But I had to burst out in laughter when I'd finished squawking to an acquaintance, an old country lawyer, who said curtly, "Every jackass thinks that he's carrying the heaviest load."

I recommend that we discard inner sobs and sighs and weeping crocodile tears over real or imagined hurts. Instead, let's work to repair the pain through positive, forward-moving action. We can take a tip from gallant actress Joan Blondell who said that when she feels herself sliding into the dumps, "I set the timer for twenty-two minutes to feel sorry for myself. And then when the timer bell rings, I take a shower or a walk or a swim, or I cook something—*and think about something or someone else.*"

For a minute or two, take a series of deep, cleansing breaths. Force a bright smile. Get up on your feet and go. *Do something*—and you'll leave self-pity far behind. You can't stagnate in a swamp if you make the effort to climb to high ground and keep moving ahead.

Don't Say It in ANGER

I commend to you three words that I use the few times in my life when I'm tempted, as you are, to erupt in anger. Just as the irrational retort is about to leave my lips, I tell myself before the torrent can emerge: *"Don't say it!"* Try that little device the next time you are about to explode in rage. Instead of blurting out invectives, block yourself: "Don't say it!" The one best way to avoid trouble, hurt, irreparable destruction through angry words is to keep your mouth shut tight: "Don't say it!"

Setting loose the harsh expressions of anger is like shooting poisoned arrows deep into the other party. After the outward evidences of the confrontation have passed, neither person involved is quite the same in feelings and attitudes toward one another. You both may have changed in love or liking or respect for each other, admitted or not. Is that danger worth the self-indulgence of a brief emotional eruption?

Time after time I've been horrified to watch the terrible uprooting of friendship, marriage, business relationships—all triggered by an angry, unnecessary, unproductive outburst. Then later: "I'm sorry. I didn't mean it." "I take back the senseless words. I was out of my head." "Please forgive me. . . ." But often it's too late, the deep hurts never fully repaired, the former good feeling weakened or smashed completely: "Don't say it!"

Ben Franklin warned, "A man in passion rides a wild horse." Losing your temper is as foolhardy as putting to sea in a wild, raging storm, risking shipwreck and worse. I've watched two people screaming at each other in vile anger, and tried to stop their inflamed accusations from shrieking through the air—and then seen love in ashes. Later: "If only I hadn't mouthed those terrible words. If only . . . too late . . ." "Don't say it!"

Yes, I've heard psychiatrists contend that it's better not to keep anger and hostility bottled up, but rather to let it all out. Years back when I suffered from migraine headaches, a physician advised, "You wouldn't have headaches if you didn't crush your resentments inside yourself, and instead would let yourself explode in anger." I answered instantly, "I'd rather have the headaches. Nothing, nothing in human relationships is worth risking just to vent a self-indulgent, mindless explosion of destructive anger—in my view."

Of course there aren't any absolutes in controlling or venting anger, applicable to each individual. You would be a vegetable if you didn't possess passions. My point is that it's foolhardy and worse to express anger irrationally. When a child is wildly upsetting, and the parent is about to scream with rage, I've cautioned, "Don't burst out at him now. The youngster is too blind with rage to see or hear sense. Wait until you both calm down, then speak reason." This system has always worked for me—with children and adults.

I realize, as everyone should, that I couldn't consider myself blameless in a quarrel since it takes at least two to cause the friction that can spark anger. I suggest this policy which I follow: Hold the words back when in anger. Then discuss the problem calmly, reasonably, after emotions have cooled and peace is restored.

Realize too, honestly, that frequently when you are actually angry at yourself, you may try to deny or conceal it by taking out your frustration on someone else. In effect, you thus are blaming the other person for your own emotional upset, refusing to accept the real cause within. Think of how often quarrels erupt when one has returned from a disturbing day at the office, or after turbulent events at home—and the day's pent-up anger is vented on the other party.

Being frank with yourself, shouldering or sharing the

261

responsibility fairly, could have averted the entire shattering blowup in such instances. And you'd feel so much better due to the cleansing quality of the act of honesty in admitting your fault. Asked whether being angry at others was related to feeling anger within at oneself, a psychologist replied, "It's the same ball game."

Participating in a controversial television debate with two physicians, the program was proceeding in high interest and increasing tension, as intelligent arguments were advanced. Then one doctor became enraged and blurted out at the other, "You're a stupid clown!" After that one mindless outburst, the speaker's credibility vanished; his further contentions were regarded as valueless.

After the show, his perspective restored, the offending physician apologized humbly, "If only I'd kept my mouth shut. If only I'd left the outrageous words unspoken." It was too late. He had disgraced himself with the audience. The show was over. The lesson: "Don't say it!"

Dickens suggested as part of his philosophy that a person should weep off by herself instead of exploding in anger. He counseled, "Weeping opens the lungs, washes the countenance, exercises the eyes, and softens the temper. So cry away." A serene woman, Mary M., commented, "That works for me. When I feel enraged, I find a place alone, think it over, perhaps cry a little. I emerge cleansed of rage. My intelligence has taken over, and I feel wonderful for the respite."

Certainly you can have strong feelings and express them vigorously. But how much more effective it is when you speak deliberately, intelligently, convincingly—rather than in a shocking blast of rage. Blake approved of expressing oneself:

> I was angry with my friend:
> I told my wrath, my wrath did end.

I was angry with my foe:
I told it not, my wrath did grow.

But—let out the reasons for the wrath after you have calmed down and can speak rationally. The greatest remedy for anger is delay, leading to constructive expression. Eisenhower said, "Never lose your temper except on purpose." In other words, seek for controlled utterance, not disorderly cries of rage.

Exploding in anger usually flames back at you, hurting you deeply. Instead, you can direct the energy of passion into useful, effective action after you have gained control. Then you let it out; as the Bible recommends: "Let not the sun go down upon your wrath." You will wind up pleased with yourself rather than shaken and distraught, perhaps grossly injuring your emotional and physical health.

Ask yourself, "If I permit little things to cause me to erupt in anger, doesn't that reveal something about my mental size?" A busy woman told an irate associate, "Go ahead, *you* get angry. I haven't the time myself." Realize this, please, that every minute you spend irrationally angry is another minute of unhappiness in your day. Blind rage and conscious happiness never live together:

"*Don't say it!*"

Self-Mutilating HATE and PREJUDICE

A psychiatrist asserted that the reasons behind hate and prejudice can be summed up in one word: *Fear*. The person filled with hatred, prejudice, or bias mutilates himself or herself. Such corrosive emotions boomerang within, and the individual hates himself for it—often unconsciously. Educator Booker T. Washington emphasized: "I shall allow no man to belittle my soul by making me hate him."

For love, decency, regard for others as well as oneself comprise an intrinsic part of the human's nature. If you go against this natural foundation, you injure and bruise yourself deep within—usually without realizing it at first. Eventually the natural contradiction to hatred causes a constant violent inner reaction, frequently resulting in serious mental harm to oneself, and sometimes in physical internal pain and destruction (such as the ulcer syndrome).

Some people tend to believe that when they put others down, they elevate themselves. It doesn't work that way. Expressing disdain or worse for others inevitably besmirches the mudslinger as it spatters the offending individual outside and inside. It has been said, "The price of hating other human beings is loving oneself less." (And a beauty expert insists that "Hate is bad for the complexion.")

If you hate, you live in a prison which you have built around yourself. If you don't free yourself of hate, and if you don't respect yourself as a whole person who doesn't need to feed on the poisonous substance of hate, then you cannot live as a self-respecting totality in peace and happiness. If you think you are better than others, the underlying reason probably is that you don't believe you are good enough within yourself.

And people tend to look down on the person who hates, recognizing the fear and insufficiency within. A woman said of her neighbor, "When she gives you a piece of her mind, it's always a long and narrow one." Gossip, bitterness, downgrading others—all such unworthy manifestations—are ruthless foes of conscious happiness. I urge you to be intolerant only of intolerance. "To speak ill of others is a dishonest way of praising ourselves."

Isn't the following inalterably true? The worth and

character of any person are matters of individuality, not what one's race or color, religion or faith may be—any more than whether people are short or tall. What one *is* has nothing to do with the color of skin, the length of hair, the shapes of features, or other such physical evidences.

Please ponder the words of a strong, thoughtful individual: "You can always be sure of this: You cannot express hatred for anything or anybody unless you make use of the supply of hatred within yourself. The only hatred you can express is your personal possession. To hate is to be enslaved by evil." Such valueless emotions as hatred and prejudice waste your time, your character, and yourself.

In seeking conscious happiness, you must understand fully that it cannot thrive without a friendly feeling toward practically everyone, including yourself. Friendliness cannot coexist with hate or prejudice, which are self-punishment—"like burning down your own house to get rid of a rat." Asserting your conscious happiness acts automatically to do away with those ugly emotions.

"The Green Sickness": JEALOUSY, ENVY

Jealousy usually embodies fear, uneasiness, suspicion, resentment about another's affections or successes. Envy includes a deeper, embittered yearning for what someone else has achieved or possesses. Both emotions contain some element of hate, anger, excessive possessiveness, insecurity, and fear. If unchecked, the "green sickness" can bring on misery and push you and your relationships to ruin.

It has been said that "Envy is the art of counting the other fellow's blessings rather than your own." When you strive for and attain conscious happiness, your wealth of blessings eliminates any need or tendency to envy another. Let others then envy your new peace of mind and contentment if they will. You'll have no room in your enjoyable way of life for envying anyone else.

You'll have no time for envy—since you realize that it could spoil your emotional and physical health, and snarl your emotions. Envy is non-productive. It wastes time that you could devote to positive action for whatever success you aim to achieve. Envy is a cancer that annihilates peace of mind.

A young writer griped continually about the plaudits won by another author. The advice I gave him applies to anyone in any field: "You can make it only by writing, by concentrating on your own work instead of glaring enviously at the gains of others. Then you'll be so busy writing the best books you can, and striving toward your personal goal, that you won't have any time or inclination left to be envious of anyone else. And then, but only then, will you produce your finest, wanted writing."

Thus, by working instead of brooding and burning about the other fellow, you wipe away envious, clogging thoughts from your mind. You become free, untainted and unscarred—for "envy's a coal come hissing hot from hell"— it can burn you and scar you for life if you seize it. Reject such unworthy obstruction. Keep your eye on developing your own greatest happiness instead.

The deadly sin of *jealousy* tends to eliminate a cherished love for another rather than preserving the caring relationship. Total love excludes jealousy since full devotion leaves no space for such wretched feelings. Jealousy puts self-love over loving another. If you love someone enough, you leave no breeding ground for personal jealousy which tends to arouse resentment and repulsion in the object of your affection. Psychologists emphasize that jealousy frequently springs from the individual's own wrongdoing or twisted desire—then directed at someone else due to the demands of suppressed guilt.

Jealousy involves a sick, narrow possessiveness, greed, selfishness—doesn't it? That's why this loathsome trait must be avoided lest it contaminate you. A teenager, runner-up in a spelling bee, seethed when a classmate remarked, "Poor you—your older brother was the winner two years ago." His wise mother calmed him, "That remark resulted from your classmate's jealousy of you. Pity him, and don't let such defeatist emotions infect you—lest his jealousy breed jealousy and worse in you."

An individual consumed by jealousy, "tyrant of the mind," loses her sense of individuality and self-esteem as she concentrates on brooding about and resenting others. The thwarting, twisting, infecting sickness of suspicion distorts her thinking. Troubles are magnified, obscuring opportunities to enjoy conscious happiness. Uncontrolled jealousy can render one impotent in mind and body, for it is bred of pernicious, usually unjustified feelings of inadequacy and insecurity.

If you will build yourself up as an individual whom you respect and honor, as suggested throughout this book, you'll be too strong to even consider being jealous. You'll replace centering on suspicion with positive action to cure a situation which might cause jealousy to erupt. You'll save much painful and destructive suffering. You'll find yourself focusing not on "Woe is me!" but on the *how* of mending or eliminating an undesirable condition. With that intelligent, corrective approach, jealousy cannot thrive.

Ineffectual WORRY: Sheer Waste and Loss

An intelligent lady, Beryl Pfizer, noted: "If I spent as much time *doing* the things I worry about getting done—as I worry about doing them—then I wouldn't have anything to worry about." Aimless, self-nagging, time-wasting worry can be obliterated by working toward a solution instead of staring blindly and fruitlessly at the problem and labeling it insoluble. Too many people, perhaps you, spend too much energy running away from something that isn't even after them.

The mind is like a sponge; squeezing out the futile worries is a cleansing process. You cannot live happily if you permit yourself to live with the fear, confusion, and pain bred by worrying. Rather, act to eliminate the fundamental cause of worry, "the sickness unto death." I have seen people worry so much that their lives will be meaningless or come to an end imminently that they never make a determined beginning toward achieving happiness and savoring the joy of accomplishment. You can cure yourself by handling the burden and getting rid of it instead of remaining crushed submissively under it.

Here's a concrete suggestion for you: It has helped me in the past to *write down my worries*. Seeing them on paper aided me in then writing down ways of positive action to replace the worry with a solution . . . and in many instances to note quickly their triviality in the total scheme of living. Why not put that little trick to work for you?

Another tip that works for me: *Do something to get the worry off your mind*. If I feel ill, instead of worrying about it, I call our doctor at once. If I have a problem, I plan a course of action to overcome it. Or I talk it over with someone knowledgeable. I don't let it grow and clutter up my thinking or get in the way of other activities. I don't let it sour my conscious happiness.

Brooding begets trouble. Doing something constructive provides relief and results. Each of us has problems—"the only permanently well-adjusted people I know of are in cemeteries." There is productive *energy* in worry when you harness it to corrective action.

A statesman said that once he'd be terribly upset—and worry about it endlessly—if he made mistakes or faced what seemed to be impossibly difficult situations. "Now I have learned that if one does the best he can in the light of his available knowledge and judgment, then that is all he can do or could have done. And there is absolutely no use in grieving or worrying about it."

Grieving? No. Worrying? No. Judging one's mistakes and problems carefully and honestly, and assessing them toward the end of avoiding misjudgments in the future, then acting to solve the worrying problems now? Yes! That's the way that makes you better and the future rosier. Torture yourself? No. Improve yourself? Yes!

There is hypocrisy in many worries. I've seen some very successful businessmen sit around a lunch table expounding on worries about their vanishing wealth—while gorging on the most costly food. That's sheer hypocrisy. Analyze the problem clearly—and use the time you would have spent worrying to correct it.

You might ask yourself as a little memory and self-analysis test: "What was I worrying about this time last year?" Then: "Is it still worrying me?" Chances are that you won't even remember what worried you dreadfully a year ago.

A friend, Ned J., agreed, "Worry can be so senseless and such a waste. I worried all last evening and through a restless night because a weather report predicted storms which would make me miss an early morning flight. The day dawned beautifully bright. I kicked myself all the way to the airport for worrying stupidly and sleeplessly all night." He grinned, "The saying is so true: 'I never met a man who gave me more trouble than myself.'"

A noted author remarked, "I worried incessantly about my last play failing."

"What happened?"

He shrugged, "It failed."

"What did you do then?"

He laughed, "I forgave myself. Then I went on to write this next play—which looks like a hit."

Working at it is, I find, the best safeguard against worrying about it. I take heart, as you may, from the story of a little city boy who tried to walk barefoot as soon as his country vacation began. He related, frowning, "It hurt a lot, and I could hardly hobble at all, and I worried about it. But," he went on, "then I stopped worrying about the hardness of the rocks, and kept walking. And you know what? The rocks get *softer* every day."

When I was away at college, my father wrote to me: "Please enjoy living today rather than worrying so much about tomorrow. Some people go through life worrying, and they increase their worrying so that they even worry if they have nothing to worry about. I would rather be called a fool and be happy—than to appear wise, and worry about something to worry about. There is neither solution nor happiness that way."

It's up to you: You can open a window and enjoy the fresh air . . . or suffocate because you worry about catching a cold from the draft. Face matters optimistically, as in the following words written by Anonymous:

"Why Worry?"

There are only two things to worry about:
Either you are well or sick . . .
If you are well, there is nothing to worry about . . .
But if you are sick there are two things to worry about:
Either you will get well or die . . .
If you get well there is nothing to worry about . . .
If you die, there are two things to worry about:
Either you will go to heaven or hell . . .
If you go to heaven, there is nothing to worry
    about . . .
But if you go to hell, you'll be so busy

Shaking hands with friends, you won't have time to worry.

Enjoy What You Are

There are other common unworthy, wasteful emotions of which we are all aware—greed, groundless fear, excess humility, exaggerated ego (excess *himility*), and others, including unreasoning obstinacy. (According to Mark Twain, "The difference between perseverance and obstinacy is that one comes from a strong will, and the other from a strong won't.")

Lest you be overly concerned if many of these traits are on your personal checklist, realize that all these are not only *wrong* feelings, but also *human* feelings. What would make them totally wrong would be if you made no effort to control and correct them.

For the most part, such destructive emotions can be restrained and even eliminated. First, you review and recognize such traits candidly and clearly—to see whether they thrive within yourself. Then, if they are part of your makeup, a dominating part, you exert efforts to correct them, as indicated here. And you keep taking action to efface them—and then continue to prevent them from marring your daily living.

Attaining and cherishing conscious happiness as a natural, functioning part of your character generally helps to exterminate such emotions so that they will not take hold of you again. If you cannot gain control, then probably you should consult qualified professional help. Any thoughtful, promising step toward winning and maintaining your supportive balance is desirable.

For most individuals, hopefully for you—as for me and many others I know—possessing the conviction of deep conscious happiness leaves no room for unworthy emotions to sprout—even if they try to get a foothold occasionally. The latter is likely to happen repeatedly in the infinite, challenging, trying variety of daily living. By and large, conscious happiness will promote the balance and resultant peace of mind plus zest in living that will uplift and sustain you—and the fortunate individuals whom your life touches.

It follows inevitably that when you improve yourself and think well of yourself, then others are more likely to think well of you. Do your best, and then you can be glad and grateful for what you have accomplished to the fullest extent of your ability. And enjoy what you have made of yourself, what you are . . . instead of worrying about what you are not.

* * *

Review the recommendations here, then act to overcome hurtful, wasteful emotions:
1. *Fight against dejection and futile brooding; remember that "all the gods are not on your side."*
2. *Analyze yourself in relation to the Character Defects chart—and work toward improvement.*
3. *Ask and answer the key questions listed to, help you combat the swamping disease of self-pity.*
4. *Do something active to lift yourself from an evil mood.*
5. *Write down your worries to aid in examining them clearly, then solving them.*
6. *Remember these three indispensable words before you explode in anger: "Don't say it!"*
7. *Cast out hatred, prejudice, and bias as deeply self-mutilating.*
8. *Shun the "green sickness": jealousy and envy.*
9. *Take positive action to correct your unworthy emotions and traits by facing them clearly and squarely; heed English statesman Bulwer-Lyt-*

ton's warning: "The easiest person to deceive is one's self."

Above all, using the suggestions in this book to attain and sustain your conscious happiness is the surest, most effective antidote to allowing wasteful, destructive emotions to oppress you with conscious unhappiness.

You'll find illuminating meaning in the story often told at Harvard about the revered dean LeBaron Russell Briggs. One day he asked a student why he hadn't completed his scheduled assignment.

The student answered weakly, "I'm sorry, sir—I wasn't feeling very well mentally and physically. I just couldn't get to it."

Dean Briggs stared him down and said, "You'll find, young man, that most of the work of the world is done by people who aren't feeling very well one way or another."

No matter how low, ill, or afflicted you may be, making an effort usually results in gratifying accomplishment for your own well-being, as well as for the good of your loved ones and others. Make the effort—it pays off.

16

Dealing Affirmatively with Troubles, Illness, Death

In a course at New York University conducted by Wallace Sokolsky, the noted historian covered problems and attempted solutions affecting people through the centuries. In the final session, he asked students to express briefly what each had learned. My summation was five words: "There are no simple solutions." Professor Sokolsky agreed, "That's been true since the beginning of time; it will always be so."

That's a major challenge we face throughout life as troubles and confrontations inevitably arise. While all the positive steps we take toward enjoying conscious happiness each day are extremely helpful and supportive, as William McFee cautioned, "Doing what is right is no guarantee against misfortune."

The key to handling troubles most effectively is embodied for me in an old proverb: "You cannot prevent the birds of sorrow from flying over your head, but you can prevent them from building nests in your hair." A former boxer explained how he kept misfortunes from overwhelming him: "I keep moving with the punches every possible way, trying to hit back. I never just stand there taking it on the chin."

You must take *affirmative action* against troubles lest they knock you out, leaving you useless to help yourself or anyone else. It helps me in times of trouble to realize that I'm not unique in being afflicted. Everybody has troubles coming, present, going. It is part of the human condition. Some people are pressed by difficulties most of the time. A woman beset by repeated trials called them "life lessons . . . I don't think of the setbacks as failures. Failure is when you don't feel or learn anything."

Many individuals have emerged from terrible adversity with greater fortitude and character. A woman of thirty, Gail F., told me, "I was a flighty time-waster until my world crashed and I had to do everything possible just to survive. Now I work at it to savor each moment to the full. I'm enjoying life as I never did before."

How does one survive the most destructive tragedies? Author Martin Gray, who lived through the tortures of Nazi death camps, then lost his wife and children in a forest fire, was asked where he found the courage to carry on with spirit and optimism, helping others with his giving support. He spoke from the heart: "No matter what life brings, one has to be faithful to it." Remember, you possess no greater gift than the fact of *living*. You must treasure and use it well.

Although the pursuit and practice of conscious happiness can't promise you a trouble-free existence, you will be able to cope far better. How well you handle reverses helps determine how much you get out of life. If you allow and even invite misfortune (as some people do) to dominate and overwhelm you, then you will suffer misery most of your waking hours—and even into nightmarish sleep. But there are affirmative ways to contain and overcome adversity . . .

★ *Keep building your strength as a self-respecting individual*—in all the ways noted in this book. Thus, you fight back instead of caving in; you apply yourself to solving the problem. A totally satisfactory solution isn't always possible, as with a fatal illness. In such cases, the course must be to fortify yourself and adapt, perhaps change, routine ways. You adjust to handle the problem since you are acting affirmatively instead of sinking into the desolate swamp of self-pity.

Being hurt by uncontrollable forces is part of living, but only part. You take vital, vigorous, continuous action to control the hurt, to keep it manageable—so that it doesn't overcome you. You keep seeking and appreciating the moments of joy available in each day—which occur no matter how profound and burdensome your troubles are. You realize that you must strive and believe: "The curse of earth's gray morning / Is the blessing of its noon."

And you never give up your drive for conscious happiness. A wonderful aging lady, Grace S., constantly beset by troubles, wrote to me: "Coming home late at night from visiting my dying husband in the hospital, the street near home was deserted due to a heavy snowstorm. I couldn't see through the thick white curtain. I stepped off the curb, fell, couldn't get up—my leg was crooked and broken. Awful pain. Nobody in sight. So—I had an intimate conversation with myself, assuring myself that somebody would appear to rescue me. I raised my face, and the soft flakes on my skin relieved the pain. Then someone appeared, and now my leg is mending. . . ."

★ *Keep fighting, never give in.* No, you can't expect to pop up smiling instantly whenever a blow knocks you down. But you have a choice of staying down, giving in to suffering, or pulling yourself to your feet and fighting back. One thing sure, you gain nothing and may lose everything, specifically yourself, by giving in. The best way to help yourself and anyone needing help is by pulling yourself together affirmatively. A ship proves its quality by staying afloat and plowing through the roughest storms and seas; the same is true of humans.

Joy in Adversity?

Educator Mary Susan Miller, who read this manuscript before it was finished, wrote to me: "May I toss in one idea about fighting deep trouble? I find sustenance in the ways you note, facing trouble as part of life, living with it, working through it, growing through fighting back. But also, when a person is in great trouble, he can gain some joy from it . . .

"We read so much in great literature about historic agonies. Then when trouble comes to us, we can share: 'So that's what it's like. Now I understand.' There is deep satisfaction, almost joy, in the experiencing and battling through against adversity." There is another consideration, hard to take perhaps but worth realizing and putting to personal use, Benjamin Franklin's truism: "The things that hurt, instruct."

Ask the unhappiest person you know who is constantly complaining about misfortune, "What are you doing about it?" The usual reply, "What can I do? I'm waiting for things to get better." Meanwhile days are wasted in dark brooding. Another individual fights back, does everything possible to alleviate the situation and *to make things better*. Exerting, climbing, you reach the light, at least see some strengthening rays if not total brightness.

★ *Keep busy.* First you fight back by doing everything corrective you can to improve the condition. Then you don't slump and mope, you occupy yourself through working, doing something constructive. Two writers I know were struck by serious illnesses of their wives. One became melancholy, refused even to try to write; he required medical treatment for depression, adding another burden to his very sick wife.

The other writer did everything possible to secure the best medical attention and comforts for his stricken wife. Then he used every available hour to research, write, keep writing. The act of working reinforced him, provided extra emotional strength to help him minister to his loved one. Both benefited as they kept fighting back—and built a sense of shared participation and joy in living.

Which of these opposite courses would you choose: Giving up? Or using all your available resources in working, making an effort? There is really only one choice for yourself, for all in trouble—living, asserting yourself, taking action: "I'll make things better."

★ *Accept others' friendship and love.* There is a human tendency when trouble strikes to shrink away from others, to run away, hide alone, lick your wounds. That leads to brooding, an excess of self-pity, tobogganing toward self-destruction. In that terrible lonely condition you help no one, least of all yourself. You must make the effort—accept friendship, companionship, love.

I was helped by a friend years back when I was in deep trouble and avoiding others. Bill T. sought me out, insisted on breaking into my privacy. He talked quietly, soothingly, opening up possibilities for my emergence. In spite of myself, my senses were coming alive, expanding. After a while, he challenged, "What are you doing to overcome your troubles?"

I sighed, "I'm doing as well as I can."

He placed his hand on my shoulder, feeding me his strength. "Not good enough," he said. "Adversity is part of growth. From now on you're going to *do better than you can.*" I did.

When you help to share the burdens of another, you feel enriched. You have touched another. You have accomplished something. Don't you owe it to those close to you to give them the joy and fulfillment of helping you, of lifting you when you're in trouble? "If you don't share your misfortunes as well as your joys with me," said my friend "then you don't love me." Giving love and solace requires sharing mutually in times of trouble as well as delight. One plus one adds up to infinity.

★ *Then try a little harder.* After you've done everything "possible," and you're still badly troubled, try a little harder—and keep trying until you have matters in reasonable control again.

Prime Minister Winston Churchill, battered, beleaguered, faced with what appeared to be certain defeat for England in World War II, exhorted all Britishers to an extra supreme effort: "It's not enough to do our best; sometimes we have to do *what is required*." The same is true in fighting all kinds of troubles. You must do what is required until you conquer and achieve some conscious happiness daily again. Your portion will grow steadily from then on.

There is no question, you will find (if you haven't learned it already from living experience), that one gains new strength from facing, handling, and exerting to overcome troubles. Each time, you emerge a little sturdier, more confident, with newly tempered, less brittle, more enduring strength. Emily Dickinson wrote: "We never know how high we are / Till we are called to rise." You learn how high you are by *making* yourself rise against adversity.

Keep in mind that conscious happiness is rarely total. It consists of recognizing and enjoying each particle of good that occurs each day. There is no day, no matter how dismal, that doesn't contain at least a brief moment of happiness to lift and sustain you. You must seek it . . . find it . . . use it. Deeply troubled over the tragedy which struck a friend, a vigilant woman, Marion Bijur, implored: "Please don't let us pass a day, an hour, a moment without the astonished and grateful awareness of our well-being, transitory though it may be."

Avoiding and Chasing DEPRESSION

Everyone has low points in moods and attitudes, periods of mild depression, melancholy, dejection. But some individuals are afflicted with deep and long-lasting depression to the point where it becomes a potentially serious illness. The latter definitely require expert medical attention and treatment since much can be done professionally to relieve and control deep depression. Severe swings from very high to very low may indicate manic-depressive problems, and an urgent need for specialized medical care.

We're concerned here primarily with learning to avoid and chase the blues as a normal part of living. In effect, switching from pessimism to conscious happiness. It can be done, as I did it. You'll find the *how-to's* in this chapter and throughout the book, for when you attain conscious happiness, periods of dejection occur far less frequently. They can vanish quite completely except perhaps for occasional temptation now and then to indulge oneself in feeling low.

It helps to realize that you're not unique in feeling low periodically. A touch of sadness now and then happens to the best of men (and women). Without some lows, psychiatrist Nathan S. Kline points out, each of us would be less, or other than, human. So don't brood about or exaggerate the normal anxieties; handle them instead. There's a tremendous lift in pulling yourself out of depression by your own volition and actions.

After I turned from pervading pessimism to conscious happiness, I wrote to a teenage friend, Amy M., who tended to feel low much of the time:

> I made a big mistake in growing up, inviting much gloom upon myself and others because I disliked myself for true and imagined faults. So I indulged myself in the bitter sweetness of melancholy until I faced reality and realized that I was permitting myself to wallow in the putrid swamp of self-pity . . .
>
> Then I forced myself to recognize that *nothing is depressing unless you decide that it is.* Now I understand that I have faults, but I exert myself strenuously to remedy them. I like and honor myself as a striving individual who tries always to be decent to others and have regard for others—*and for myself.*
>
> Now I try to live at peace and to draw the fullest possible joy from each day, each hour, each minute (my name for that is "conscious happiness"). Life can't be a drag if you don't make it so. I'm totally convinced and committed to the certainty that it wastes the precious gift of life .to gloom the days away.

There are specific steps you can take, as I have, which are effective in avoiding, relieving, and chasing the blues:

★ *When you start feeling low, change what you're doing—at once.* Depression is a poisoned well—spit out the first swallow. At the first indication of the blues besieging you, get up, change the scene. Take a walk, admire flowers or birds, savor the beauty of nature. Talk about something interesting with someone in person or on the phone. Read a gripping or amusing book. Get a cup of coffee or whatever you enjoy—do something you like.

A woman suggests that "Noble deeds and hot baths are the best cures for depression." Planning something desirable helps also—an evening in the theater, a party, luncheon or dinner date. Any event to look forward to is a definite antidote to brooding.

My primary cure is to tackle something I enjoy most—the act of writing anything, a letter, article, book, just writing and thus immersing me in something other than my gloomy mood. What excites and delights *you* most? Do it—the instant you feel your spirits dipping, to swing yourself upward in a hurry. Depression is like a runaway horse. Grab the frantic animal early, and you can calm, soothe, control the creature. Similarly with the beast of depression: check it before it gallops away with you. Apply the effort—it works.

★ *See someone you like very much.* Hundreds of years ago, John Gay advised: "If the heart of a man is depress'd with cares / The mist is dispell'd when a woman appears." Sex isn't involved necessarily—see a friend, an acquaintance, an associate. Share the time—and you're likely to forget soon that you were feeling low.

★ *Tackle the problem that brought on the blues.* Ask yourself, "Why?" Then correct it. Frequently it's because you're angry with yourself for certain reasons, or about something another has done. Facing it helps wash it out of your mind, especially after you've taken specific steps to correct and eliminate the cause. Some people act depressed in order to win attention and to appear interesting and profound. Realize how phony that is, and you'll laugh at yourself and the worthlessness of being dejected.

★ *Don't talk about feeling blue.* I walked into a little gift shop in Washington, D.C., one day. As I browsed, the young attendant sat in a chair, hands in lap, head lowered. A disheveled man walked in, blurted, "Oh God, Bonnie,

I'm feeling low. Got the blues. But the blue blues. Know what I mean?"

"Yeah, Ralphie. Me too. Low low low."

They moaned on, drenching themselves and each other in self-pitying bathos. Finally I asked the girl to handle my purchase. The man glared at me, then left. The girl came over reluctantly, wiping her sleeve across her reddened eyes.

I said with a smile, "Sorry to interrupt your sentimental feast. What's the big trouble?"

She glared, then shrugged, "Just feeling low."

"A lot lower since your moaning, groaning session—right?"

She stared resentfully, my smile broadened. Then she burst out laughing as she realized how ridiculous the act was. She handed me the package. "Thanks," she said, "I feel better after that deserved slap in the face."

"Good. What were you really feeling blue about?"

She thought, then grinned, "I can't remember." Her lips tightened, "Next time that stupid Ralphie starts moaning the blues to me, I'll kick him right in the teeth. It's not only depressing, it's *boring!*"

Despair is an evil adviser—give it a deaf ear, and turn away to the light. When you build yourself up, respect and like yourself, the blues can't take root and smother you. Don't let them get a grip. Strengthen your individuality. Take the steps listed here. Then if depression tries to push you under, kick the worthless, tiresome devil right in the teeth—*hard and instantly*. For there just isn't enough time in living to indulge in gloominess and brooding.

★ *Count your pluses instead of the debits.* Philosopher Thomas Fuller said that "blessings are not valued until they are gone." I've found that it helps to list side by side on a sheet of paper my pluses and minuses. Then I cross off many of the negatives by thinking about and eliminating them by counterattacking. Your assets tend to look bigger and better as you list what you have rather than dwelling on what is lacking. Right at the top of all the blessings, I'd write: "Hallelujah, *I'm alive!*" And all you have to do is make the most of it to the best of your ability.

Handling ILLNESS: Yours and Others'

"There is no mortal whom sorrow and disease do not touch," Euripides wrote. When illness strikes, there are two courses we can take: Give in and suffer . . . or fight the sickness in every possible way in order to recover most quickly, undertaking corrective measures until the illness is conquered or at least contained.

Instead of letting sickness take over and lay you low, hoping it will "go away," do something about it at once. The first obvious step is to get competent medical attention, of course. Yet a surprisingly large percentage of people never take that basic, essential step. Do you? If the doctor tells you that it's a minor illness that will run its course quickly, isn't the assurance and relief worth the cost of the visit? Again—what price peace of mind?

After considerable medical research over the years, along with coauthoring eight books with eminent physicians, I must emphasize to you here the stern necessity of a preventive medical checkup annually. It's not a guarantee against illness, but an extremely valuable measure that can make the difference between life and death.

A close friend, about to skip her annual checkup, was driven to the doctor forcibly by her husband. The examination uncovered early indications of cancer of a lung. The tiny growth was removed, otherwise she might not have lived another year. "And to think," she said, "that wanting to save a little time and money could have killed me . . ."

Another lady feared for months that her stomach cramps were signs of cancer. She was afraid to find out. Finally she learned during a routine checkup that the problem was a slight digestive disorder which cleared up quickly with proper medication. The resultant freedom from fear lifted her spirits and her overall well-being.

Even in long-lasting illness, there can be increased strength of mind and body eventually if you fight back and consciously determine to gain every available benefit from the trying experience. Doctors I've interviewed have stated repeatedly that individuals who recover from heart attacks and other severe setbacks frequently live happier, more fulfilling, more rewarding lives than before the attack.

Patients affirm this, as Pauline C. told me: "I learned the value of living as I'd never appreciated it before my long illness. I gained a better, healthier, more effective way of using time and enjoying life, because I became aware of and valued every moment of possible happiness each day."

A neighbor, Dr. David M., back from a month in the hospital following a severe heart attack, said, "It's the most beautiful Spring I've ever seen. The flower colors have never been so vivid, the sky so clear. I have a new dimension of appreciation for all the little things." He paused. "I wonder why I never noticed such available wonders before. . . ."

No, I don't mean that sickness is a blessing. Existence is far better without any illness. But when it invades, it makes a crucial difference if you face it positively, hopefully, even aggressively instead of yielding to self-pity—and possibly compounding the physical ills with mental depression. And you don't have to wait until adversity strikes to enjoy the "available wonders" to the full, do you?

285

The Will to Live Better

Actress-dancer Lisa Kirk struggled back from multiple bone and nerve damage which threatened to keep her from ever performing again. She fought back during four long years of intense physical suffering: "I couldn't face the idea of not being able to perform. I kept thinking of Cole Porter who had both legs crushed in a riding accident ten years before. . . . It was seeing his determination to get better that made me work so hard."

She'd gone to a party back then on the opening night of a Cole Porter play. . . . "At the entrance, there was a big, long staircase. He was walking with a cane and was in great pain. . . . The producer who had just read the first review, a rave, appeared at the top of the stairs and shouted down, 'Cole, we've got a hit!' And Cole Porter threw away that cane and walked up that flight of stairs." Lisa Kirk too rejected the dread predictions that she'd never dance again—and became a star once more.

"What makes such recoveries possible?" I asked a doctor friend.

"Simple," he said, "even though scientifically 'impossible.' It's compounded of desire, determination, fighting back—making 'miracles' happen by never giving in."

Blind singer-composer Stevie Wonder was smashed up badly in a car accident. When he had struggled back to full recovery, he expressed deep regret for his previous trivial, improvident ways: "I think that when you come close to dying, you realize the importance of life, and what you have to do with whatever time you have."

There's a striking lesson in answering the searching question: *Do you have to come close to dying to appreciate the value of living?* Do you have to experience severe sickness and suffering to prize good health and enjoy it every day?

Will *you* try, consciously, vigilantly to esteem the act of living from now on? Accomplishing just that is a big part of attaining conscious happiness.

When illness, like any other misfortune, strikes loved ones, there is only one course we can take: *We can cope* instead of collapsing and making a bad situation worse for the afflicted as well as oneself. The New Testament states: "Be not overcome by evil, but overcome evil with good." That applies to dealing with sickness too. It isn't easy. But there is no alternative.

A deep-thinking man who endured many operations said before further surgery, "For myself I am not afraid. . . . I know that you suffer a little, that you bear it, and that you are happy at having eliminated a peril." Although he had been marked as doomed many years before, he lived to eighty-two, crediting his unflagging will to look forward to the good, not backward to sickness and miseries suffered. This attitude is sustenance and comfort, and a must for the loved ones as well as the afflicted.

One Is Not Alone

Always, you are not alone, not the only one to experience suffering. That truth was imprinted on me when attending a political rally. One volunteer, a beautiful young woman, impressed me with her hard work and strength of character. I found out later that her husband had died suddenly, and that she supports and spends weekends with her teenage, schizophrenic son who is in a mental hospital, perhaps for life.

I complimented another lady for her efficient running of the affair with such an air of serenity. Then I learned from someone else that she limps due to polio, and that she works long hours as a hospital supervisor to support her two kids and invalided husband. Seeking her out again, I asked, "How in the world do you manage to stay so composed?" She smiled slightly, "I cope. There is no other course but to make the effort day after day, every day, optimistically, hopefully. I cope. Period."

She refused to talk any further about her troubles, explaining, "Medical science hasn't ever figured out a way to make ailments as interesting to others as they are to those who are ill or surrounded by troubles—and go on about it incessantly."

You make the effort also to find new interests and work that you can do within your physical and perhaps emotional limitations. A twelve-year-old boy, paralyzed in both legs, was confined to a wheelchair. Despairing at first, he decided that he could live a useful and enjoyable life nevertheless. He told another wheelchair patient, "We can't stand up—but there are so many things we can do sitting down." He became an expert, valued woodworker.

A woman who had endured much suffering from chronic back injury explained after hospitalization that she was running her household once more. Although she couldn't return to her favorite sport of bowling ... "I'm taking a ceramics class and I make candles. The pain still keeps me from doing a lot of bending and lifting, but otherwise I think I'm pretty normal again ... I'm out in the world, seeing friends. I'm able to enjoy life again. *I'm living.*"

Much depends on one's will to get well, the will to live. An honored physician, Dr. Judd B., told me, "There's no question—the will to live, and to live better, may produce unexplainable 'miracles' in medicine. Like me, practically any doctor can describe cases where the patient was dying clinically but lived subjectively—and left the hospital alive and relatively well. Cheerfulness too is an invaluable aid to recovery and functioning." Dr. Paul Dudley White agreed that "An optimistic and determined mental outlook is almost as important as physical recovery."

The greatest enemy of illness is you yourself, as patient or caretaker, if you refuse to succumb to fear, despair, defeat. A religious leader, Professor Wolfson, who fought his own serious physical incapacity over a long period and conquered, asserted: "I wish I had been sick thirty years ago—I would have been a better man. I've learned that 'who best can suffer, best can do.'" Not illness but conscious desire and sustained effort can make you "a better man" right now—and from now on.

Two Sides of DEATH

There are two sides of death: Facing it oneself ... and dealing with the death of a loved one. There is a saying— "Where life is, death is not / Where death is, life is not." As long as life is, death is not—and there is no possible benefit in wasting a moment of life through fearing death of oneself or another. Dealing with death most effectively, yes. Fearing, no. Professor I. A. Richards of Yale, at eighty, said flippantly, "Death seems to me the most interesting set of undetermined possibilities, so I'm rather curious."

In respect to the imminence of death for oneself, Hubert Humphrey expressed a fortifying attitude when faced with the possibility that he might have a terminal affliction: "What can be done by medicine, surgery or radiation, I'll have it. And if it can't be, then I'll have had it, you know, and that's it. And I really don't worry about it. I say in my mind, 'To hell with it, I have something else to do!'" For me, the best attitude toward death is to try to enjoy life to the fullest. Mark Twain advised: "Let us endeavor so as to live that when we come to die, even the undertaker will be sorry."

I've found sustenance in Leonardo da Vinci's words: "Just as a day well spent brings happy sleep, so a life well spent brings happy death." I haven't feared death at all since I gained conscious happiness. I believe that if you dwell on death, you are already half dead. So I concentrate on making each day well spent. That brings joy to me, and leaves no time for useless morbidity. Sir Winston Churchill quipped: "I am ready to meet my maker. Whether my maker is prepared for the great ordeal of meeting me is another matter."

Regarding the loss of loved ones, the past should never be permitted to affect the present so that there seems to be no future. When a loved one has died, I've always been comforted by continuing to feel the presence of our love together, and the proved conviction within me that the good memories remain and become richer with time. I agree with Sir Noel Coward's lines about friends who have died. "How happy they are I cannot know / But happy am I who loved them so." In my will is the request to my family: "Please live with happiness, and think happily of me and of us."

Speaking out your love and showing it, as urged throughout these pages, is part of being able to handle the other's death with greatest personal solace. We were vacationing with a young woman, Joan S., when a phone call came from across the country that her father had died suddenly. When she gained control after weeping, she said, "My biggest regret is that I didn't tell my father how wonderful he always was, the best father there possibly could be for me. I was too inhibited, afraid of seeming oversentimental. I was on the verge of telling him of my love and supreme admiration just before I left on this trip—but I didn't. And now it's too late. . . ."

I said, "I'm sure he knew."

Joan shook her head, "I wish I could be that sure. . . ."

Making It

I met Steve and Doris Moran (disguised names) every year at the annual dinner of a lively writers organization. Steve had been a leader, bright, cheerful, effective—everybody had liked him and clustered around him and his beautiful, gay Doris. He died suddenly at fifty, and I met Doris again at the annual dinner almost a year later. . . .

She stood next to me at the side of the ballroom, apart from the others. She looked twenty years older. Her drooping posture ruined her formerly lovely, proud figure. Her once exquisite face sagged with sadness and self-pity, her eyes shifting and lusterless. She turned to me glumly, "There's no spirit of fun here tonight. The people have changed. The affair has lost its dash. It's drab . . ."

I hesitated, then took the plunge. I said gently, "The dinner hasn't changed, Doris. You've changed. With Steve gone, you've given up and forsaken the individual you were in your own right. You sag all over—your face, your figure, your spirit. You've deserted the friendly, optimistic person you were, the beautiful lady Steve was so proud of. You're doing him and yourself a terrible disservice. . . ."

Her head was lowered—I forced myself to go on, "Steve would be ashamed of the dejected woman you present to his friends now. You're letting him down, as well as yourself. You've got to pick yourself up, or there's no future for you. Look, darling, there's a lively, happy world of people around you, wanting to help you, to be with you, with the bright giving person you were. Pick yourself up and let them love you, as they loved you and Steve before—"

I stopped, my arm around her shoulder now. She was weeping silently. "I'm sorry," I choked, my throat tight with pain, "I've hurt you. Because I care about you. Please forgive me."

291

She looked up. Her shoulders straightened, her youthful bosom lifted. "You're right," she said, her voice clearing, gaining strength. "Thank you—for bringing me to my senses. Steve would be grateful too—" She leaned to me and kissed me, her lips warm, alive. I clutched her hand, pressed it hard.

My wife appeared from nowhere, kissed her impulsively. Doris looked around the room, her still moist eyes twinkling. "It *is* a nice party," she said.

A friend at a nearby table caught her alert glance. He arose and came toward her, both arms outstretched in warm greeting. She hugged him. Over his shoulder she looked at me through damp lashes, smiled slowly, and winked.

She breathed deeply, gave a small shudder, and murmured, "I think I'm going to make it. . . ." I walked away as other people crowded around her. The sage advice of Thomas Jefferson echoed in my mind: "The earth belongs to the living, not to the dead."

The experienced wisdom of Schweitzer is nourishing truth for each of us: "As long as someone is kept alive in the heart, he is alive."

* * *

Review again and again the details of these basic, proved ways to help overcome adversity:

1. *Keep building your confidence as a self-respecting individual.*
2. *Go on fighting, never give in.*
3. *After doing everything "possible," then try a little harder.*
4. *Take action: "I'll make things better!"*
5. *Accept others' friendship, love, and help.*
6. *Keep busy, keep active, be involved.*

To avoid and help chase depression:

1. *Realize that everyone has low points; you are not unique, not alone.*
2. *When the blues invade, change what you're doing at once.*
3. *See someone you like very much, right away.*
4. *Tackle the problem that brought on feeling low.*
5. *Don't keep talking about feeling depressed.*
6. *Count your pluses instead of your debits.*

Handling illness—yours and others':

1. *Take preventive steps regularly with medical check-ups.*
2. *Get medical attention fast instead of hoping the illness will "go away."*
3. *Never lose your strong will to recover and live.*
4. *Appreciate the value of good health and recovery—from then on.*
5. *Accept the attention and aid of others gratefully.*
6. *Realize that your worst enemy is despair.*

Dealing with death:

1. *Enjoy life to the fullest—and fight back with unflagging determination.*
2. *Don't dwell on death; heighten your interest in life.*
3. *Keep active, more than ever: Do something!*

"DO SOMETHING!" Those simple words are the urgent exhortation of actress Doris Day who clearly tries to live her days with conscious happiness—in spite of tragedy in her life. Her beloved husband of seventeen years, Martin Melcher, died suddenly. Shocked, stricken, she picked herself up, carried on more energetically than ever before. She is involved in many fine causes which help others—and help her.

To those stunned by death, serious illness, or other adversity—especially women—she insists passionately: "Do something! Go to work in a store. Wrap parcels if you can't sell things. But don't sit around moping." And she is bolstered by realizing about her husband: "He would have wanted me to keep busy."

Dread troubles need not be the end, but can be a productive beginning. Best-seller novelist Dr. A. J. Cronin, whose books are enjoyed by millions, tells how his life seemed smashed as a young man. As a successful London physician, about to move into a promising specialist's practice, his health broke down. He was told that he had to take at least a year's rest—and even then he might not be able to resume the demanding life of a doctor.

Crushed, Dr. Cronin felt bitter at the dirty trick played on him by fate. He expressed his resentment to an old Irish woman who was Revered Mother of a small order of nursing sisters known as Bon Secours. She was silent after his outburst, then she spoke quietly:

"You know, Doctor, we have a saying in Ireland— that if God shuts one door, He opens another."

Cronin shrugged off her statement. But months later, instead of going on brooding idly, he followed an impulse to write a novel. Then he devoted himself to that work day after day. That's how his first very popular book came to be—Hatter's Castle—which may have brought pleasure to you, as to so many others. The opening door—his new career—probably has been more fruitful in many ways than his medical practice would have been.

If you strive, if you reach, then doors open inevitably to enduring, increasing conscious happiness. You can conquer . . . if you will.

17

Making the Most of Marriage, Children, Family Life

WHEN WE WERE discussing getting married, I wrote a letter to my girl in which I noted my basic premise of one of the key fundamentals for a fulfilling, enduring partnership:

> My one primary concern about marriage is that each of us must remain an individual—as well as being partners. And that would have to continue for the rest of our lives. If one of us loses individuality by submerging into the identity of the other, our marriage will fail. Our aim must not be, as wife and husband, to think alike always—but to improve ourselves continually as thinking individuals, yet always thoughtful of each other. . . .
>
> You must never lose your personal identity in becoming totally "wife" or "mother." I must never permit myself to become more "husband" or "father" than myself as a whole person. Otherwise each of us will lose respect for self and for each other. We want to join together by marrying the *individuals* we are and will be—and we must determine and function always to keep it that way. . . .

It's not a question of how much love we have for each other; the amount is total or we wouldn't be considering marriage. I've seen too many marriages and relationships crash because the woman loved herself more than she loved her husband and her children—and vice versa. [Psychiatrist Harry Stack Sullivan stated the point this way: "When the security of another person becomes as significant to one as one's own satisfaction or security, then a state of love exists."]

Nor do we want total *possession* each of the other. Love not only thrives but grows on the individual strength of each one involved. Whatever crushes individuality tends to destroy happiness in being married. And without achieving greater happiness individually and together, there would be no point in getting married.

Natalie agreed completely. That was over thirty years ago at this writing. During that time, both of us have gained and grown as individuals (and as partners and parents). When there is mutual esteem, one can disagree without being disagreeable. The marriage has survived and flourished—it gets better every day. That is true mostly, we know, because we have retained respect and pride as well as love for each other, by working—yes, *working*—toward that end through the years, and now each day, and always.

Peace, trust, excitement, honesty, openness, joy—all are among the elements of marriage at its best. And you must remain alert each day to act to make the union not just good enough, but the *best* it can possibly be. The continuing feeling in an alert, thriving, fulfilling relationship is inevitably that the best is yet to come—"you ain't seen nothin' yet!"

No Deception

Honoring oneself as an individual embodies discarding all duplicity and self-deception for both parties. Recognizing your own imperfections, you don't expect faultlessness or the impossible from your partner. If one wants to dominate—such as a man insisting on having a submissive, subservient wife, in effect a slave—this should be clear and acceptable to both before marriage. If the woman wants no part of running a home and having and raising children, this must be plain to both before the commitment.

An honest beginning is a favorable augury for a successful, lasting marriage or any union. This is attested by the following excerpt from the diary of a man, Herbert B., who has long lived with integrity and conscious happiness:

> I can hardly believe it—today is our thirty-eighth wedding anniversary. I remember the first time I saw Marion, her compelling brightness, her radiant beauty. And today she is lovelier, fresher, more alive and stimulating than ever. How did we gain this boon, this enduring gain? I think by beginning with candor, by banning deception. And by loving and caring more about the well-being and joy of the other than for self—as we still try consciously each day, and I believe always will. I can hardly wait for tomorrow. . . .

One-to-One Commitment

It must be emphasized that a marriage is between two individuals, not between types or classes of "people." An attractive black woman, Lena Smith, was a member of the Panel of American Women of Kansas City, Missouri, which fights prejudice. She was asked: "Do you believe in intermarriage between different races and religions and cultures?"

She retorted, "There is no such thing as marriages between races or religions or cultures. Marriage, and any other relationship, is between two *individuals*. And whether there are any special problems about race or religion or culture must be handled by those two individuals—nobody else. . . .

"If Joe, of Italian-Catholic background, is marrying Joan, from a German-Jewish culture—the decision isn't up to the world's Italians, Catholics, Germans, and Jews. It is the choice and responsibility of Joe and Joan. And the success or failure of their marriage or other relationship is also their personal concern."

The intelligent woman concluded, "No, I wouldn't marry the white race or the black race. If I marry, it will be to a man—whatever his race, religion, or culture—with whom I agree that this would be the happiest, most rewarding existence for both of us until the end of our days."

Popular male movie star Clint Eastwood, who had been married for twenty years, was asked by an interviewer, "Why do you think your marriage has lasted this long?" The gist of his answer is a sound platform for a gratifying, enduring, ever-improving marriage:

"There's always a certain respect for the individual in our relationship," he said thoughtfully. "We're not one person. She's an individual. I'm an individual. And we're friends. We're a lot of things—lovers, friends, the whole conglomerate—but at the same time."

A woman who had suffered through a painful divorce, and was now undertaking a career in broadcasting, said that she intended to "teach my ladies not to make their husbands their whole lives. . . . If you're just a reflection of a man, maybe he can't stand that reflection right up against him. So don't be a mirror for him. Be a portrait of yourself!"

Someone recommended that the common marriage proposal be changed from "Will you be mine?" to "Let's be ours."

"Work" for Marriage Success?

On a television discussion show, I was confronted by a strong-willed, glamorous young author. During the wide-ranging conversations, I mentioned that "One *works* to make a marriage good."

She retorted, "If making a marriage succeed is *work*, then it's not for me. I'd find it either good or bad, but working at it would drain off all the romance and ruin the whole deal for me. As a woman, I demand the right to *enjoy* marriage, not toil over it. I'm for women's rights, and one of them is the right to conduct a marriage without *working* to make it good."

I responded quietly, "I've been for women's rights— which means *people's* rights to me—all my life. I'm for the rights and respect of the individual, women and men of every age. Of course a marriage must be enjoyable. But you work at it to make it most pleasurable—just as you work at anything worth building and having. You name it, you *work* for it—or you lose it. You don't wait for anything good to fly in through the transom—or expect to improve something without making a continuing positive effort."

One of the most disastrous elements causing a marriage to flounder and fail is that the man and/or woman let up instead of paying attention, working at the relationship to keep it joyous and always better. Too many who marry then decide that the "courting days" are over as soon as the ceremony is completed. They pay less attention to the other person, often growing fat and lazy in body as well as mind. Their attitude, spoken or withheld, is: "I don't have to impress her (or him) any more. I can let up— after all, we're *married* . . ."

But after the ceremony is when love and caring and attentiveness must really begin—for you have chosen this one individual above all others. If you think enough of the other person to want to join for life (legally or otherwise), then life should really begin and improve. And therefore, *more* attention must be paid.

Concern, care, sharing chores, acts of love and regard and respect should expand. The partnership should really begin flowering and accelerating *after* the first moments —not decline or end at that point. If attentions deteriorate, so does the joy and fulfillment of the total joining. (A reported "Personals" ad in the *Dallas News*: "Alice, I love you more than duck hunting. Dave.")

"Why do I have to keep telling her I love her?" one man asked. "I proved it by marrying her, didn't I? Okay, that says it all—enough is enough." It's never enough. Each day should be an affirmation of love. It must never end. Believe it. Show it. Speak it . . . not every hour on the hour, but often enough for thorough corroboration.

If the partners don't talk up, give, communicate, then a marriage or other union falters, remains static, fails to grow. A happily married, exquisite woman, Eve M., said, "My husband keeps telling me, 'You're beautiful.' It means much more than hearing it from other men. He's the one I love. He's the one I want to hear it from. He told me so on the first day we were married. And he tells me so now—twenty-four years later. He makes me believe it, and I return his love manyfold."

That's one basic tip for both parties toward thriving on a joyous marriage: *Be as attentive, caring, and expressive always as on the first day you were married.* If that day was an unhappy one, then probably you should have sought an annulment at once.

Support? or Spoil?

The recommendations on earlier pages for the *"Don't"* system about unleashing anger apply specifically as well to supporting and sustaining a marriage joyously. "Happy anniversary," said a husband at breakfast to his wife . . . "and, damn it, why did you overcook this lousy egg?" If what you are about to say is going to hurt the other person, *don't say it.* It has been said that to be a good marriage partner, you should make molehills out of domestic mountains—instead of the other way around, as happens too often.

If one isn't going to take great pride in marriage, in a mutually respecting partnership, it shouldn't be considered in the first place. Any woman can be proud of running her home—or another in working outside the home—if that is part of the strong, cooperating relationship. The same applies to the man.

There isn't much hope for a happy marriage in the situation where a sloppy young woman explains to an equally desultory friend, "Marriage is really a grind. You wash the dishes and make the beds. And then in a couple of weeks you have to do it all over again!" The saying is that "pride goeth before a fall," but more pertinent is the consideration here that marriage goeth with the fall of pride, in one's participation in making the partnership a supportive one for the other and for oneself.

A cartoon showed a wife waving to her husband leaving for work in the morning, as she called out: "Have a nice day. And good riddance!" A comedian commented, "That's the kind of woman who believes that the only way to hold a man is down." The opposite is the case of a wife complaining to a friend: "When I told Roger I needed an outside interest, he bought me a lawn mower."

Funny? Yes—and sad and hurtful. For humorists frequently probe to the heart of an existing problem—in this instance, wife and husband diminishing and even despising each other. A character in a novel by F. Scott Fitzgerald asserted bitterly, "I think that the faces of most American women over thirty are relief maps of petulant and bewildered unhappiness."

I don't agree with the "most," but certainly too many women and men fail to reflect the conscious happiness that should exist whether one is married or not. A good marriage can be the most fertile ground for constant joy to root and grow for a full and fulfilling lifetime for both. Much depends on showing, proving, telling of your increasing love. We are advised to "love thine enemy," but shouldn't we always remember to love our so-called loved ones—and prove it daily?

"She knows I love her (or him)," many will comment impatiently. Does she? Does he? Why take it for granted when it's so easy to say it—if you feel it? If the love doesn't exist, then should the relationship continue? "The greatest enemy of man is man" when he or she fails to love, to prove it, to give and receive eagerly, totally, in any association—especially in the weighty commitment of marriage. The most damaging blows are often struck by silence.

Your undertaking to exert every effort to keep the marriage fortifying and growing doesn't mean giving up your individuality. On the contrary, the stronger and happier each one becomes, the sturdier and more fulfilling the partnership. Each lends strength to the other in such a union—not one draining from the other and thereby weakening the total two.

The commitment to love and show and prove love to the other doesn't mean that the husband and wife must give up finding anyone else attractive and interesting. A *person is not a possession.* Marriage is basically sharing rather than possessing.

Of course the alert, lusty individual looks and finds enjoyment in all about him or her. Whether such interest permits other sexual relationships depends on the attitudes and promises of wife and husband to each other and to the partnership. All aspects of the alliance are worked out between the two partners—yes, *partners.*

The definition of partnership is clear: "a relationship (in this case between two people) in which each has equal status and a certain independence but also implicit or formal obligations to the other." The rules of the partnership are made by the participants in joint approval, not written documents. The purpose of the marriage partnership is to attain the happiest, most rewarding life for each, and for any offspring. Each participant must contribute productively toward achieving that goal—or the enterprise fails. *You* are the decisive factor—not the institution of marriage.

Divorce? Separation?

A cartoon in *The New Yorker* showed a young man proposing to a girl, beseeching her: "Alice, will you be my first wife?" If the commitment isn't intended to be enduring and total, why marry? You might as well mail proposals to a thousand people saying, "I love you passionately. Marry me." And signed—"Guess Who."

If the marriage becomes less than 51 percent enjoyable and desirable to one or both parties, it probably will and probably should end in divorce or separation—depending on the decisions of the individuals involved. Often the seeking for grounds for divorce results from a failure to establish and support the grounds for gratifying marriage beforehand. Beyond that, people change—for better or worse.

Before deciding on a breakup, one might consider the conclusion of W. H. Auden: "Like everything else which is not the result of fleeting emotion but of time and will, any marriage, happy or unhappy, is infinitely more interesting and significant than any romance, however passionate." But if not, then probably the union is doomed.

Separation or divorce should not eliminate the ability of either or any party involved to maintain a sense of conscious happiness—since that consists of enjoying whatever moments of pleasure may be drawn from each day, whatever the circumstances. That probability persists in spite of any troubles, including those that tend to arise in marriage or any other relationship or state of existence.

Unfortunately, divorce generally brings out the ugliest elements in those involved, rather than the best. This should not be, need not be—if each party will retain respect if not love for the other, at least for the person he or she regarded and loved enough to make the marriage commitment originally. If one has built a strong reinforcing individuality and sense of conscious happiness within oneself, then she or he can best handle and survive divorce or separation, as well as all other problems and crises in life.

Sex in Marriage

Sex should be a joyous, exultant actuality in marriage, especially because both individuals have committed themselves and are bound with the closest ties by mutual accord. Sex can never be everything in marriage or in living, but it can contribute enormously to the closest kind of man-woman relating with each other. Sex can "solace the fatigues of life." In the happy union, sex is of the intellect, emotions, and spirit in the full, as well as being physiological and physical.

In the "good" marriage, sex is generally free, uninhibited, ecstatic—for truly, as stated by a leading authority, Mary Calderone: "The body is a valid source for pleasure and enjoyment." The sexuality encompasses the same regard for the other individual as in all other phases of the happy marital state. It is lived, not just performed, seeking intimacy rather than orgasm solely. In later years, sex can improve with the deepened love and experience, and the increasing knowledge and freedom with each other. By caring so much for the other, and sharing increasingly, the spirit of venture and adventure is sustained.

As touched on, sexual "faithfulness" when married, whether essential or not, is a determination that must be made by the individual, in some cases by the two individuals who have chosen marriage as their preferred way of living. There may be problems with self-induced "guilt" (physicians relate some heart attacks to remorse in having sex while "cheating").

A doctor points out that if attitudes are strictly "anatomical, physiological, mechanical—like in a laboratory—the participants might as well be rabbits or dogs" rather than intelligent human beings. But is *love-making* as contrasted with just *coupling* limited or restricted only to married couples? You, each individual, must answer that for yourself. Others may comment and advise, but no one else can be your own conscience and guide. Fundamentally, sexual fulfillment is a participation, not a performance.

In essence, all the qualities and personal contributions which go into building and maintaining a happy, most fulfilling marriage are true for enjoying sex in its fullest variations and completeness. In or out of marriage, a noted researcher has concluded that "In most people, interest in sex lasts as long as they want it to."

Giving and Receiving

It is an eternal truth, voiced long ago, that a truly happy marriage is one in which the woman gives the best years of her life to the man who makes them the best years. Another definition of a "good" marriage, by Oliver Wendell Holmes: "Four feet on a fireplace fender." Keeping a marriage fresh and most gratifying for both is an ever-extending, never-ending joy. The continuing, renewing endeavor has been likened to running a farm where you have to start over again each morning—and each morning can be another pleasurable experience, if you regard it so.

A study conducted by psychologist Norman M. Bradburn of the University of Chicago, based on interviews of over one thousand women and men, reported that "Tension in marriage was most often attributed to the other partner *'not showing love.'*" A further point of interest: "Men in the prosperous communities reported the most marital tension and unhappy marriages, indicating that economic problems are not necessarily associated with marital problems"—so far as general living standards are concerned. (This is not to say that money troubles may not bring on lots of other problems—for married or unmarried persons.)

What is clear to me is that the basic elements that contribute to the individual's building conscious happiness for himself or herself are also embodied in making a happy marriage. The art of giving and receiving love is one of the fundamental assets. It may be that in a successful marriage, each of the parties strives to build up the other as "the better half." My recommendation is that each build up himself and herself equally as a loving, giving, receiving individual—with no "better half" involved in any sense.

The Joys of Family and Children

Don't trust anyone who claims that he or she has the precise formula for you with all the right answers about bringing up children: "Ten Easy Rules For Raising Your Child." There are some excellent guidebooks, and many poor ones. Insights for thought, as you find here? Yes. But only *you* can follow through most effectively, for—like you—each child is an individual, and must be guided and treated accordingly.

Whether you have children at all, or how many, can be determined only by your personal views and desires. I've seen both happy and troubled marriages with one to sixteen offspring—and similarly, joyous and failing marriages with no children at all. You've probably noted research proving that having one child is better for the happiness of the marriage and offspring than two or three or more—and exactly the opposite. You can't go by the numbers and data, only by what you feel is best for the pair of you and your progeny, if any.

Fundamentally, the same attitudes and actions that are proposed in this book for gaining conscious happiness within yourself apply in your relationship with your children: Decency toward others. Self-respect. Giving and receiving love . . . and so on down the list. I believe strongly that the best chance of having your child enjoy happy, fulfilling years from birth and throughout growing up and adulthood is *through your best example* in dealing with the world as a whole, and with your offspring.

On a couple's thirty-fifth wedding anniversary, this message arrived from their grown son who was undertaking his own pursuits on another continent: "Congratulations on a continuing life of love and commitment, which is a magnificent accomplishment for me as well as for you. These have always been enormously sustaining values for me—as for you." For a parent, that result becomes one of the greatest of life's rewards.

A supreme boon of being a parent is that you can return to all the growing-up years again—but better. When your child is one or three or five, and on and on, you can be each of the ages once more. But this time around you gain far deeper pleasures because you are conscious of all the wonderful miracles and adventures a child encounters, seen through his eyes as well as your own.

But this, one of the greatest available thrills of living, happens for you only if you love fully, are aware, and thus participate in the delightful, sparkling, and vulnerable joys of being four or whatever. You view life afresh through his or her eager, questing, widening eyes. . . .

Then, if there is a grandchild, you have your *third* life, your second reliving of childhood—but still better—because you have the fun without the primary responsibility of parenthood. How enchanting for you—if you will grasp, use, enjoy the opportunity, with brimming conscious happiness.

Good, Bad, but Never Indifferent

No parent needs to be told that there are downs as well as ups in raising children—as there are for the youngster, and all through life. A father quipped, "We named our child Helen Joy, and that's what life with her has been ever since—hell and joy." Some youngsters tend to blame all their troubles on their parents. Similarly, some adults charge most problems to the younger generation. Both are wrong, of course. Both must share the responsibility.

The primary cardinal sin of a parent is *indifference* toward the child. Another blunder is *overprotectiveness*. Only you, as parent, can find the right midpoint for your situation. But you must realize, above all, that a five-year-old hasn't a twenty-five-year-old mind; a fifteen-year-old hasn't the maturing wisdom or the experienced attitudes of age forty. I always tried to see and think of their viewpoint through the five- or fifteen-year-old eyes and minds of our children. Frequently I failed. I kept trying always. Trying is at least half of succeeding. Not trying hard is failing.

Always you give love. You strive for mutual understanding. You endeavor day in, day out to set a commendable, inspiring example. Then you hope for the best. If you fail, you have the fortifying assurance that it wasn't due to lack of attention, giving love, trying. And it helps a little to realize that in similar circumstances, John reacts differently from Jim, Ann's response may be totally unlike Mary's.

Each growing being is an individual with his or her own characteristics, thought processes, decisions, actions. If there is failure, the fault may be primarily the youngster's, not the parents'. Your sustenance is in being able to tell yourself honorably, "I did my best." Then you don't squander time and effort and emotions fruitlessly in self-blame and regret. You exert every continuing, unceasing thought and activity to *make things better*.

And Always—Communicate

Another essential between parent and offspring at every age is to *communicate*: Make known. Impart. Transmit. Receive. Tell. Listen. Interchange. Connect. The lines must be kept open or all else may fail. A cooling threatened to develop in our family because our son of twenty-six, Jeff, advised that he and his wife and infant were breaking the lifelong tradition of Christmas dinner at the parents' home—in order to enjoy the holiday at their own home. I thought the matter through long and hard, then wrote this letter:

We don't feel "sunk" that you're not coming for Christmas dinner, even though we'd love to have you all here as in the past. So discard any concern about that. We're immeasurably grateful that we've had the wonderful emotions and rewards of past holidays together, along with all the other pleasures of your growing up. . . .

As for your life now and in the future, we're concerned, as always, about the happiness and well-being of all of you. But again, we can only stand and watch, ready to help as much as you want us, and as much as we're able to help in any way. And, as always, you have our love and respect. We're totally proud of you as a fine, decent, thinking, caring, seeking individual. . . .

We couldn't and *don't want to* overly influence or "run" your life—as you don't want us to and wouldn't let us. We honor you and your ability—but we don't want the responsibility that is your own. It's tough enough handling the challenge of living our own lives most fully and effectively, gaining the most that we can from the days, helping others as much as possible, being careful not to hurt others—within the limits of our knowledge and abilities. . . .

This you must realize too about me: Beyond being a father and husband, I'm an individual in my own right. I have always believed fully that, fundamentally, *if I am not myself, then I am nothing*. Nothing for myself, nothing to and for those I love. I have tried and will do anything and everything I can for you—within the boundaries that you permit and that you may want my help and love and me. . . .

Help you, always. Interfere unwanted, never. I try

to do best and be best for you, and for all I love, and for myself. I'll never stop trying to be better in every way that helps others and myself. I'll never succeed fully—but I don't think that achieving the ultimate would be very satisfying. Go well. I love you.

As the result of that letter, the entire family achieved a far greater warmth and depth of understanding and love. They communicated. They never stopped touching. And as parents we received from our son the most fulfilling accolade one could hope for: *"You instilled in a stubborn son a sense of belief in living—a trust in the enriching promise of adulthood and continued growth."*

One tries. One never stops trying. . . .

A sensitive parent, Ronald Russell, observed some years ago in *Lessons from Life:* "A child that lives with truth learns justice . . . A child that lives with distrust learns to be deceitful . . . A child that lives with sharing learns to be considerate . . . A child that lives with antagonism learns to be hostile . . . A child that lives with happiness will find love and beauty."

That's as good a guide as any—combined with your own perceptions, intelligence, and always attentive endeavors in bringing up and being brought up by children.

* * *

Give thought to these basic precepts of an increasingly rewarding marriage:

1. *Honor your partner as an individual, and foster that individuality throughout.*
2. *Make a clear, candid statement of what each wants and expects from marriage well before-hand—and live up to it continually.*
3. *Face the marriage ceremony as the beginning of a lifetime courtship, not the end.*
4. *Be as attentive, caring, and expressive always as the first day you were married; work to keep*

311

the marriage not only good but better each
year.

5. Speak out your love, and prove it with your actions year after year—no letdown.

6. Retain your personal sense of conscious happiness
in spite of any problems in the relationship;
this will help to rectify them if that's at all
possible.

7. In sex, never forget that the body is a valid source
for pleasure and enjoyment for love-making, not
just coupling.

8. Respect, give, and receive fully so that there is
never a "better half."

9. You help children best through your best example of respect, self-respect, and decency in daily
living.

10. Partake of the full wonder of growing up year by
year with your children.

11. Always strive to give love, share responsibilities,
and to communicate, interchange, connect with
your children as well as with your partner.

12. Act each day to reflect to your family a feeling of
optimism and the great joys available in living;
this will reflect back happiness for all of you.

Misunderstandings with your children, as well as your
partner, can result from not probing actions and motivations thoroughly—resulting in a lack of mutual understanding. For instance, it's a fact that Thomas Gains-
borough who became Britain's most renowned portrait
painter (Blue Boy, for example) was a difficult youngster. He often skipped school sessions in order to go out
and sketch the countryside.

Once he gave the teacher a faked note stating: "Give
my son Tom a holiday."

His father raged, "That boy will be hanged!" But

when he saw the sketches Tom had drawn that truant day, he cheered, "That boy will be a genius!"

Each marriage partner must establish sound values and responsibilities. At the height of his winnings, golf champion Johnny Miller turned down invitations to several important, big-money tournaments because he felt that he should be home when his wife was expecting a baby imminently. Why? His simple statement is a sensible guide for the foundation of a solid, enduring marriage:

"No amount of success can compensate for failure in the home."

Always you must be aware and strive to make a good marriage better. The results are enormous, forming a prime factor in enjoying deep, fulfilling conscious happiness for your adult lifetime—for all your family's lifetimes.

18

How to Grow Older Enthusiastically, Exultantly, Ecstatically

SOME MODERN DOOMSAYERS make much ado about something mysterious and threatening called the "Youth Culture" taking over the world. I reject the fallacious concept completely—in favor of the "Living Culture" encompassing everyone. The latter means being alive, alert, striving to make the most and best of every minute and every hour at any and every age. The purpose is to enjoy to the fullest the exhilarating, enriching sense of conscious happiness as much as possible each day.

For I believe beyond question that living exultantly is not an age but an intelligent, unremitting attitude of striving for joyous discovery and participation totally in everyday living.

You are as young as your enthusiasm, as old as your disinterest. It was first said years ago by Marie Dressler but is just as true today: "It's not how old you are, but how you are old." Happy aging is just a further extension of happy living—and all the suggestions in this book for gaining conscious happiness apply increasingly to the later years.

A lively lady in her mid-sixties, Ruth C., was involved in a busy schedule of political, community, and social activities which kept her on the run. Her married daughter scolded her, "For goodness' sake, Mother, slow down. Why don't you grow old gracefully?"

The older woman retorted brusquely, "Because I want to grow old enthusiastically, exultantly—yes, even ecstatically! That's exactly what I'm doing—and I love it. That's what keeps me vigorously alive and in there punching every minute."

Relating this story in a living room setting a few days later, it aroused controversial opinions instantly. A handsome young woman in her early thirties asserted, "I couldn't agree more with the daughter that the mother ought to calm down and grow old gracefully. The person reaching the later years has to recognize and accept the fact that she's aging and slowing down—instead of fighting it unnaturally. Such yielding to the onslaught of the years is the proper, healthier attitude."

I disagreed completely. "Innocuous as it sounds, when one person tells another to 'grow old gracefully,' what she or he really means is, 'Give up your interest in life—lie down and get ready to die.'"

Another guest who was a noted psychiatrist, Dr. Joseph K., listened to all the arguments silently. Then, taking his pipe from his mouth, he stated emphatically, "The underlying meaning that the younger person aims to convey, even though she may not realize it when she tells the older one to 'grow old gracefully,' is this: '*Forget your sexuality*. Realize that you are no longer a fully functioning sexual being. Give up on that score and on most other activities. In short, *you're through!*'"

On the point of sexuality, the medical profession is in overwhelming agreement that the enjoyment of sex can continue into the eighties and longer. The average individual never loses his or her sexual feelings, never ceases

315

to be a sexual being at any age—if he or she cares. In fact, generally the more sexual activity, the greater is the pleasure and enduring capacity. ("I'm not a dirty old man," said an energetic gentleman in his late seventies. "I'm a sexy senior citizen.")

Dr. Sallie Schumacher, head of a sex therapy program at Long Island Jewish–Hillside Medical Center, summed up: "One cause of poor health among the elderly is despondency resulting from a loss of interest in life. They feel that everything of value, including physical love, is over for them. So they let themselves just wither away. Some are ashamed to even think about sex, and that is all wrong. . . . Sexual activity can help keep you young; it's a normal function to be enjoyed at any age, if one is in reasonably good health."

Ever-Expanding Time

Sexuality is only one facet, and generally not one of the most important, in growing older. *Aging successfully* is just an extension of volition for *living successfully*. Fundamentally, the best years of one's life can be after fifty. The greatest enjoyment and fulfillment in living can start right then, or later, or earlier of course. My hope is that the best years of your life will start right now—whatever your age. What *you* do about it is the most significant factor.

Many of the fears, hangups, uncertainties of youth are behind you after forty—good riddance. Probably if you had to pay money now for the total value of your experience, you couldn't afford it. But you own it now, as one of your most valuable possessions. As Henry Adams wrote: "All experience is an arch to build upon." You are better equipped—thanks to your experience and maturing—to plan and use time as you prefer, instead of time using you.

It's never too late (or too early) to learn to live joyously with conscious happiness, to follow all the provocative suggestions on these pages, and wherever you find them. Today, at any age, can be the first day of the best days of your life—if you determine to make them so, and follow through persistently. "Old age is not so bad," said Maurice Chevalier at seventy-two, "when you consider the alternative."

The number of years you live doesn't determine how old you feel and act. You age badly by deserting your interests, your ideals, your exertions. Dr. Hans Selye pointed out that while old age wrinkles the skin, giving up enthusiasm and eagerness for living and participating wrinkles the soul.

"Growing old" hinges to a considerable degree on your attitude, no question about it. Jack Benny, gagging as throughout his career, said he wasn't bothered at all by his eightieth birthday: "Age is strictly a case of mind over matter. If you don't mind, it doesn't matter."

Not only shouldn't it matter that you're growing older, it *doesn't* matter if you will consciously feel and exhibit a zest for life, for every new day. It isn't really a matter of being old, but of some individuals being younger than others—and probably lacking in the deeper wisdom obtained from fuller growth. And you never stop growing mentally if you make the effort. Supreme Court Justice Oliver Wendell Holmes, at ninety-two, was reading in his library. A friend entered and asked, "What are you doing?"

Holmes looked up and answered matter-of-factly, "Improving my mind."

How lucky one is to be living in the challenging, forward-moving world of today! Not very long ago, the cutoff time for "really living" was set at sixty-five, the general legal point of retirement in big firms and, in the minds of many, the "drop dead" marker. But, think of it, between 1960 and 1970, the number of persons aged seventy-five

317

and over increased three times as fast as the number aged sixty-five to seventy-four—and the figure multiplies each year now.

Today, for all who will look forward, and *act forward*, there is no cutoff time—there is only and always the beginning. If you care to look far, far ahead—a study of the very aged, quoted on a television program, reveals that individuals who live to one hundred, and are still working, are likely to live until at least one hundred and twenty. Encouraging?

Today! Tomorrow! How fortunate to be and feel alive—with opportunities to use time best, to welcome and enjoy each approaching, present, and passing moment. Again, how much you gain depends on your personal attitude, will, exertions. Philosopher Soren Kierkegaard asserted: "Life can only be understood backward, but it must be lived forward."

The only regret about dying—which is generally hidden remorse about not having lived fully enough at any stage—was stated by a thoughtful character in a novel by John MacDonald: "Should a man reach eighty, he has had only eighty Septembers. It does not seem like many, said that way. It seems as if there are so few, each one should have been better used." Are you using each day the best way? If not, why not?

Sid O., a friend imbued with conscious happiness, told me, "When my wife turned fifty, we had a wonderful, gay party. But when we went to bed about 3 A.M., she broke out into weeping and wailing, 'I'm fifty! I'm fifty!' I couldn't stop her. . . .

"Finally, in desperation, I snapped, 'Were you crying at one minute before midnight—when you were forty-nine?'

"Her sobbing let up, and she squeaked, 'N-o-o.'

"I pressed, 'So did *one minute* in time make that much

difference that you have to cry because—one minute later—you're fifty?'

"She hesitated, then blurted, 'No . . .' She took a deep breath, stopped crying, even managed a faint smile—then sat up and extended her open arms to me."

So time marches on—one minute, then another minute. And the one sensible and possible course is to use and try to enjoy every minute rather than waste each valuable, irreplaceable sixty seconds by bewailing its passing. Ben Franklin challenged: "Does thou love life? Then do not squander time, for that's the stuff life's made of."

Life Secret: Keep Active

A fundamental tip for enjoying conscious happiness at any age, to the end of life, is to *keep enthusiastic and active* mentally, physically, lovingly—active in mind and body to your fullest possible extent. Work. Think. Read. Play. Walk. Exercise. Participate. Keep involved. Seek to use and gain some pleasure every moment. Thus you are living, functioning, thriving to the ever-expanding boundaries of your capacities.

You become so busy discovering, using, and enjoying life that there is no time or room for laments or self-pity. Sydney J. Harris called the later years a perplexing time when one hears two voices, one saying, "Why not?"—and the other uttering drearily, "Why bother?" A two-letter word can be your answer for moving ahead with the years, using your potential instead of letting yourself dwindle into lassitude and hopelessness. That tiny, potent word is: *Do!*

Can life begin at seventy? When I first met Dr. Irwin Maxwell Stillman, who became one of the best-known doctors in the world, he was in his very late sixties. He had cut down his large, busy practice in order to give the valuable diet information he had gained through about fifty years in medicine to the world's overweights. He hadn't succeeded in conveying what he knew—up to the time of our meeting. I found him disappointed, quiet, retiring.

Together we went to work and wrote *The Doctor's Quick Weight Loss Diet.* As it became the best-selling diet book in history, Dr. Stillman was in tremendous demand for TV, radio, newspaper and magazine interviews, speeches, personal appearances everywhere. His liveliness, new energy, and brilliance emerged fully—and expanded further. *Activity* made him more "youthful" at seventy-nine (as this is written) than most people in their thirties and forties.

One is never old enough to give up. Author J. B. Priestly at eighty, working on three projected books, said, "When you get to my age, if you stop writing you may die." Grandma Moses, whose paintings are exhibited in museums and galleries worldwide, said at eighty-nine, "I felt older when I was sixteen than I ever did since." She kept painting until one hundred, and then was stopped only by having to leave for what she had referred to happily as "up yonder."

When he was approaching his eightieth birthday, Pablo Picasso stated that he figured he had earned the privilege of *choosing* his own age for the rest of his life: "I have decided that from now on I shall be aged thirty." And he continued to paint at an energetic, unflagging "thirty" pace until he died eleven years later.

Sculptor Louise Nevelson asserted, "I treasure each moment of each year because—last year, at seventy-three, I saw things a certain way. . . . So I'm eager to use every minute of this year for working—since I'll work a little differently next year at seventy-five. . . . I could never do at thirty or forty or seventy-three the quality of work I can do now. And I'll do even better next year, so I'll be glad about being seventy-five."

But you don't have to be an artist or celebrity to grow older actively and productively. A general physician who still attends patients daily, at ninety, as he has done all through his career, explained why he keeps working. He said that he didn't need the money but "Work is my philosophy—it keeps me going." A study shows that men who work past sixty-five, staying physically and mentally active, live longer than others on the average.

Five women, all of them past seventy-five, were interviewed for a *New York Times* article titled "Old Age: A Case of Spirit, Not Chronology." All were "plain citizens." Stella Fogelman keeps going to college, after attaining a Ph.D. in education. She explained, "I just like people . . . I'm not going to live bottled up." Judith Epstein takes piano lessons, stays active daily in a worldwide women's organization, and said that one of her "great joys" is keeping busy and participating in "good conversation, intellectual stimulation."

Ida Martus, in spite of having severe arthritis and having to use a metal walker to get around, does her shopping, goes to the theater, keeps occupied with many pursuits, and entertains a good deal . . . "There's no old age when your mind keeps going." Of the other two, Rosalba Joy is a busy professional lecturer; Estelle Frankfurter tutors handicapped children during the school year as a volunteer, and spends the nine weeks of summer vacation in traveling the world—mostly by bus.

One of these active ladies, Mrs. Joy, summed up the basic attitude: "I'm too interested in the things I'm doing to have time to be old." Still another involved lady of seventy-eight said she was at her work in an office every day, and was better than ever: "I'm going through rebirth!"

It's vital to keep physically as well as mentally active—

321

walking, exercising, keeping busy at whatever interests one most. It may be a vocation or avocation, a hobby such as handicrafts (which many turn into an earning occupation), amateur radio participation which brings in others from different cultures everywhere, or a multitude of other undertakings, available for the using.

A gentleman of seventy-six, Raymond Haulenbeek, pursues his birdwatching hobby of the past fifty-five years, walks at least three miles a day, spells out his outlook: "You can derive pleasure from the mere beauty of birds . . . and you see trees, clouds, and the sky—and all the things that make life worthwhile." A very fit ninety-two-year-old grandmother also goes for outdoor sports: "I fish almost every day . . . it only takes me fifteen minutes to row my twelve-foot boat out to where the fish are biting."

Dr. Paul Dudley White, the eminent heart specialist, advised at eighty-seven: "Get real exercise. Keep your weight down. Keep moving, and keep thinking. Don't let your brain atrophy. Too many people die from disuse of their bodies. It is your thigh muscles, your leg muscles, that squeeze the artery and vein pipes and push blood to your chest again."

A bright, energetic lady of seventy-two, actress Molly Picon, who keeps very busy with varied interests, observed: "One thing that happens when people grow older is that some are afraid to keep doing things. I walk at least five miles a day. In the summer I swim every day. . . . When in doubt, do a somersault, that's my philosophy." Well, everybody can't do somersaults—whatever the age—but other simpler exertions are available.

Another active woman of seventy-five exercises, maintains a busy career as always, asserting, "To wake up in the morning and not have a challenge, well . . . that's death to me." Again, all these vital older individuals echo the keynote word: *"Do!"*

"I'm Younger than I Used to Be"

Some years ago I taught, and learned, a lesson about happier living in the later years which has been a great help to me (and others) in maintaining a vigorous, most optimistic outlook. It came about from hearing nine little words that you have probably heard dozens, even hundreds of times. Perhaps you've said them yourself. If so, I hope you'll never speak them again, pessimistically at any rate, after reading this.

Waiting for a train at a suburban station, I was chatting with two men well up in their sixties, whom I knew only slightly. One remarked to the other, "I hear that you're expanding your business. Sounds very promising."

"I'm not sure," the second man replied with a sigh. "I've been thinking that maybe I'm not up to it any more, much as I'd like to do it. Y'know," and here he stressed the nine ruinous words, "*I'm not as young as I used to be.*"

There was an unhappy pause. Then I found myself saying, "You never were!"

The man who had just spoken looked puzzled, "I never was?"

"That's right." I explained, "You've never been as young as you used to be. On your ninth birthday, you weren't as young as you used to be at eight, one day before. At twenty, you weren't as young as at nineteen. So why discourage yourself with those gloomy words, 'I'm not as young as I used to be'? You never were—why let the thought drag you down now?"

Both men thought a few seconds, then laughed heartily. "That's right," one echoed. "Even when I was two days old, I wasn't as young as I used to be the day before. . . ."

323

The train pulled in, and we were separated. Visiting a friend's dinner party several months later, I saw again the man whom I had addressed on the train platform. He looked bright, optimistic, successful. I told him so.

He grinned and stated, "Thanks for telling me off that day at the train. It changed my negative outlook. I went ahead with my business expansion—and it's going great, even better than I'd hoped. Y'know," his eyes twinkled, "I'm much younger than I used to be!"

If you're discouraged about trying something new because you feel you're too old, consider A. J. Marshall's comment: "The fellow who says he's too old to learn new tricks probably always was."

Never-Ending "Mental Gymnastics"

It's more essential than ever in the later years to keep the mind active, exercised with every possible type of mental gymnastics—observing, thinking, caring, learning. It's a great gain when you find learning, as Cicero called it, "a sort of food for the soul in cultivating your mind." And one is more fit than ever to have the mind expand effectively since—as just one more benefit of living into the later years—you have learned from past mistakes which you will try not to make again.

In addition to working, becoming involved in all kinds of undertakings, more and more older people are finding the joys of exercising the mind through *formal learning*. Local adult classes in schools, library and community centers, and universities offer many different types of education for all ages. Some universities enroll people over sixty at little or no charge. And practically all educational facilities above elementary school welcome older people enthusiastically and most cooperatively.

A university student of sixty-five explained eagerly, "College is good for me. It makes me do intellectual gymnastics." All kinds of mental gymnastics are good for the intellect and the ego—at every age. "A wise man will be master of his mind—a fool will be its slave." By exercising your mind whatever your years, using it, you master it and handle better any problems that concern you.

This educational upsurge is occurring throughout the world. In France, the Third Age College serves only people of "the third age"—past sixty. About half of the students are in their sixties, about 35 percent in their seventies and eighties, and a few students are in their nineties. This is just one division of the University of Toulouse, and the Third Age students get along excellently with the younger ones.

Learning adds much to living at any age. It can certainly be a great aid in fostering and enjoying conscious happiness. I recommend continued learning strongly and wholeheartedly, however old or young you are. I have attended classes at four universities (along with teaching at several colleges), and despite a very busy schedule, I now spend at least one night a week as a student in university courses on varied subjects.

The continuous process of learning stimulates, excites, expands my mind and imagination. One is never too old to learn more—"a learned man (or woman) has always wealth in himself." Worth investigating classes for yourself? Chancellor Ernest L. Boyer of the State University of New York stated that "education is much too important to be left only to the young."

Looking Forward to More Wonders?

At age seventy, famous songwriter Richard Rodgers listened to his enduring hit song "Where or When." Then he remarked, "I never look back. I only look forward to what will be—where or when." He was busy with the demanding, exhilarating challenge of writing the songs and music for yet another Broadway show.

All about you in the world, everywhere, individuals of your age and younger and older are enjoying conscious happiness from being *alive*. They are not simply surveying the scene, but eagerly acting and using the days for their ongoing pleasure and benefit. Each dawn can be a new opportunity, a revivifying, fresh challenge—if you will greet and grasp it as such.

If you will exert yourself, strive, work at it—then at any age, at every age, you will be one of the joyous company who hail the morning enthusiastically, exultantly, ecstatically.

Perhaps the inspiring poet Archibald MacLeish described best the joys available to each individual in the later years: "Now at sixty what I see / Although the world is worse by far / Stops my heart in ecstasy / God, the wonders that there are!"

* * *

Short summary on how to stay alert, eager, enthusiastic at any age:

1. *Refuse to "grow old gracefully" if that means giving up excitement for living. Disraeli advised: "Get excited, and you stay young forever."*

2. *Realize that you are better equipped by experience, and put your knowledge to use creatively. Note the sage conclusion of psychiatrist Theodore I. Rubin: "I firmly believe that creativity makes for longevity, and longevity makes for creativity."*

3. *Keep active in mind and body: Work. Think. Play. Walk. Exercise. Participate. Keep involved. Heed the seasoned wisdom of writer May Sarton: "You stay alive by living"—by living to the full.*

4. *Consider courses of study at school or at home:*

Learning contributes to living always. You can never know enough ... the great sculptor and painter Michelangelo, on his death bed at eighty-nine, cried out, "I am dying just as I am beginning to learn the alphabet of my profession."

5. Greet each day as a new beginning; look forward to the wonders that exist if you look for them and appreciate them. That's an integral part of enjoying conscious happiness at any age. Take a tip from actress Angie Dickinson who, asked to tell her age, said: "I really don't know—it keeps changing from minute to minute."

6. Never lose your sense of humor, like actress Billie Burke who said in her later years: "Age doesn't matter ... unless you're a cheese."

I learned an inspiring lesson when I attended services in a chapel for a close friend, one of my editors, Evonne Rae, killed in an auto accident. She was a bright, sparkling woman. At the end of the devotions honoring her, an associate was asked to say a few words about Evonne. She spoke briskly:

"Recently we were having dinner and I told Evonne about a parlor game I'd played the night before—because she loved challenging games. 'The point of the game,' I explained, 'was for each person to state what she'd like others to say about her if she walked out of the room ...'

"One gracious lady asserted, 'I'd like them to say— there goes Mary Daley, a fine mother, a loving wife, but above all a strong, intelligent individual in her own right.'

"The next person, a prominent businessman, spoke up: 'I'd like people to say—there goes George Monroe, an effective executive, but always a sensitive, caring gentleman.'

"After that," the speaker went on, "I asked Evonne, 'What would be your answer?'

"She stated without a second's hesitation: 'I'd like people to say—there goes Evonne Rae ... and I wish she'd hurry back!' "

Whatever your age, are you striving consciously to live every moment to the full? Will you from now on?

19

Welcome to Your Future
of Conscious Happiness

WITHOUT THE SLIGHTEST doubt, I'm convinced that conscious happiness is a way of living better that can uplift and work for everyone—of every age, class, status, type. It can be part of every individual who wants to possess it, for *you*—if you will welcome it, use it, strive always to improve it for the benefit of yourself and others about you from now on.

In a *New Yorker* cartoon, a king ordered his court magician: "For tomorrow, Wizard, I want you to conjure up a nice, sunny day in the seventies, with perhaps a gentle southwesterly breeze. I want to be in a happy frame of mind, and I want happy, smiling faces all around me and throughout my entire kingdom."

No wizard can produce happiness to order for you or anybody else. But you can create it for yourself to a considerable degree—by the way you think, act, and react to the world about you—as illuminated throughout this book. Your personal volition and actions can help determine whether you will live dispirited and melancholy, or in a generally happy frame of mind in the future—regardless of the past.

Is the latter your dream? It can be effective to dream —if you then do what is necessary to make it come true. If you will it and work on it, you will find that your dream can become an actuality—or at least close enough to it so that you are happy with the result. Most of the gain is in trying cheerfully, energetically: "Better to believe too much than nothing at all."

Living TODAY

A college professor noticed that one in his audience was yawning and half-asleep during class. He snapped at the student, "What are you thinking of—if you are thinking?"

The confused young man bluffed, "I was wondering if I should believe in an afterlife ... "

The teacher snorted, "What makes you think that you're alive right now?"

It is the simplest folk philosophy that we had better act alive and happy now—since we are a long time dead. If you don't exert every effort to be happy today—if you keep waiting—then you will lose both your todays and tomorrows. Take a tip from a system which has worked for many troubled individuals, alcoholics, melancholics:

> I will try to be happy TODAY—I will work at making the day pleasurable and productive. And then when tomorrow becomes today, I will try again to be happy TODAY . . . one day at a time.

A business associate noted for his driving force, as well as for his pervading irritability and recurring ulcer, said to me, "The trouble with you is that you act too damn nice to people. That way, they take advantage of you."

I shrugged. "I enjoy being 'nice' to others. It makes them happier and keeps me happier. I have to be happy today, every day, or I'll lose the day—never get it back. I can't permit any day to be ruined by being nasty to others."

He frowned. "The word will get around that you're a pushover—"

"Doesn't bother me. You can be grouchy and mean, grow another aching ulcer. So your days are difficult and depressing. What does it get you?"

He snapped, "A bigger income, a better office than you."

"Granted. And people don't 'take advantage of you,' as you put it. But neither do you take advantage of joys available by being decent and enjoying others—"

The phone rang. He groaned, "Oh, God—another problem!" He reached for his indigestion pills. . . .

I keep remembering Mark Twain's advice: "Always do right. This will gratify some people—and astonish the rest." No one can always do right, but trying helps to make you feel good. And it saves lots of concern about not doing right—and therefore is very good for your peace of mind. Aren't those enough good reasons for trying to do "right"—and striving to be happy about it?

Cheerful or Cheerless?

A grim advocate of gloom contended, "To be cheerful is to accept—and one who accepts is forever without hope." On the contrary, to be cheerful is to face and assess a situation as it exists—*and use that as a starting point for moving forward.*

Which is preferable for you? To be cheerless is to give in, to yield in despondency to the presumption that there is no way you can remedy and improve your condition. To be cheerful is to look ahead eagerly, and work toward your wanted goal optimistically, vigorously. In that upward direction lies your best chance of attaining the gratifying results, the expanding happiness you seek.

Some people complain incessantly about not having enough money to meet their ever-accelerating desires ... "The more money I make, the more we want, damn it!" You have to build the conviction that beyond living comfortably, money is not of prime importance. You must realize that the most valuable thing one has in life is *time* to use each day—and the conscious appreciation of making the most of each hour of every day.

Conscious happiness embraces the concept that you search out the good and the real in living—carefully, eagerly, but without voracious hunger and frenzy. As you handle your responsibilities, you are ever reaching to discover and uncover life in its truest meaning. Living exactly as you wish is never easy since problems and troubles arise inevitably. But the trying can be enormously joyous and fulfilling.

On the Way to Wisdom

A philosopher wrote: "We are none of us wise, we are all on the way to wisdom." I would amend that to affirm that we are all of us wise to some degree, but we must never stop striving for greater wisdom. In the trying, searching, and discovering lie increasing conscious happiness.

William James recommended: "Believe that life is worth living, and your belief will help create that fact." You must do more than believe, you must endeavor indefatigably to help make life worth living. Thereupon it becomes more likely that "if you love life, then life will love you back."

There have undoubtedly been times—and there may be again—when you, like myself, have almost lost hope. When a challenging, controversial book I'd written (*The Permissible Lie*) was suppressed and attacked by conglomerate pressure, as had happened to no other book in history, I let a little hopelessness leak in. I wrote to a friend high in Government, FCC Commissioner Nicholas Johnson, a volatile fighter for people's rights, that I wondered if the battle was worthwhile. He shot back: "If we don't fight, who will?"

You, I, all of us are in it together—living, trying, exerting for a happy life for ourselves and our loved ones. If we don't fight, who will? If we don't discover, search, strive for the best life—a consciously happy way of living— who will?

Wisdom dictates that the supreme results we want never come easily, swiftly. As a gardening writer attending the All-America Rose Selections annual awards luncheon where the year's prize-winners and newest developments in rose-growing are presented, I said to a nurseryman in his seventies, "People here emanate a special serene quality, a lack of frantic competitiveness."

He nodded agreement, "Nurserymen have to be patient. We've learned from nature that all development and growth are gradual. The most beautiful rose bush grows by pushing upward persistently. It can't shoot up overnight."

Nor can we humans. But if we "push upward persistently," we are more apt to grow and flourish and bloom exultantly. It's worth the struggle. A gallant lady, Bette Davis, who survived many defeats, said, "Life becomes a bore if you lose your appetite for the future." Bucking harsh winter storms, the rose plant knows by nature that spring will come, no stopping it. And eventually it will flower again. G. K. Chesterton asserted: "To hope means hoping when things look hopeless, or it is no virtue at all."

Want to know the secret of what everything in life is really about? The answer is that *one never knows*. You will never know even if you live past one hundred. The important meaning is to keep seeking, questioning, trying to unlock the secret of the happiest, most fulfilling way of life for yourself. You will never know it all, but there is great and enduring joy in trying to find out.

If you stop seeking, then you lose much of the zest and deep inner reward of living. Whatever else, "no person is a failure who enjoys life." And the converse is true also, that no one is a success who fails to enjoy life.

The Future in Your Hands

Many people complain in these terms: "It's awful the way the hours and the days slip away—and nothing is accomplished—such a waste."

This morning I received an invitation to an affair months away. I lifted a stack of empty pages on my desk calendar until I found the correct date, and made the notation. Then I riffled the blank sheets reflectively—all those days, weeks, months ahead beckoning to be used, to fill and fulfill ...

It struck me that every empty page is the future offering challenging opportunities for us—for "the future is not in the hands of Fate, but in ours." What a multitude of chances ahead for involvement, accomplishment, enjoyment! Will you try to use each day best? One way is not to be afraid to venture, to look into all the possibilities. Let's not be like the unyielding woman who insisted, "You couldn't get me to go to the moon if it was the last place on earth!"

Will we remember too to recognize and enjoy the pleasures in the smallest things? I learned from hearing a survivor of a tragic plane crash in the Andes. Passengers who lived were subjected to a grueling seventy-day ordeal without adequate shelter, clothing, food—in freezing temperatures. Despite the terrible experience, he was able to assert, "It helped me a lot—I find more confidence in myself and what I can do."

He related that the group talked about small wonders they'd never appreciated at home ... "like turning a tap in the sink and taking it for granted that life-giving water will flow out. Now every time I turn the tap I'm grateful for this and hundreds of other daily miracles as simple as walking freely in the warm sun ..." That made me more aware and appreciative of the little "daily miracles" —and the importance of valuing them consciously.

Working at It

Is it necessary to pound the repetition that one must "work at" living in order to make it worthwhile? I believe it essential: We must "work at it" to attain and retain practically anything valuable—in the double sense of being awake to what is occurring, and doing something active about it. Conscious happiness is primarily a do-it-yourself endeavor and triumph.

You must *go* to your window if you want to gain from looking out. Then you must be *aware* of what there is to see and enjoy—grass, birds, shapes of buildings, a graceful cloud in the sky, whatever. And then you *do something* to multiply your pleasure—touch the grass, plant a flower (or none will grow), take a walk, feel—with full appreciation. Yes, you "work at it" and the rewards are colossal, enhancing your personal thrilling enjoyment of your world through conscious happiness.

In its fullest development, you will find that conscious happiness draws an extra dimension of enjoyment from each day's happenings. You are not just living but are more conscious of all that goes on. You recognize all phases, good and bad. And you glean all the possible good for your well-being and support.

Furthermore, conscious happiness is contagious. You will find that it not only enriches you but is catching for those with whom you come in contact. You don't *preach*. In effect, you *teach* by your personal example about the joyous gains to be had from an attitude of decency to others and yourself, of looking up instead of down. Just by enjoying conscious happiness yourself, the effects help convey to others the pleasures of possessing an optimistic outlook.

An interviewer asked me, "What do you believe?"

After thought, I said, "I believe in today and tomorrow and in hope and possibilities. Along with multitudes of other searching humans. I believe that progress for all is the sum of small victories won by individuals. I believe in working to make that come true."

Does Conscious Happiness Endure?

Will your conscious happiness last? That's up to you, for much as we seek to make the good permanent, even we change—our bodies, minds, attitudes. And people and things about us are constantly evolving, so we must handle inevitable change as best we can. Without variations, life would be dull—no expectation of new developments and challenges. Far better to anticipate, recognize, and make the best of change rather than denying or regretting it. By accommodating and progressing always, you sustain and increase your conscious happiness.

Don't forget my earlier admonitions: No hard and fast rules. No encumbering formats. No rigid, impossible demands on yourself. As life offers opportunities, grab them, use them. Exert to respect and improve yourself—loving, sharing, seeking, giving. Perhaps it boils down to one ultimate course: *Enjoy!* Others are ready to respond, to touch—you are never alone except when you want to be.

My one reasoned, soaring hope is that the precepts and suggestions here will help *you* to live the happiest possible, most fulfilling life from now on. Toward that end, this book is ultimately dedicated to *you*—with the reminder that "the only limit to our realization of tomorrow will be our doubts of today."

Writing this volume has made me even more conscious of all that life offers—more than I thought possible. Filling the pages with intense meaning has increased my conscious happiness in striving "to see beyond the range of sight." I fervently hope that reading this book will do the same for you. But remember that "a book tight shut is but a block of paper." I trust that you will reread often (as I will) for refreshment and inspiration.

For each day is a new beginning, and "all glory comes from daring to begin." *Dum spiro, spero*—"While I breathe, I hope." My hope is that you will develop and use your conscious happiness to find the best direction for yourself—and then act soundly and determinedly to achieve your personal, most fulfilling goal.

Please tell yourself: "I shall exert unflagging effort to explore and enjoy the wonderful possibilities, the endless facets of living. And each day I will work to bring to fullest fruition my conscious happiness credo: *'I'll make things better!'*"

* * *

Now to you . . . I say the last words that I whispered to my children in their growing up, each night before sleeping . . . a kiss on the forehead, and:

"Happiness come to you."

ABOUT THE AUTHOR

SAMM SINCLAIR BAKER has written twenty-three books including some outstanding bestsellers. His books cover many topics: diet, art, creative thinking and gardening. He and his wife, Natalie, a professional artist, live in Mamaroneck, New York.